Rome, Season One

For Flavia

optimae sorori

Rome, Season One: History Makes Television

Edited by
Monica S. Cyrino

Blackwell
Publishing

BLACKWELL PUBLISHING
350 Main Street, Malden, MA 02148–5020, USA
9600 Garsington Road, Oxford OX4 2DQ, UK
550 Swanston Street, Carlton, Victoria 3053, Australia

First published 2008 by Blackwell Publishing Ltd

1   2008

Library of Congress Cataloging-in-Publication Data
Rome, season one : history makes television / Edited by Monica S. Cyrino.
      p.   cm.
   Includes bibliographical references and index.
   ISBN 978-1-4051-6776-5 (hardcover : alk. paper) – ISBN 978-1-4051-6775-8 (pbk. : alk. paper)   1. Rome (Televison program)   2. Rome–On television.
I. Cyrino, Monica Silveira.

   PN1992.77.R557R66 2008
   791.45′72–dc22

                                                                              2007032666

A catalogue record for this title is available from the British Library.

Set in 10.5 on 13 pt Minion
by SNP Best-set Typesetter Ltd., Hong Kong

For further information on
Blackwell Publishing, visit our website at
www.blackwellpublishing.com

Contents

Illustrations

Notes on Contributors

Alena Allen is Instructor of Latin at Cathedral Catholic High School in San Diego, California. Her most recent publication explores the image of Briseis in the Homeric poems, Ovid's *Heroides*, and the film *Troy*. A lifelong student of Roman and Italian art, she is interested in the depiction of the ancient world in contemporary visual media.

Antony Augoustakis is Associate Professor of Classics at Baylor University in Waco, Texas. He has recently completed a book, *(M)otherhood and the Other: Fashioning Female Power in Flavian Epic*. He has also published scholarly articles on Plautus, Pliny the Younger, Lucan, Statius, and Silius Italicus. His current project is a commentary on Plautus' *Mercator*.

Barbara Weiden Boyd is Henry Winkley Professor of Latin and Greek at Bowdoin College in Brunswick, Maine. She is the author of *Ovid's Literary Loves: Influence and Innovation in the Amores* (1997) and the editor of *Brill's Companion to Ovid* (2002). She has written several textbooks on Vergil's *Aeneid*, and numerous articles on Augustan poetry. Her current project is a book on Augustan Rome.

Lee L. Brice is Associate Professor of Ancient History at Western Illinois University. His current book project is *Holding a Wolf by the Ears: Mutiny and Unrest in the Roman Military, 44 BC–AD 68*. He is also a contributor to the forthcoming *Oxford Handbook of Warfare in the Classical World c.700 BC–AD 602*. He currently serves as the President of the Society for Ancient Military Historians.

Ward Briggs is Carolina Distinguished Professor of Classics Emeritus and Louise Fry Scudder Professor of Humanities Emeritus at the University of South Carolina. He is the editor of *The Biographical Dictionary of North American Classicists* (1994) and *Soldier and Scholar: Basil Lanneau Gildersleeve and the Civil War* (1998). At present he is completing a biography of the American classicist Basil Lanneau Gildersleeve and beginning a book on classical myth in American film.

Brian Cooke is Senior Leader of Iris Learning, an international consulting group that focuses on leadership development and teambuilding. Prior to founding Iris Learning, Brian taught history and classics at Deerfield Academy and Milton Academy in Massachusetts. He is the author of *Frank Boyden of Deerfield: The Vision and Politics of an Educational Idealist* (1991).

Monica S. Cyrino is Professor of Classics at the University of New Mexico. She is the author of *Big Screen Rome* (2005) and *In Pandora's Jar: Lovesickness in Early Greek Poetry* (1995). She has published numerous articles on Greek poetry, mythology, and classics and cinema. Her current book project explores the ancient and modern popular significance of the goddess Aphrodite.

Gregory N. Daugherty is Professor of Classics and Chair of the Department of Classics at Randolph-Macon College in Ashland, Virginia. He is interested in the reception of classics in American popular culture, especially Homer, Cleopatra, and the depiction of ancient battles. He is currently the President of the Classical Association of the Middle West and South.

Alison Futrell is Associate Professor of Roman History at the University of Arizona. An abiding interest in the symbols and rituals of power led her to explore Roman spectacle in her books *Blood in the Arena* (1997) and *Roman Games* (2006). She is also fascinated with the way the ancient Mediterranean is reconfigured in popular culture and has published articles on *Spartacus, Xena: Warrior Princess, Troy,* and *Rome*.

Holly Haynes is Assistant Professor of Classical Studies at The College of New Jersey. She is the author of *The History of Make-Believe: Tacitus on Imperial Rome* (2003). She specializes in the historiography of the early Roman Empire. Her current projects focus on memory and trauma in the post-Domitianic period and on Petronius' *Satyricon*.

Kristina Milnor is Associate Professor of Classics at Barnard College in New York. She is the author of *Gender, Domesticity, and the Age of Augustus: Inventing Private Life* (2005), which won the American Philological Association's 2006 Goodwin Award of Merit. She has published articles on Roman comedy, elegy, and the use of history in marketing Barbie™. She was a Rome Prize Fellow at the American Academy in Rome (2003–2004).

Stacie Raucci is Assistant Professor of Classics at Union College in Schenectady, New York. Her research specialty is Latin poetry, in particular the elegies of Propertius, and she has presented several conference papers on the topics of gender and the gaze in the Roman poets. Her current book project is entitled *Vision in Roman Love Elegy*.

J. Mira Seo is Assistant Professor of Classical Studies and Comparative Literature at the University of Michigan. She specializes in Latin epic and post-Ovidian Latin poetry. Her most recent publication explores the ideas of divinity and prophecy in the television series *Alias*. She is currently working on a book entitled *Allusive Characterization in Latin Literature*.

Jon Solomon is Robert D. Novak Professor of Western Civilization and Culture and Professor of Cinema Studies at the University of Illinois, Urbana-Champaign. He is the author of *The Ancient World in the Cinema* (2001) and *The Complete Three Stooges: The Official Filmography* (2002). His current projects include an edition of Boccaccio's *Genealogy of the Pagan Gods*, a volume on the influence of *Ben-Hur*, and several volumes on the Greco-Roman tradition in opera.

Anise K. Strong is Visiting Assistant Professor of Classics at Northwestern University in Evanston, Illinois. Her most recent scholarly publication examines the 'don't ask, don't tell' enforcement of incest laws in Roman Egypt. She has presented several conference papers on the topics of ancient prostitution, motherhood, pornography, and cannibalism.

W. Jeffrey Tatum was until recently the Olivia Nelson Dorman Professor of Classics at the Florida State University, Tallahassee. He has now joined the Department of Classics and Ancient History at the University of Sydney. He is the author of *The Patrician Tribune: Publius Clodius Pulcher* (1999) and *Always I am Caesar: Eight Perspectives* (2008), as well as numerous articles on Latin literature and Roman history. He is currently completing a commentary on the *Commentariolum Petitionis.*

Margaret M. Toscano is Assistant Professor of Classics at the University of Utah. She specializes in gender, myth, and religion. She is currently working on the Cupid and Psyche story in both its literary and visual representations, and she is co-editing a volume of essays entitled *Hell and Its Afterlife: Historical and Comparative Perspectives.*

Episode Guide
Rome, Season One

Episode 01 "The Stolen Eagle"
written by Bruno Heller, directed by Michael Apted

Episode 02 "How Titus Pullo Brought Down the Republic"
written by Bruno Heller, directed by Michael Apted

Episode 03 "An Owl in a Thornbush"
written by Bruno Heller, directed by Michael Apted

Episode 04 "Stealing from Saturn"
written by Bruno Heller, directed by Julian Farino

Episode 05 "The Ram Has Touched the Wall"
written by Bruno Heller, directed by Allen Coulter

Episode 06 "Egeria"
written by John Milius and Bruno Heller, directed by Alan Poul

Episode 07 "Pharsalus"
written by David Frankel, directed by Tim van Patten

Episode 08 "Caesarion"
written by William J. MacDonald, directed by Steven Shill

Episode 09 "Utica"
written by Alexandra Cunningham, directed by Jeremy Podeswa

Episode 10   "Triumph"
written by Adrian Hodges, directed by Alan Taylor

Episode 11   "The Spoils"
written by Bruno Heller, directed by Mikael Salomon

Episode 12   "Kalends of February"
written by Bruno Heller, directed by Alan Taylor

Introduction

Monica S. Cyrino

At Cinecittà Studios in Rome, where the series *Rome* was filmed, the exterior set of the Roman Forum is staggering in both sheer size and visual impact. Sprawling across the famed studio backlot, the Forum set comprises only about 60 percent of the size of the ancient original, but still appears jaw-droppingly huge at first sight. As my students and I peak through the open gate, on a rare, special-*permesso* visit arranged by some well-connected friends in the Italian film industry, our handsome tour guide cheerfully reminds us, "No photo!" – the second season DVD of the series has yet to be released, hence the studio employee's protective caution. But at this moment, cameras are not necessary. Before our astonished eyes, scenes from the series seem to come alive: to the right we see the brightly painted exterior of the Curia, or Senate House, where Caesar climbed the steps surrounded by his lictors; in the distant background stands the tall marble expanse of the Roman municipal calendar, where a black-robed woman moved the markers to chart the swift passing of time in the series; to the far left, incongruously, is the gilded façade of Cleopatra's Alexandrian palace, where Atia and Octavia waited in the hot sun to be received by Mark Antony, who never emerged. We blink in amazement as the enormous structures glitter in the mid-morning sunlight.

    Rome is the first English-language series shot entirely in a non-English-speaking country, in this case, Italy – yet now it seems instinctive that the series creators decided to do so. James Madigan, who supervised the visual effects for the series, notes: "Being on location where all this history can still be seen was incredible . . . Anytime I wanted to get a feel for what the real Roman Forum was like I could just walk down the street

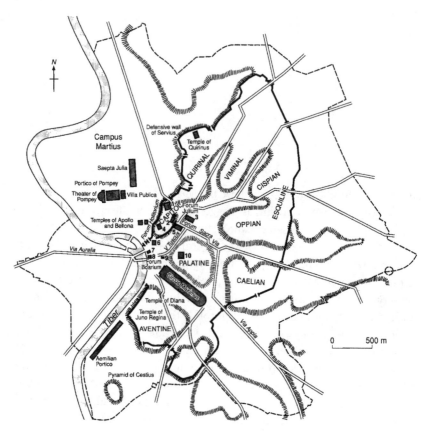

Figure 1   The city of Rome at the end of the Republic.
1 Temple of Juno Moneta 2 Tabularium 3 Basilica Aemilia 4 Temple of Jupiter
Capitolinus 5 Basilica Iulia 6 Temples of Fortuna and of Mater Matuta 7 Temple
of Portunus 8 Temple of Hercules Olivarius 9 Ara maxima 10 Temple of Cybele
or Magna Mater.
Source: Le Glay, M. (2005). *A History of Rome*. Oxford: Blackwell Publishing.

and look at it. It's all still there. The ruins of the temples show us exactly where everything stood in 50 BC."[1] My students and I experience a similar sense of the merging of temporal levels as we peer into the new ancient world so vividly reconstructed on this restricted space of the legendary cinematic landscape. In the foreground, nearest to where we are standing just inside the gate, a team of shirtless Italian workmen are busy setting up what looks like a sound system and building various platforms around the vast set. "They are preparing for a party tonight," our guide says to me in a stage whisper, as he – unintentionally, I surmise – echoes the words of Posca, one of the characters in the series. "A very fancy list of people."

Rome, Season One: History Makes Television is a collection of essays that responds to the critical and commercial success of the first season of the television series *Rome*, a sumptuous co-production by HBO (Home Box Office) Entertainment and the BBC (British Broadcasting Corporation).[2] The series was filmed, in partnership with RAI (Radiotelevisione Italiana), on massive outdoor sets covering five acres and six sound stages at the celebrated Cinecittà Studios, and at other locations around the Italian countryside. At a cost of over $100 million, the series *Rome* offers exceptionally high-quality, bigscreen production values, with a visual spectacle of sets, props, and costumes both opulent and highly authentic, as well as the most intelligent scripts, gripping plots, and brilliant acting seen on screens of any size in many years. The series, which unfolds in twelve weekly episodes, first aired in the United States on the cable channel HBO starting in August 2005; the pilot episode attracted a solid four million viewers, with cumulative viewership for each episode increasing over the course of a week's worth of rebroadcasts.[3] In the United Kingdom, *Rome* premiered on the BBC in November 2005 in eleven episodes: the BBC had decided to edit the first three episodes down to two, allegedly because British audiences were more familiar with the historical background than their American counterparts.[4] Later, however, in April 2007, the original uncut version of the first season – in all twelve episodes – was shown in the UK on the satellite/cable channel UKTV Drama. HBO released the first season DVD in August 2006 to great popular response: *Rome* is a series that demands repeated viewings, in order to digest and savor the complex political and social structures as well as to appreciate and enjoy the lavish details of sets and costumes. And as the online chat-rooms and blogs will attest, access to the DVD allows fans to repeat more accurately their favorite one-liners from the series. As Julius Caesar coolly informs Mark Antony: "It is only *hubris* if I fail."

The first season of *Rome* focuses on events that take place between Caesar's return to Rome after his conquest of Gaul in 52 BC and his assassination by Senatorial conspirators in 44 BC. As the series opens, Caesar is planning to return to Rome after eight years of warfare to seek his political fortunes, together with his battle-hardened, plunder-rich, and intensely loyal soldiers. The series features a broad array of characters, including both historical figures and invented ones. Such a combination of real and fictional characters can be found in virtually all films based on ancient Roman history, from *Quo Vadis* (1951) to *Gladiator* (2000), and it is also a creative hallmark of other historically themed television programs on HBO, such as the acclaimed Western drama, *Deadwood* (2004–2006). Yet it was the genius of Bruno Heller, creator and executive producer of *Rome*, to interweave with his "great" historical characters, like Caesar and Antony, two "regular guy" protagonists who are actually mentioned by Caesar in his military commentaries. The characters of Titus Pullo and Lucius Vorenus, the heart and soul of *Rome*'s narrative trajectory, are thus able to manifest both the realism of historical authenticity and the thrill of dramatic originality. Moreover, as "ordinary" Romans, Pullo and Vorenus more easily invite the audience into the grand historical account that might otherwise have been difficult for some viewers to access. Here's what Caesar himself had to say about these two men in his commentary on the campaign in Gaul:

> In this legion there were two centurions, both men of great courage, and close to reaching senior rank. Their names were Titus Pullo and Lucius Vorenus. There was always a dispute going on between them as to which had precedence over the other, and every year they clashed in fierce rivalry over the most important posts. While the fighting at the defences was at its height Pullo shouted: "Why are you hesitating, Vorenus? What chance are you waiting for of winning praise for your bravery? This day will decide the contest between us." With these words he made his way outside the defences and launched an attack where the enemy ranks were densest. Nor indeed did Vorenus remain within the rampart, but followed his rival for fear of what men would think of him. Then Pullo cast his spear against the enemy at close range, and transfixed a Gaul who had run forward from the ranks. He was knocked senseless, so they covered him with their shields and all together threw their weapons at Pullo, giving him no opportunity to withdraw.
>
> Pullo's shield was pierced, and a dart was stuck in his sword-belt – this knocked his sheath and hindered his attempt to draw his sword. While he was in difficulties the enemy surrounded him. To the rescue came Vorenus, his rival, who helped him out of trouble. Straight away the Gauls turned their attention from Pullo to Vorenus, thinking the former had been killed

by the dart. With his sword Vorenus fought at close quarters. He killed one man, and drove the rest off a short way. But he pressed forward too eagerly, tripped, and fell into a hollow. Now he was surrounded, and Pullo came to his aid. They killed several Gauls and both returned safely within the defences to great acclaim. Thus fortune played with them both in their rivalry and struggle, so that despite their enmity each helped and saved the other, and it was impossible to decide which should be considered the braver of the two.

(*Julius Caesar*, The Gallic *War* 5.44)[5]

Rome captures well the complex blend of rivalry, camaraderie, and allegiance shared between the "real" Vorenus and Pullo as described by Caesar in the above passage. But then the series takes each character further and grants him his own distinctively expanded role in driving the narrative of the drama. Vorenus, the strict and dour centurion who embodies old-fashioned Republican virtue, stands as a figure for Rome itself. As Vorenus' fortunes evolve over the course of the series' first season, the audience watches as the destiny of Rome also develops. Vorenus returns from war and learns – not without effort – to be a family man, gentle to his wife and children. While his focus grows more domestic, his soldierly loyalty to Caesar and Antony pays great dividends as he is promoted in rank; soon he is rewarded with high political office, and even becomes a Senator. The focus in *Rome*, too, changes from external war to internal politics. Yet as Vorenus is seen compromising his principles to follow his commanders into dangerous political territory, the viewers also see the fate of Rome unfold in rapid, inexorable steps. In the final episode, as Caesar gasps his last breath on the floor of the Senate and the city disintegrates into chaos, the camera cuts to a parallel shot of Vorenus cradling the dead body of his wife in the courtyard of his home, where his own world has collapsed around him. As the narrative of the first season charts a rising and falling arc of tragedy for Vorenus, his cascading fortunes serve as a metaphor for the grave crisis and loss of security in Rome.

While Vorenus wears the tragic mask, his friendly rival, Pullo, dons the twin mask of comedy. Pullo represents a type of Everyman figure, in particular, the indestructible spirit of the Roman people: in more contemporary cinematic terms, he is like the character Forrest Gump in his role as an incidental agent of high politics and history.[6] In *Rome*, Pullo is assigned a lower status than Vorenus, both in his servile origins and in his military rank, perhaps to emphasize his more popular association with the common people of Rome: Pullo is a regular *Publius Civis*. Like the average, everyday Roman, the series suggests, Pullo is brash, courageous, trustworthy, flexible, and kind-hearted; he is also superstitious, greedy, over-sexed, and prone to outbursts of murderous rage. Like Forrest Gump, Pullo is either present at or the direct cause of several momentous occasions during this most bracing period of Roman history: one episode is even titled "How Titus Pullo Brought Down the Republic" (Episode 02). Most importantly, the character of Pullo is shown to be a survivor, and so presents the optimistic flip side to the tragic coin of Vorenus. As the audience watches Pullo go from loyal legionary soldier to jobless veteran to condemned criminal, it seems that all hope is lost; but in the final two episodes, Pullo is redeemed by his indissoluble bond with Vorenus and his own powerful instinct to survive. Even as Rome falls into turmoil with the assassination of Caesar, the final shot of Pullo walking hand-in-hand with his beloved Eirene, whose name means "Peace," offers a visual promise of the ultimate survival of the Roman people.

Rome utilizes this technique of cutting between the "high" and "low" worlds to extraordinary effect: this rubbing together of the two worlds, between the elites and the plebs, between the historical personages and the invented ones, creates a unique dramatic friction that is unlike any other representation of the ancient world on screen. Although *Spartacus* (1960) was the first film to give a realistic impression of the world of lower-class people in antiquity, the film unabashedly branded the world of the rebellious slaves as "good" and set it starkly against the lush, decadent lifestyle of the Roman aristocracy, which was duly marked as "evil."[7] The series *Rome* resists such simplistic oppositions, and offers a much more nuanced view of how the two worlds are inextricably entwined to make up the authentic, multivalent fabric of Rome in the last days of the Republic. From the opening titles of the series, which luridly signal the themes of sex, violence, and power combined with evocative images from ancient mythology, *Rome* assures the audience that we will see the high and low worlds of the city mingling together at street level. Several instances of this dramatic parallelism occur throughout the first season of the series, with the characters of Vorenus and Pullo, as noted above, providing the most opportunities for narrative analogies between themselves and their elite leaders. In Episode 04, for example, while Atia hosts an elegant soirée to welcome home her uncle Caesar and to bolster the growing political power of the Julian family, the camera cuts back and forth to the more modest festivities at the home of the recently returned Vorenus, who also embarks on a new business venture. In this way, *Rome* visually underscores the connection between the elite characters and those of the lower classes, without casting any value judgment as to the relative morals of either: instead, their equality of purpose is emphasized, the very nature of what makes them all Roman.

About the Book

The contributors to this volume are all experts in their various subfields of ancient history, literature, and culture, whose scholarly work also engages both enthusiastically and astutely with popular culture appropriations of classical antiquity. In so doing, these scholars are actively creating a new charter for the study of classics, one in which we realize and appreciate the significance of how and why the ancient world is recreated by contemporary artists, writers, and filmmakers. New meanings are conceived, generated, and transmitted to current audiences every time the ancient world is represented on the modern page, stage, or screen. Popular culture recreations of antiquity, particularly those depicted in the powerful, ubiquitous, and pervasive visual media of film and television, articulate for us the value of understanding the ancient world in a modern context, and studying these contemporary recreations should rightly be seen as the natural occupation of modern classicists. The contributors to this volume all accept that challenge as a starting point to their discussions of the television series *Rome*.

The essays collected in this volume all endeavor to highlight the essential aspects of the artistic, historical, and popular contribution of the first season of *Rome*, as they investigate the series from a wide range of thematic and disciplinary viewpoints. The intersection between television and history forms the subject matter of the first four chapters. The opening chapter, "Televising Antiquity: From *You Are There* to *Rome*," is a comprehensive survey of the ancient world on the small screen, providing a much-needed history of broadcast feature films and original television programming set in antiquity. The second chapter, "Making History in *Rome*: Ancient vs. Modern Perspectives," explores how the creators of the series echo the methods of the ancient historians in combining pure facts with sensationalized bits to spice up their historical accounts for both entertainment and educational purposes. Historical accuracy is also the concern of the third chapter, "What I Learned as an Historical Consultant for *Rome*," as the author recounts a few days' work on the set of *Rome* and the conflicts inherent in the process of creating an authentic, but not always accurate, onscreen portrayal of antiquity. The fourth chapter, "*Rome*'s Opening Titles: Triumph, Spectacle, and Desire," examines the point of contact between television as spectacle and the use of spectacle in ancient Rome, where the interaction of message and audience occurs in a similar way in both the opening titles of the series and in the Roman military triumph.

The next four chapters deal with significant aspects of the series' representation of late Republican Roman history, the place of the Roman military in society, and individual historical characters. The fifth chapter, "The Fog of War: The Army in *Rome*," offers a thorough evaluation of the multifaceted and visually credible depiction of the military in the series, both on the battlefield and in camp life. The sixth chapter, "Caesar's Soldiers: The *Pietas* of Vorenus and Pullo," explores how the series uses the two quasi-historical characters to delineate the ideal virtues of the Roman soldier and citizen, such as loyalty, duty, and patriotism. The seventh chapter, "Becoming Augustus: The Education of Octavian," follows the future emperor's process of maturation throughout the series, as the young Octavian carefully observes and is observed by those around him in his attainment of Roman manhood. The eighth chapter, "'Not Some Cheap Murder': Caesar's Assassination," surveys the ancient sources and later traditions that inform the account of Caesar's death, and suggests how *Rome* depoliticizes and so undermines the traditional "script" of the murder by dramatic reference to personal betrayals.

While as a genre the epic film set in antiquity is not well known for the portrayal of strongly drawn female figures, the series *Rome* breaks the mold by showcasing several powerful women characters, as the next three chapters demonstrate. The ninth chapter, "Women's Politics in the Streets of *Rome*," considers how the representation of the fictional feud between Servilia and Atia rewrites the highly competitive politics of the late Roman Republic to highlight the importance of women in securing dynastic power. The tenth chapter, "Atia and the Erotics of Authority," continues in this project as it scrutinizes the way the character Atia uses her sexual and political influence in the series specifically to advance the goals of the Julian clan. The eleventh chapter, "Her First Roman: A Cleopatra for *Rome*," examines the series' innovative depiction of the Egyptian queen, and reveals how it both derives from and challenges the historical reality and later reception of her celebrated life on stage and screen.

In the following four chapters, scholars investigate several important thematic, aesthetic, and cultural issues as they are presented in *Rome*. The twelfth chapter, "Gowns and Gossip: Gender and Class Struggle in *Rome*," explores how the series utilizes social categories to create and assign power, in particular through the use of costume and the trope of gossip as privileged communication. The thirteenth chapter, "The Gender Gap: Religious Spaces in *Rome*," analyzes the various religious rituals associated with men and women in the series, and how their depiction creates an impression of gendered devotional space, both public and private. Space is also the topic of the fourteenth chapter, "Staging Interiors in *Rome*'s Villas," as we take a walk through the homes and apartments of several important characters in the series, and see how each domestic space visually reflects the identity of its particular owner. The fifteenth chapter, "Latin in the Movies and *Rome*," examines one of the most extraordinary and intriguing features of the series: its extensive and colorful use of Latin – and other languages – to heighten the effect of historical and cultural authenticity.

The final two chapters of this volume explore aspects of sexuality as portrayed in the series *Rome*. The penultimate chapter, "Spectacle of Sex: Bodies on Display in *Rome*," looks at the way the male characters in the series are presented as observable sex symbols, and how their prowess in the bedroom is shown to be more important in constructing an image of masculine political power than their battlefield exploits. The final chapter, "Vice is Nice: *Rome* and Deviant Sexuality," considers how the incest motif in the series substantiates the notorious sexual decadence evident in earlier cinematic representations of the ancient Roman world, while it also reveals the recent tendency towards boundary-breaking depictions of sex on network and cable television.

As the editor of this volume, my primary gratitude goes to the contributors who agreed with great passion, collegiality, and commitment to participate in this project and who worked so hard to see it to its fulfillment. Like veteran members of the Thirteenth Legion, I feel honored to have served with them, and I would gladly save any one of them from the arena. I am grateful to HBO for their generous permission to use the images from the series that are reprinted in this book. At Blackwell Publishing, I am indebted to Al Bertrand for his support of this project from the beginning, to Hannah Rolls for her help in the production process, and to Leanda Shrimpton for her tireless efforts in picture research. As always, this volume is dedicated to my friends and family who indulge me in my obsession with popular culture.

NOTES

1   Wes Beckwith, "Interview with James Madigan, VFX Supervisor for HBO's *Rome*," www.cgfocus.com.

2   HBO and BBC had previously teamed up on the production of the Emmy
    Award-winning miniseries, *Band of Brothers* (2001).
3   Denise Martin, "HBO *Rome* Ratings Not Built In A Day," www.variety.com,
    August 31, 2005.
4   This claim has been disputed in private conversations with individuals involved
    in the production of *Rome*, who suggest the BBC's decision to edit was driven
    more by the economies of scheduling than by any evaluation of the relative
    education levels of Anglo-American audiences.
5   Translation by Hammond (1998).
6   In the film *Forrest Gump* (1994), the title character influences the course of
    recent history and popular culture, for example, by teaching Elvis Presley how
    to dance, and by meeting with several Presidents.
7   Cyrino (2005), 104–117.

1

Televising Antiquity: From *You Are There* to *Rome*

Jon Solomon

Chronologically and generically speaking, the HBO-BBC series *Rome* is the result of a half-century's development of broadcast special events, made-for-television films, and miniseries. This chapter surveys the various experiments the television industry developed for making classical antiquity palatable to millions of viewers and profitable for producers, broadcasters, and sponsors. It begins with the concept of "event-status programming" and early attempts at broadcasting Hollywood films on television and creating original television programming. It then proceeds to the importation of miniseries from Great Britain, the production of in-house made-for-television films and miniseries, and the expansion of venues from network and then public television audiences to syndication, basic cable, and the home video market. And it culminates with the contemporary solution on premium cable in the United States, namely, the series *Rome*. Along the way this survey will help identify prototypes for many of *Rome*'s notable features.

In its infancy as almost exclusively a broadcast medium, television in the 1920s, 1930s, and 1940s began (not entirely unlike film in the 1890s) as a medium confined for the most part to the representation of actual, that is, live, contemporaneous events. Broadcasts often provided a distant window to events which, because of the novelty of the medium, could be described as "special."[1] These events included musical and dramatic performances, speeches, and athletic contests. But even the initial World Series broadcast – Game #1 of the 1947 Yankee/Dodger series – was viewed by only an estimated 3.9 million viewers, most of them in public venues.

The postwar boom changed television's demographic breadth and geographical coverage rapidly. Most popular shows of the period – game shows, soap operas, variety shows, dramatic anthologies, and sitcoms – were broadcast live, and the broadcast of a unique live event like the hotly contested six-day Democratic National Convention in the summer of 1952 attracted 70 million viewers.[2] Soon thereafter came the 1953 coronation of Elizabeth II (film of the live UK broadcast was flown in overnight by charter flight), the first color broadcast of Pasadena's New Year's Rose Parade (1954), a series of live events transmitted across the Atlantic via Telstar (1962), live images from Apollo 7 (1968), dozens of Super Bowls, the O.J. chase, and the bombing of Baghdad, just a few highlights of the thousands of events watched live by tens of millions of viewers.[3]

As of 2006, the top ten network telecasts recorded by Nielsen include five live sporting events, the two premiere television broadcasts of *Gone With the Wind* (1976), the eighth and final episode of *Roots* (1977), the "Who Shot J.R.?" episode of *Dallas* (1980), and the final episode of *M.A.S.H.* (1983). As an accounting that tallies up the victors of the entire history of American television, this list demonstrates the persistent lure of "special" television events. And the presence of the eighth episode of *Roots* as the third top-rated network broadcast of all time reminds us that television producers and executives periodically strive to recreate this kind of success by making enormous expenditures not just on acquiring the rights to major sporting events, but also in supporting expensive multi-evening broadcasts of miniseries. Whether live or taped/filmed, and whether intended as a loss-leader or not, "event-status programming" continues to create successful television. Though neither live nor a single-event broadcast, *Rome* derives from this same television stratagem. Prohibitively expensive and limited in duration, *Rome* in the historical scheme of television works like a special event.

The miniseries (or "limited series") genre to which *Rome* belongs was not born along with the medium, nor was the made-for-television movie, of which *Rome* is a derivative. In fact, except for a few early broadcast experiments, Hollywood feature films were not broadcast – even as special events – on national television in the early 1950s.[4] Hollywood studios had distanced themselves from the television industry as a dangerous competitor apt to steal away their audience, despite television's smaller screen, dimmer, blurrier image, and considerable startup costs.[5] But ABC's Leonard Goldenson, eager to woo Hollywood studios into the business of producing television shows, signed an agreement with Walt Disney,[6] and just the second episode of *Disneyland* (November 3, 1954) offered an edited version of the studio's theatrical film, *Alice in Wonderland* (1951).[7] *Alice in Wonderland* had not been a box-office success, but its draw on television was considerable, as would often be true for films broadcast on television. A few weeks later, two episodes (January 5 and 12, 1955) featured Disney's full-length feature film, *Treasure Island* (1950), in two one-hour segments. Interspersed into that same season were three installments of the first film produced for television broadcast, which were edited together for the subsequent theatrical release of *Davy Crockett, King of the Wild Frontier* (May 1955).[8]

Although Disney, Warner, and several other film studios had set up separate television production studios and established a solid foothold in the television industry, a labor dispute delayed the television broadcast of Hollywood feature films. The dispute over making residual payments to actors for repeat broadcasts created the legal and financial resistance spearheaded by such Western luminaries as Gene Autry and Roy Rogers. The opposition succeeded in banning films made after August 1, 1948 from television exhibition.[9] Meanwhile, only B films from "Poverty Row" studios as well as British films were being exhibited on local channels.[10] The logjam was broken in 1956, when MGM agreed to have *The Wizard of Oz* (1939), which had just failed to generate much income from its 1955 theatrical re-release in a pseudo-widescreen version, broadcast as the final episode of CBS's *Ford Star Jubilee*, which normally featured live performances by popular entertainers, on November 3, 1956. But despite the success of that historic broadcast, there would be no second broadcast of the film until it was rebroadcast as a two-hour Christmas special on December 13, 1959.[11]

The first regularly scheduled prime-time network program devoted entirely to showing post-1948 feature films was *NBC Saturday Night at the Movies*, which premiered on September 23, 1961, by broadcasting Fox's *How to Marry a Millionaire* (1953). The advent of color television, the celebrity of Marilyn Monroe, and living memory of the first widescreen film ever produced helped make this premiere successful.[12] Soon after, ABC created *The ABC Sunday Night Movie*. CBS, the leading network at the time, did not clear a timeslot for feature film presentation until the fall of 1965 with its *CBS Thursday Night Movie*, but by 1968 there was a prime-time network movie every night of the week. Relatively few of these broadcast feature films were set in antiquity. Rental fees were very high for the best of them. But when MGM's *Ben-Hur* (1959) finally had its television premiere on February 14, 1971, it attracted the third largest rating (37.1) and share (56) of any prime-time movie to date: some 86 million people watched it.[13] Similarly, a few years later, DeMille's *The Ten Commandments*

(1956) earned the second highest audience share (54) of any program in 1973. Of course, B films like the hundreds of European sword-and-sandal films of the late 1950s and early 1960s had already been playing on local channels throughout the period.

The profits generated from frequent broadcasts of televised films, along with the now well-established synergies between the film and television industries, encouraged the major networks to produce in-house a fresh supply of previously unseen films tailored to the television audience. In fact, the first made-for-television film, an adaptation of Ernest Hemingway's *The Killers* (1964), was so violent that NBC refused to air it. (The first made-for-television film actually broadcast, *See How They Run*, aired on October 7, 1964.) Some of these made-for-television films were pilots for potential series, as was *Hercules and the Princess of Troy*, the second TV movie that ABC aired (September 12, 1965). This film, also known as *Hercules vs. the Sea Monster*, was the creation of Joseph E. Levine, who had introduced *Hercules* (1957) and thereby the Italianate sword-and-sandal/ muscle-man cinematic genre to the US market. Attempting to create a regular peplum series on network television, he produced this film as well in Italy and Yugoslavia, yet, ironically, it seems to be the only example of the genre which was not dubbed into English. But Fox's *Cleopatra* (1963) had already come and gone, and the genre of films set in antiquity was rapidly withering on the vine.

Previous to this unsuccessful pilot and the broadcasting of feature films set in antiquity, relatively little original television programming exploited the contemporary popularity of theatrically released films set in antiquity. Since 1949, the year in which Paramount released DeMille's *Samson and Delilah*, all the major studios had released at least one major film of the ancient genre. But in the early 1950s, there were only three television programs that featured episodes set in antiquity. One was *You Are There*, a television version of the successful 1947–1950 radio program originally titled *CBS Was There*. More a docudrama than a melodrama, and aired on Sunday afternoons rather than during prime time, *You Are There* placed a CBS news correspondent amidst unfolding historical events. The show offered such episodes as #6: *The Assassination of Julius Caesar* (March 8, 1953), #14: *The Death of Socrates* (May 3, 1953), #30: *The Death of Cleopatra* (October 18, 1953), #39: *The Fall of Troy* (December 20, 1953), #70: *The Return of Ulysses* (September 2, 1954), #74: *The Burning of Rome* (October 24, 1954), and #95: *The Triumph of Alexander the Great* (March 27, 1955).[14] The second was the long-running *Hallmark Hall of Fame*, a weekly dramatic anthology in 1952–1955, then sporadic thereafter. Episode

#54, *Socrates' Wife* (January 25, 1953), featured Katina Paxinou as Xanthippe and Berry Kroeger as Socrates; episode #93 offered *Aesop and Rhodope* (December 13, 1953). Similarly, the Ford Foundation's aptly named humanistic anthology *Omnibus*, hosted by the same Alistair Cooke who would later give his British imprimatur to *I, Claudius* (1976), included dramas based on ancient literature, for example, the 1955 season opener which offered a 90-minute *Iliad* (April 1955), and Sophocles' *Oedipus the King* (January 1957).[15] As is evident from this brief accounting, Greco-Roman antiquity for television in the 1950s signified vivid history and traditional drama, not programming worthy of the moniker "vast wasteland" that FCC Chairman Newton Minow would soon bestow upon television programming in 1961.

Even the chronological center of the ancient film vortex at the turn of the decade produced only two failed television projects. *Rivak the Barbarian* had a relatively large budget of $750,000 and was shot in Italy. NBC aired the 90-minute pilot, directed by Rudolph Maté (who later directed *The 300 Spartans* in 1962) and starring Jack Palance (*Sign of the Pagan*, 1954), on October 4, 1960. *The Centurion* seems never to have gotten beyond the planning stages, even though the successful oil and television mogul Jack Wrather (*The Lone Ranger*) had planned to produce this "'Ben-Hur'-type Roman western shot in Europe."[16]

The Hollywood studios that were producing half-hour and hour-long television programming were not for the most part those producing films set in antiquity. MGM, Paramount, and Fox, for instance, did not invest heavily in television production until the 1960s, while Warner and Universal had been producing a steady diet of successful Westerns in the action genre since the mid-1950s. As a result, even in the 1960s there were very few episodes of regular TV shows set in antiquity.[17] Every Friday during the 1966–1967 season, Irwin Allen's *Time Tunnel* placed James Darren and Robert Colbert in a different period of history. But only one of this time-traveling anthology's thirty episodes, *Revenge of the Gods*, took place in antiquity – the seventh episode, aired October 21, 1966, which took the two American time travelers back to the Trojan War where they were thought to be Olympian gods. Several episodes blended historical personages and eras, one of which was episode #19, *The Ghost of Nero* (January 20, 1967), wherein the ghost of Nero possesses Mussolini in 1915. Only occasionally during the 1960s did dramatic anthologies feature plays set in antiquity. The only distinguished example is the *Hallmark Hall of Fame*'s 1966 presentation of Maxwell Anderson's *Barefoot in Athens*, featuring Peter Ustinov as Socrates, for which he won an Emmy.[18]

One potential 1960s television show set in antiquity was *Alexander the Great*. The pilot featuring the Battle of Issus was shot in Utah in 1964 but shelved until 1968. By then, both William Shatner (Alexander) and Adam West (Cleander) had become household names thanks to their roles in *Star Trek* (1966–1969) and *Batman* (1966–1968). In fact, Shatner remarked later: "The nine months I spent working on *Alexander the Great* came in handy for *Star Trek*. Capt. Kirk is, in many ways, the quintessential hero and the Greek heroes in literature have many of the same qualities I wanted to explore."[19] Of course, both Shatner and West were obligated to other projects, so there was to be no series forthcoming, but ABC decided at least to air the film as an episode of their Friday night, MGM-produced family anthology, *Off To See the Wizard*, on January 26, 1968. Not coincidentally, just seven weeks later, on the Ides of March, 1968, Shatner appeared in *Bread and Circuses*, a *Star Trek* episode (#43) in which Planet 892-IV looks very much like ancient Rome and is under the control of Proconsul Claudius Marcus, who conducts gladiatorial contests to amuse the planet's inhabitants. Later that year, on November 22, Shatner starred in *Plato's Stepchildren* (#65), and on December 20 in *Elaan of Troyius* (#57), which updated the story of Helen of Troy. *Star Trek* episode #31, *Who Mourns for Adonais?*, featuring Mark Forest as Apollo, was broadcast on September 22, 1967. But all this was futuristic science fiction, not newly created drama set in Greco-Roman antiquity. The correct formula for portraying antiquity on commercial television still eluded the industry.

The period of the mid-1960s is erroneously said to have produced the American television miniseries. In 1966 David L. Wolper, a pioneer in distributing films to television stations in the late 1940s and then an award-winning documentary producer, produced a program based on William L. Shirer's *The Rise and Fall of the Third Reich*, which, because ABC aired it over three consecutive nights, has therefore been regarded as the first miniseries.[20] The film, however, is not a drama but a documentary narrated by Richard Basehart; its uniqueness lies not in being a dramatic miniseries but in its run-length and clustered broadcast.[21] More accurately, it was Great Britain that would provide the model for the American miniseries, and this model was not delivered via the commercial networks. In 1969 the BBC produced *The Forsyte Saga*, a dramatic series packaged into an irregular number of episodes serialized over a number of weekly viewings. This kind of limited dramatic series did not fit easily into the typical American scheduling grid of discrete episodes ideally extending over at least several seasons, and the commercial networks did not foresee the potential popularity this kind of limited series would have in the United States.

But in that very year American public television was in its final stages of being redefined as an alternative, differently constituted kind of network – the result of the Carnegie Commission Report and the resulting Public Television Act of 1967.[22] The resulting Public Broadcasting Service (PBS) did not create its own programming but instead purchased it from a variety of sources, and, despite the lack of regularly scheduled commercial interruptions, obtained ample funding from corporate sponsors.[23] It was the Ford Foundation that provided sponsorship of this British adaptation of the John Galsworthy novels which, along with *Sesame Street* (which all three networks had rejected), could now attract several different devoted segments of the non-commercial viewing public. PBS followed *The Forsyte Saga* with *Masterpiece Theater* in 1971, an anthology of British dramatic series which ranged from just a few episodes to several seasons in length.[24] It was here that television turned for the first time to an ancient setting for a miniseries, though tellingly, not until the 1977–1978 season, which saw the broadcast of the thirteen episodes of the BBC's dramatic adaptation of Robert Graves' *I, Claudius* and *Claudius, the God*. Before airing in the United States in November 1977, Les Brown in the *New York Times* predicted that the series would "test the boundaries" of PBS, and this would not be the last time a television show or series set in antiquity would challenge the moral code of television viewing.[25] Fittingly, the "gorgeous malevolence" of Graves' Livia (Siân Phillips) would set a standard for future *femmes fatales* in ancient settings,[26] not the least of which are Atia and Servilia in *Rome*.

The first genuine and successful miniseries to premiere on any of the American commercial networks was not broadcast until the mid-1970s. First was the lengthy presentation of the Leon Uris bestseller *QB VII* (1974), although this did not attract much of an audience.[27] Then came *Rich Man, Poor Man*, produced by Universal TV. This ground-breaking serialization of the 1970 Irwin Shaw novel aired on ABC in six two-hour segments in February and March 1976.[28] The first two hours aired on a Sunday night – the most popular night of the week for family viewing – and then the subsequent two hours aired the next night; this scheduling strategy of showing episodes on consecutive nights would become a common scheduling format for miniseries broadcast on commercial networks. However, using the pattern established by the BBC and PBS, ABC aired all subsequent episodes on successive Monday nights. By the end of the second night millions of viewers were "hooked," and the success of *Rich Man, Poor Man* spawned not only a repeat broadcast the next spring but also a sequel the following fall. In doing so, *Rich Man, Poor Man* also established a memorable precedent for the many novels-for-television that would follow. By far the most successful and well regarded of these was Wolper's *Roots*, from the novel by Alex Haley, which aired January 23–30, 1977. Because Wolper and ABC feared a ratings disaster, they decided to cluster the eight episodes over eight consecutive nights from Sunday to Sunday so only one week's ratings would be "lost."[29] Far from being a disaster, *Roots* was the most watched dramatic show in American television history, and the viewing audience grew as the week proceeded, with approximately half the entire population of the United States watching the final episode on the concluding Sunday night. The multi-evening clustered miniseries would now become a regular part of the American television landscape.

Even so, the flurry of miniseries that followed throughout the next decade included only a handful of high-profile projects set in classical antiquity. The first was Franco Zeffirelli's *Jesus of Nazareth* (1977). Not unfamiliar with recreating ancient settings, Zeffirelli had been responsible for designing Samuel Barber's *Antony and Cleopatra* – the inaugural opera at New York's new Metropolitan Opera House at Lincoln Center in September 1966. He co-wrote the teleplay with Anthony Burgess and others, and like so many miniseries of the era, the cast featured a number of aging but well-known actors (e.g., Laurence Olivier, Rod Steiger, Anthony Quinn, and James Mason), most of them in lesser parts or cameos. The budget which producer Lew Grade's ITC – a flourishing British production and distribution company in the 1970s – poured into this lavish miniseries was reportedly $18 million.[30] Co-produced with RAI and filmed in Tunisia and Morocco, the final cut, which NBC aired in two three-hour segments on Palm and Easter Sundays, 1977, attracted some 91 million viewers and garnered two Emmy Award nominations.[31] Even today, *Jesus of Nazareth* is heralded by some as one of the better miniseries ever produced. Of course some of the current praise is due to the film's devotional posture, but before its airing on April 3 and 10, 1977, there was a considerable outcry of impiety and irreverence inspired by Bob Jones III – so much so that General Motors, responding to thousands of angry letters, withdrew its $3 million sponsorship.[32]

Jesus of Nazareth followed a series of religious films produced in the pre-*Roots* period of the early/mid-1970s. Michael Cacoyannis, who had in the previous decade directed such notable cinematic renditions of Greek tragedies as *Electra* (1962) and *The Trojan Women* (1971), directed *The Story of Jacob and Joseph*, which aired on ABC during Easter week (April 7, 1974). The next year ITC, RAI, and many of the same talents combined again to produce the six-hour *Moses, the Lawgiver*, starring Burt Lancaster, which aired on CBS in six one-hour segments on consecutive Saturday nights from June 21, 1975. A version edited from 360 minutes down to 141 minutes was given a theatrical release the following fall, and during the following Easter week (April 9, 1976), ABC aired the four-hour *The Story of David* featuring Timothy Bottoms and Keith Michell as the younger and older David. Insofar as *Rome* is concerned, *Jesus of Nazareth* differed from its Old Testament predecessors in that it is set in the Roman province of Judea. Zeffirelli and Burgess took advantage of the Roman setting not just by costuming the *de rigueur* Roman soldiers for the Passion episodes but, for instance, by creatively inserting into the court of Herod a Roman advisor, called Gaius Gracchus, as well as a fictitious Roman consul, Marcus Naso. These two togaed Romans force Herod (Peter Ustinov) into conducting the census that returns Joseph and Mary to Bethlehem before the birth of Jesus, and, when Herod resists, they remind him that the divine Augustus would not appreciate "any lack of cooperation." Such Roman-specific dialogue fans out to the people of Jerusalem, who mistrust Augustus and Roman motives for conducting the census. Then even Joseph includes Augustus in his praises, believing that Augustus obeys god, fulfilling the prophecy (Matthew 2.6) that Bethlehem will produce a shepherd of Israel.

Jesus of Nazareth confirmed in the miniseries genre the renewed viability of producing a big-budget film set in antiquity, which had not happened in the feature-film genre since the mid-1960s. But it still took four years to air a second ancient miniseries, Universal TV's *Masada* (1981). To create this 394-minute drama, Joel Oliansky adapted Ernest K. Gann's novel, *The Antagonists*, which contrasts two complex principals, the Roman General Cornelius Flavius Silva (Peter O'Toole) and Eleazar ben Yair (Peter Strauss). Aired in two-hour segments on ABC on consecutive nights from Sunday to Wednesday, April 5–8, 1981, the $22 million film drew nearly 50 percent of the inaugural Sunday audience, was well regarded by critics, and was nominated for thirteen Emmy Awards. For authenticity's sake, Universal and veteran television producer George Eckstein and several partners opted to spend the money on location shooting at Masada despite the problems generated by the intense desert heat. They also spent the time and effort to reconstruct Roman siege apparatus and reenact the building of the ramp.

Audiences treated *Masada* as educational and inspirational drama, and so these two initial ancient successes helped to generate two additional and equally ambitious miniseries set in antiquity, 1984's seven-hour, $19 million *The Last Days of Pompeii* (ABC, May 6–8, 1984) and 1985's enormous twelve-hour, five-night, $30 million *A.D.* (NBC, March 31–April 4,

1985). Like *Jesus of Nazareth* and *Masada*, both of these subsequent films had a Judeo-Christian element. The former, like most of the more than half-dozen previous film renditions of the 1834 Edward Bulwer-Lytton novel, featured the second-generation Christian character Olinthus (Brian Blessed). As for *A.D.*, its production was unlike anything previously attempted in television filmmaking, with over 400 speaking parts, nearly 20,000 extras, seven different production sites in Tunisia (including the gladiatorial arena at El Jem), and sets of Jerusalem and the Roman Forum which covered six city blocks in Monastir. More comprehensive in chronological scope than *The Last Days of Pompeii*, much like *Jesus of Nazareth* (with which it shared Anthony Burgess and others) and more so than *Rome*, *A.D.* surveys several decades of history, namely the paleo-Christian movement through the Neronian period.

Europe also produced an additional miniseries set in antiquity, Franco Rossi's *Quo Vadis?*, which was an RAI co-production presented on Italian television in February 1985. Like *The Last Days of Pompeii*, *Quo Vadis?* was another nineteenth-century historical novel that had been rendered into more than a half-dozen film versions since the early decades of the twentieth century, and it too takes place in paleo-Christian Rome of the first century. It is particularly interesting that Rossi turned to such a text late in his career, for he had been one of the first Italian directors to work on a television miniseries, two of which had been set in Greco-Roman antiquity. But both *L'Odissea* (1968) and *Eneide* (1971) were huge projects that attempted to realize on film two ancient epic poems. The Homeric epic was rendered into 446 minutes of film; the Vergilian, 311.

As a veritable historical sequel to *Jesus of Nazareth*, *A.D.* seemed to have had the same effect on the genre of the television miniseries set in antiquity as *Cleopatra* did on the equivalent genre of the feature film. Its $30 million budget brought it more ridicule than praise – it was nominated for only a single Emmy Award. There would not be another ancient made-for-television film until the 1990s. It has been common for critics and film historians, myself included, to denigrate these lengthy, over-produced, relatively ephemeral enterprises (DVD releases have been very limited, and severely edited). For those of us old enough to remember watching them night after night, it is easier to remember the incessant commercial interruptions and network promotions, the disheartening reliance on Hollywood cameos, and the marathon endurance required to watch them than it is any artistic achievement or historical/intellectual satisfaction. Nonetheless, twenty to thirty years later, they should now be reevaluated as examples of a unique and high-profile, albeit limited, media experiment.

Considering the relative dearth of Greco-Roman-type programming in the first two decades of popular television broadcasting followed by the nine-year gap between the airing of the *Alexander the Great* pilot and *Jesus of Nazareth*, we now have the perspective to note that the four high-profile 1970s–1980s American miniseries, all of which were quite costly to produce, represent important rarities emerging from the few thousand made-for-television films and numerous television miniseries of the last half of the twentieth century. These rare creatures had to conform to the cumbersome constraints of network television: framing the narrative and editing segments to function between commercial interruptions, dividing the entire story into larger segments for serialized viewing over a series of evenings, targeting the dialogue and intellectual level for a broad audience spectrum, avoiding any offense of religious or parental watchdog organizations, and confronting interference from sponsors and network executives. It is now time, a generation later, to understand them at least as noteworthy phenomena in the history of American film and television. And when we look at the costuming and set designs, consider the multi-faceted but intertwining storylines as well as the segmentation of evening viewings, we are seeing many of the same elements we see in *Rome*. Then and now the television screen is enlivened with human activity both central and incidental to the plot and the principal players, or it is blackened behind a single lamp beside which two major characters carry on a nocturnal or clandestine conversation. Then and now the tableaux alternate from ceremonious pomp and dazzling imperial architecture to dusty streets and impoverished dwellings. Then and now the characters range from powerful emperors, generals, and kings to manipulative females to loyal servants to weasel-like villains. These miniseries are clearly the ancestors of *Rome*, albeit now without most of those network constraints.

The 1980s provided many challenges and rivals to commercial network television in the United States. Both cable television (basic and premium) and home video players/recorders were enabling viewers to access a much wider variety of programming and time-shift their viewing, and the expanding home video market and the availability of commercial free movies on cable were changing consumer viewing habits. The impact on the genre of films set in antiquity was to provide a fresh availability of films from the 1950s and 1960s, making such films as *Ben-Hur* (1959) and *Spartacus* (1960) fresh in the minds of both viewers and filmmakers and introducing them as classics to a new generation. Sales of VHS and later DVD copies considerably increased profits from films that were now decades old, and motifs from and allusions to *Ben-Hur* would appear in a wide array of films

from Mel Brooks' comedy *Robin Hood: Men in Tights* (1993) to Oliver
Stone's *Any Given Sunday* (1999), as well as in *Forget Paris* (1995), *Titanic*
(1997), and *Star Wars: The Phantom Menace* (1999). Similarly, the "I'm
Spartacus" motif from the 1960 film appeared in Tom Hanks' *That Thing
You Do* (1996) and *Punchline* (1998), and it was featured in a Pepsi com-
mercial aired first during the network broadcast of the annual Academy
Awards ceremonies on February 27, 2005.[33]

This revived currency gathered such momentum by the mid-1990s that
several producers, taking advantage of the new television landscape, determined to retest the ancient waters. The first was Sam Raimi, who had
broken into the film industry by forming Renaissance Pictures to produce
a series of horror and comical productions. Along with partner Rob Tapert,
Raimi devised a television pilot film, *Hercules and the Amazon Women*,
which premiered in the United States on April 30, 1994. The film did not
represent Hercules as a state-of-the-art muscle man, as had been the tradition since the 1957 Joseph E. Levine *Hercules* through the two Lou Ferrigno
Hercules films of 1983 and 1985. Instead, Raimi's Hercules (Kevin Sorbo)
had a softer look thanks to long hair and a more rounded musculature, he
displayed a casual, less musclebound manner with modern sensitivity, and
he spoke in contemporary dialogue, not a stilted pseudo-ancient concoc-
tion. In addition, the visual landscape of Raimi's film abandoned the traditional Mediterranean scrub for lush New Zealand scenery peopled with
half-naked bodies for the older demographics and innovative special com-
puter effects for the younger. Raimi used this comprehensive formula to
produce another four films in 1994 (*Hercules and the Lost Kingdom*, *Hercules and the Circle of Fire*, *Hercules in the Underworld*, *Hercules in the Maze
of the Minotaur*), after which he launched the most popular television show
in the world with *Hercules: The Legendary Journeys*, which premiered on
January 16, 1995.

Raimi released *Hercules: The Legendary Journeys* in first-run syndication,
which allowed him to bypass network interference and scheduling conflicts. Syndication had played a significant role in television broadcasting
since the 1950s, but larger profits and greater international exposure – in
no small part because of recently launched satellite downlinks – enabled
Raimi to reach a worldwide audience with his hit show. It ran for six
seasons until November 1999, and along the way inspired the very popular
syndicated spin-off *Xena: Warrior Princess*, which ran from 1995 to 2001,
as well as *Young Hercules*, which aired in 1998 and 1999.

The tremendous success of Hercules in television syndication revived
interest in at least one network boardroom. On May 18–19, 1997, NBC

premiered *The Odyssey*, a project produced by Francis Ford Coppola's American Zoetrope, Hallmark Entertainment, and several other companies. This 176-minute, two-part version of Homer's *Odyssey* (with Armand Assante in the title role) was co-written and directed by the successful Russian film and theater artist Andrei Konchalovsky. *The Odyssey* was not particularly well received by critics, nor was it a ratings success, but it has found some favor today among consumers.[34] In addition, in that it was contemporaneous with Raimi's series and the most current Disney animated feature-film release, *Hercules* (1997), *The Odyssey* helped blaze the path for the subsequent renascence of the ancient made-for-television film and miniseries that would eventually inspire *Rome*.

Only two years later Hallmark Entertainment again, along with the once legendary Babelsberg International Film Produktion, produced a new version of *Cleopatra*. Following such memorable screen Cleopatras as Helen Gardner (1912), Theda Bara (1917), Claudette Colbert (1934), and Elizabeth Taylor (1963), Chilean actress Leonor Varela now starred in the fifth major American film based on the historical romances of the Egyptian queen. The $30 million budget paled in comparison, allowing for inflation, to the budget for the 1963 Fox feature version of *Cleopatra*, but it was more than adequate for the two-part, 177-minute made-for-television film, which ABC broadcast on May 23–24, 1999, during a sweeps period. The impetus behind the production was Robert Halmi, Sr., a Hungarian resistance fighter during World War II, a *Life Magazine* photographer in the 1950s, and subsequently the chairman of Hallmark Entertainment, which has become the leading supplier of such miniseries and made-for-television movies. That same year under his guidance Hallmark produced *Mary, Mother of Jesus* (with Pernilla August as Mary, and Christian Bale as Jesus), and the following year *Jason and the Argonauts*, which NBC aired on Sunday and Monday, May 7–8, 2000 – not coincidentally the same week in which DreamWorks' *Gladiator* was scheduled for theatrical release. The production was not unlike the 1963 Columbia *Jason and the Argonauts* in that Zeus (Angus MacFadyen) and Hera (Olivia Williams) observe, control, and comment on human events, and the film features a plethora of Emmy Award-nominated effects, albeit now computerized *à la Hercules: The Legendary Journeys*. Thanks in no small part to the latter, the ancient genre had once again found a home on television.

These successes were followed by another miniseries set in antiquity, the four-hour *Attila*, but unlike its predecessors this series was broadcast not on any of the traditional commercial networks but on the most widely watched basic cable channel, the USA Network, on Tuesday and

Wednesday, January 30–31, 2001.[35] Airing on USA Network meant that the film was available to the USA's 80 million viewers, and also that it could be rerun more frequently than had ever been possible on the major three commercial networks. Robert Cochrane, previously a reasonably successful television writer, wrote the screenplay for *Attila*, after which he joined in the production of the extremely popular Fox show *24* (2001–current).

Ancient miniseries began appearing at the rate of approximately one per year. The next was *Julius Caesar*, which aired first in Germany on December 27, 2002, and then in the United States on Sunday, June 29, and Monday, June 30, 2003. *Julius Caesar* featured a combination of such film and television personalities as Richard Harris (Sulla), Christopher Walken (Cato), Jeremy Sisto (Caesar), and Chris Noth (Pompey). But the storyline, scripted by the otherwise unheralded Peter Pruce and Craig Warner, created some expanded roles not only for Pompey, but also for Julia's slave, Apollonius (Christopher Ettridge), Calpurnia, Cornelia, Julia, and Cleopatra. This concentration on the condition and treatment of a slave and the importance of women reflects something of the postmodern spirit which pervades *Rome* and its fleshed-out Pompey, competent slaves, and influential patrician women. Moreover, one of the co-producers of *Julius Caesar*, the DeAngelis Group, specified in press releases that they wished to portray Caesar as a populist: "[Caesar] fights the corrupt aristocracy that dominates Roman politics. He declares that, for the Empire to have real meaning, all of its subjects – of whatever race, creed or color – should be offered Roman citizenship. His populist politics and unprecedented military victories raise Caesar to Roman Emperor."[36] The production of this innovative version of the Julius Caesar saga was shared by several American and European companies, most notably the German Degeto Film, hence its early airing in Germany, and Five Mile River Films, which has specialized in producing over a half-dozen Biblical made-for-television films since *Abraham* (1994), *Joseph* (1995), and *Samson and Delilah* (1996). All of their films were aired on Turner Broadcasting's TNT network, another popular basic cable station, and Turner was a co-producer and original broadcaster of *Julius Caesar* as well.

The following spring USA Network returned to the genre by airing its *Helen of Troy* on April 20, 2003, a full year before the American premiere of the feature-film *Troy*. The original script, which includes some inventive un-Homeric moments, was written by Ronni Kern, whose credits also include Showtime Networks' version of *Solomon and Sheba* (1995). Branching out even further on basic cable was the horror film *Cerberus*, which Cinetel Films, Inc. produced for the Sci-Fi Channel, aired first on October 29, 2005 as part of some aggressive Halloween programming.

This considerable if belated popularity of the ancient world on television was meanwhile extending out as well to such basic cable channels as Arts & Entertainment, the History Channel, and the Learning Channel. They had begun to produce and/or air a number of documentaries on such widely recognizable ancient historical personages as Julius Caesar, Cleopatra, Helen of Troy, and Alexander the Great. Meanwhile, almost all of this recent material from the late 1990s and early 2000s – the made-for-television films, the miniseries, and the documentaries – was soon made available for the home market. *Cleopatra* was released on DVD two years after airing, in October 2001, and *Julius Caesar* a little less than a year after its airing on TNT, in October 2004. The DVD release of *Jason and the Argonauts*, however, followed its original May 2000 airing closely on August 15, 2000, and then on January 1, 2002 it was bundled into a boxed DVD set with *The Odyssey* and other Hallmark made-for-television films. In fact, home market sales (now mostly in DVD format, even more profitable than the VHS format) so helped to make made-for-television antiquity a booming business that a European consortium including EOS Entertainment of Germany and Lux Vide of Italy began producing a series of six direct-to-video films on the Roman emperors. The first two releases were *Imperium: Augustus* (November 30, 2003) and *Imperium: Nero* (September 6, 2005), although the latter seems to have been telecast in Europe.[37]

During this same period bridging the late 1990s and early 2000s, HBO, the leading American premium cable network, was simultaneously developing ground-breaking original programming. One of its stimuli was the need to attract new monthly subscribers (and to entice casual viewers to more regular viewing), but an additional stimulus was the profitability of DVD sales, which, depending on the number of seasons included, can generate $15–30 per disk, and sales often number in the millions for the most popular television series releases.[38] Following the success of such comedies as *Sex and the City* (1998–2004) and *Curb Your Enthusiasm* (2000–current) and of such dramas as *The Sopranos* (1999–2007) and *Six Feet Under* (2001–2005), among many others, HBO set to work on *Rome*. Much like most of the television series set in antiquity produced over the past seven years and, for that matter, those of the 1970s and 1980s, *Rome* is an international co-production with the BBC and RAI. Unlike most of its predecessors except *I, Claudius*, however, it was designed not as a miniseries to be aired in a cluster of evenings, but as a regular series to be aired on a specific night (Sunday) over consecutive weeks.

After decades of experimentation, development, successes, and failures, television is now once again providing a select but sizable segment of television viewers with a weekly series of made-for-television antiquity. While

the innovations of *Rome* will be made clear in the following essays, the huge
budget, the multi-layered narrative, the enormous cast of characters, the
sexual titillations and contrasting extremes of morality, the densely packed
and constantly varied screen visuals, and the segmented broadcasts as well
as the pre-broadcasting and post-broadcasting promos, trailers, and teases
all have their precedents in the earlier examples of the genre – minus the
Hollywood cameos.

NOTES

1   The first public demonstration of synchronized pictures and sounds transmit-
    ted by the Charles Jenkins television system in 1925 was actually of a film of
    a model windmill. Nonetheless, 1928 audiences in Massachusetts and New
    York saw variously a tennis match, Al Smith's acceptance speech at the Demo-
    cratic Convention, and *The Queen's Messenger*, a drama, all live. See Jeff
    Miller, "A US Television Chronology, 1875–1970," in *History of American
    Broadcasting*, online (members.aol.com/jeff560/chronotv.html).
2   Lang and Lang (2002), 59–96.
3   For the chronology, see Wheen (1985).
4   An early attempt at showing a film on television was W2XBS's infamous
    May 31, 1938 broadcast of *The Return of the Scarlet Pimpernel* (1937), which
    terminated twenty minutes early after the projectionist played the final reel
    prematurely.
5   Williams (1990), 58–62.
6   See Barnouw (1970), 61–63. As a result of 1948's "Paramount Case" (*United
    States* v. *Paramount Pictures, Inc.*), Goldenson had been forced to divest the
    Paramount theater chain, of which he was head, from Paramount Studios.
    Banned from Hollywood, he achieved success at ABC.
7   Disney charged $50,000 per episode, which included capital for building
    Disneyland; see Goldenson (1991), 121–125.
8   Similarly, Paddy Chayefsky's *Marty* (1953) and Rod Serling's *Requiem for a
    Heavyweight* (1957) were adapted from their original television format for
    theatrical release, as would be in decades hence *Moses, the Lawgiver* (1974)
    and *Jesus of Nazareth* (1977).
9   Segrave (1999), 13–15, 21–43.
10 Cook (2000), 409–410.
11 In 1959 the timeslot was moved up to attract younger viewers. Thereafter as
    annual events, broadcasts of *The Wizard of Oz* earned five of the top nine
    all-time ratings until 1971.
12 The year 1961 was the first that brought a profit of more than $1 million to
    RCA for its color televisions. *How to Marry a Millionaire* was produced before

The Robe (1953), also filmed in CinemaScope, but *The Robe* was released first.

13　Segrave (1999), 82. *Ben-Hur* trailed *The Bridge Over the River Kwai* (1957) and *The Birds* (1963), broadcast in 1966 and 1968, respectively.

14　In addition, *The Assassination of Julius Caesar* was repeated as episode #104 on May 29, 1955.

15　Christopher Plummer starred in *Oedipus the King*, as he would in the 1967 feature film directed by Philip Saville.

16　Goldberg (1990), #364: *Centurian* [*sic*]; #76: *The Ten Commandments*, inspired by DeMille's film of the same year (1956), was set in modern times; its pilot, written by Ben Hecht (*Ulysses*, 1955), aired on NBC on February 8, 1959.

17　Excluded from this discussion is the Trans-Lux cartoon series, *The Mighty Hercules*, broadcast first on Saturday mornings in 1963. Note that the Petrie living room used for the first several seasons (1961–1963) of CBS's *The Dick Van Dyke Show* displayed a copy of a segment of the Parthenon frieze above the couch.

18　For a detailed survey of television scheduling and demographics during this period, see Ozersky (2003), 1–59.

19　Goldberg (1990), #750.

20　On Wolper, see Marc and Thompson (1995), 285–300.

21　The Wikipedia article on "Miniseries," for instance, identifies *The Rise and Fall of the Third Reich* as the first miniseries. This has helped spread the misidentification to a variety of online resources. In contrast, Umphlett (2006), 140, describes *The Rise and Fall of the Third Reich* as a documentary.

22　For a detailed description of this period, see Witherspoon and Kovitz (1987), 67–72.

23　Despite the reluctance of the Nixon administration to fund the service, the US Congress funded the Corporation for Public Broadcasting; see Sterling and Kittross (2002), 425–427.

24　For a historical critique of *Masterpiece Theater*, see Ouellette (2002), 155–163.

25　Brown (1977). According to Hal Himmelstein (*The Museum of Broadcast Communications*, online, www.museum.tv), WGBH made a number of cuts to edit out nudity and sexual activity.

26　O'Connor (1977), 74.

27　See Levinson and Link (1986), 137–138.

28　See Papazian (1991), 91–94.

29　Wheen (1985), 152.

30　"Late-Blooming *Jesus* May Become A Perennial," *Variety* (April 6, 1977).

31　BFI *screenonline* (www.screenonline.org.uk). Subsequently the film was expanded to eight hours shown over four nights; see Marill (2005), 1, 115.

32   See Ostling (1977). Procter & Gamble assumed sponsorship, carefully provid-
     ing a video border before each commercial break. Pope Paul VI ultimately
     gave the film his imprimatur.
33   On this scene, see Winkler (2007), 6–8.
34   See O'Connor (1997).
35   On cable's adoption of event-status programming in the 1990s, see Caldwell
     (1995), 160–164.
36   From the synopsis at www.deangelisgroup.com/film/julius_caesar. The same
     sentiment can be found in such contemporary scholarship as Canfora (2007),
     340–341.
37   According to IMDb, *Imperium: Nerone* aired in Italy on May 23, 2004.
38   During the Christmas season in 2004, for instance, consumers purchased
     some four million copies of the first three seasons of *Seinfeld*.

2

Making History in *Rome*: Ancient vs. Modern Perspectives

W. Jeffrey Tatum

The HBO-BBC series *Rome* wins over its viewers not least through its cunning combination of fantasy and truth. Episodes of striking violence or graphic sexuality are depicted in historical settings remarkable for their accuracy in various and numerous details, the totality of which lends every moment a high degree of plausibility – even believability. It can only be difficult for a viewer unfamiliar with the events of the late first century BC to discriminate reality from fiction. And the series' writers know where best to exercise their imaginations. Consider Atia, a pivotal and robustly delineated character who is never far from the center of the plot in all its multiple strands. Of the historical Atia we know very little, a vacancy the screenwriters were able to annex for their own dramatic purposes and with obvious success. Invention shrewdly and gratifyingly situated in an exciting yet genuinely historical framework – that is one of the keys to the captivating quality of the series *Rome*. These were also the ingredients of ancient historical composition in Rome, a society that relished its past and demanded its representation in truthful but also stimulating manifestations. Roman authors of history, as we shall see, although they could never ignore the facts of the past, were nevertheless encouraged to elaborate it – to tart it up – in exciting and even sensational style, if they hoped to find readers in anything like an adequate supply.

The Romans made history – in more than one sense of the expression. The reality of Rome's lengthy domination of the ancient Mediterranean, like her formative influence on subsequent European societies, is a topic far too familiar to require rehearsal here. What may be less familiar to readers outside the circle of classicists, however, are the resourceful methods the Romans used to recover or invent their past. Some of these techniques are by no means alien to the sensibilities of modern historians but, in their actual practice, are sometimes remarkably similar to the creative operations we associate with historical fiction or historical drama.

European historiography begins with the Greeks, with Herodotus, who described the wars between the Greeks and the Persians, and Thucydides, who dealt with the Peloponnesian War. War and politics, the natural arenas for glory in both ancient Greek and Roman societies, remained the central concerns of Greek historians, for whom history served as a sort of prose epic based in the reality of the past but indebted in its presentation to its Homeric antecedents. Any reader of Herodotus will recollect how many amazing tales he includes, how many aetiologies, how many geographical excursus, and how many fabulous stories he borrows from mythology – however distilled by the reagent of rationalism – stories often redolent of private intrigue and sexual adventurism. Not that he believed in all that he reported: he simply believed that what he recorded was worth preserving because of the pleasure it gave his reader. Thucydides claimed to be less interested in entertaining his reader, offering instead an exact account of men's actions and motivations, each always presented as fact instead of surmise. Nonetheless, his work is replete with dramatic representations and challenging orations, the very kind of literary effects that made it a lasting classic. The historians Herodotus and Thucydides were active in the fifth century BC. The Romans did not take up historical composition until the third century BC, by which time the genre of historiography was well established throughout the Greek world.[1]

For the Greeks and, once they came to it, for the Romans, history properly composed ought to do three things. It must inform, edify – and gratify. It was by reading history that one learned the truth about the past. As Cicero put it, and his view is representative: "To be ignorant of what took place before you were born is always to remain a child. For where is the meaning of one's own life unless it is woven into the lives of our ancestors through the records of the past?" (*The Orator* 120).[2] History becomes nothing less than "the witness of past times, the light of truth, the vital force of memory, the guide to life" (*On Oratory*

2.36). By way of examples, wholesome or otherwise, and through its predilection for explicit moralizing and exhortation, history was designed to make its reader a better person. It was a true guide to life. On these principles there was universal agreement. More controversial, however, was the element of pleasure. That history must please was all well and fine, but by what means and at what levels? A record of the past distinguished only by preciseness or by its moral elevation may have been sufficient to gratify some readers, but, so far as we can tell, not many of them. They insisted on much more: a narrative that won them over both by way of entertaining content and by way of a stimulating literary style. This is why ancient historiography remained a category of literature. The success of any work was as much determined by its narrative technique – the focus of most appraisals – as by its scientific merits. It is in composing his narrative that the Roman historian made history.

How far a historian ought to go in order to render his narrative pleasurable was controversial among Greek historians working in the third and second centuries BC, the period in which the Romans took up historical composition. Duris of Samos, who in the early third century BC combined the occupations of tyrant and historian, criticized his most distinguished fourth-century predecessors for neglecting the element of pleasure in historical writing:

> Ephorus and Theopompus fell far short of the events [they reported in their histories] because their narratives lacked naturalism and pleasure. Instead, they cultivated an artificial style of writing.[3]

Not enough of Duris survives for us to learn how he believed pleasure was achieved in the recording of history. Was it by way of a plausible and realistic – and full – description of engaging events? How important were the emotions of human experience, as history's central characters were confronted with crisis and reversal as well as achievement and victory?

The extent of this controversy, and its relevance to Roman historiography, emerges into view when Polybius, a Greek historian of Rome's conquest of the Mediterranean writing in the second century BC, attacks the work of Phylarchus, a third-century BC predecessor (Polybius, *Histories* 2.56). Polybius is explaining why he rejects Phylarchus as a source. In part, Polybius claims, this is owing to Phylarchus' carelessness. His principal deficiency, however, is his excessive commitment to pleasing his readers through sensational and, to a large degree, fabricated narrative. For instance, in describing the misfortunes of the city of Mantinea at the hands of the Macedonians, Phylarchus endeavors:

> to provoke the pity and compassion of his readers by means of graphic depictions of women clinging to one another, their hair disheveled and their breasts bared, or again crowds of men and women, along with their children and elderly parents, weeping and lamenting as they are dragged away to slavery.[4]

According to Polybius, this was typical of Phylarchus, who was "always trying to put horrors before his readers' eyes" (Polybius, *Histories* 2.56.7). This is an approach to history that the sober and reliable Polybius rejects outright. In his view, it was not the job of the historian to thrill his reader by resorting to sensationalism.

Phylarchus did not have at his disposal an accurate account even of the horrors he described. Instead, he relied on his intuition to tell him what was probable or at least plausible in such circumstances, largely because his purpose in describing the miserable fate of Mantinea was to indict the conduct of the Macedonians. To put it differently, he made stuff up. By contrast, a proper historian "should simply report what actually happened and what actually was said, however ordinary this happened to be" (Polybius, *Histories* 2.56.10). In Polybius' estimation, "it is the responsibility of the historian to teach and to persuade serious students by means of the truth of the actions and the speeches he narrates" (Polybius, *Histories* 2.56.10). Polybius' brand of historian eschews fabulous stories and contrived narrative strategies,[5] or anything that is untrue or unnecessary to the reader's comprehension of the facts and the causal relationships that give genuine meaning to historical events.[6] Polybius, then, was obsessed with historical truth more or less in our sense of the term. From his perspective, Phylarchus and his ilk were content to gratify their readers by offering them something not unlike the truth but so amplified and sexed up that it can, in contemporary terms, only be described as *truthiness*.[7]

It would hardly have been necessary for Polybius to make such a strong case against Phylarchus if his own standards for historical composition had been the prevailing ones. It appears, however, that *truthiness* enjoyed a comfortable edge over truth and that serious students constituted a distinct minority amongst the readers of history in antiquity. The majority wanted vivid and exciting narrative, stretched out with geographical or mythological or aetiological digressions. And they wanted speeches, orations in direct speech that were patently the work of the historian and not a transcript of what was actually said at the (past) moment. Now some historians endeavored to include speeches in their accounts only where they knew a speech had been delivered. Some went even further and attempted to recreate the basic sentiments of the original speech. That this was Polybius' practice will be clear from the citations in the previous paragraph. It will be just as clear, from his attack on Phylarchus, that for too many historians this attempt at "accuracy" was an irrelevant expectation. The sensational theatricality of historians like Phylarchus could come to a peak in a patch of direct oratory, at which moment in the narrative historical characters could come to life, as it were, and perform for the reader like actors in a drama.

The Romans were not immune to the attractions of sensational historiography. This is not to say that they were keen to jettison the truth – even the likes of Phylarchus did not believe that they were violating the truth of the past, but instead were convinced that they were elaborating it by means of an engaging and stimulating presentation. Still, historical amplification for the purpose of creating pleasing effects distinguished a Roman historian, as did a fluent and sophisticated literary style. In the late first century BC, when Romans like Cicero looked back on the Latin historiographical tradition, these were the criteria they stressed in their assessments. Now, Cicero was a serious student of the past and an unsurpassed intellectual. Nevertheless, the Roman historians whom he singles out for praise are his contemporary, Lucius Cornelius Sisenna, and the second-century BC historian Lucius Coelius Antipater. Sisenna's literary model was the Greek historian of Alexander the Great, Cleitarchus,[8] who was notoriously unreliable but extraordinarily popular owing to his proclivity for depicting striking scenes of violence and suffering. The surviving bits of Sisenna are evidence of a vivid and fetching style employed in the representation of affecting speeches, diverting digressions, omens, and even dreams. Of Coelius Cicero was fonder still. Rome's earliest chroniclers, Cicero complains, failed to elaborate their material, instead limiting themselves to excessively concise narration, all of which was pretty lifeless and dull.[9] Coelius, however, who wrote about the Second Punic War, employed a range of sources – Roman, Greek, and Carthaginian – in order to construct a narrative conspicuous for its sensationalism, including orations, digressions, dreams, and prodigies, all offered to the reader in a somewhat extravagant style. On the last point, Cicero observes,

Coelius could have done better. Nonetheless, he showed his countrymen the way to write proper history. That these are the opinions of no less a figure than Cicero, whose commitment to historical accuracy is observable in many contexts (including the composition of his own literary dialogues), can only be revealing about the Romans' notions of history and historiography. A century later the politician and philosopher Seneca could complain that too many histories were little more than entertainment.[10]

Let us consider an example of the Roman historian, or in this instance, two Roman historians, at work. Rome was sacked by invading Gauls around 390 BC and the early fourth century recorded frequent conflicts with Gallic intruders onto the Italian scene, including several duels between the inevitably heroic Romans and the gigantic Gauls (who did in fact tend to be physically larger than the Romans). The most famous such battle was fought by the youthful Titus Manlius, destined for multiple consulships and eternal fame, in 361 BC. Having slain his enemy, Manlius claimed as his prize the torque which the Gaul wore about his neck, and for this reason he received the honorific nickname Torquatus, which he bequeathed to his descendants. The tale itself is of dubious historicity, but it retains credibility even amongst some modern researchers. When the Romans turned to the writing of history, what will they have known of this episode? The fact of Manlius' deed was unquestionably famous enough to be familiar to them – the Manlii Torquati remained a living presence in Rome – and it will have been preserved in family history[11] and rehearsed over the generations at the family's public funerals. Still, Rome's first historians can have had little more than that at their disposal when it became their job to recover this element of their past. Yet a concise and bald report of the event, no more than a single sentence, remained a far from satisfactory specimen of history: in order for the episode to deliver pleasure along with instruction and edification, it had to be worked up into a fitting narrative.

We have frequent references to this episode in the ancient historical writers. Two versions are illustrative of Roman practice, the first one composed by Quintus Claudius Quadrigarius, a historian working early in the first century BC (as quoted by Latin grammarian Aulus Gellius in the second century AD), and the second by Livy (59 BC–AD 17), writing about fifty years later, and for whom Quadrigarius was his principal source for this story. This means that we can put their accounts side by side:

Then a Gaul advanced, naked apart from his shield and two swords, adorned by a torque and by bracelets. He excelled the rest in might and mien as well as youthful vigor and courage. . . . He called out loudly that if anyone wished to do battle with him, he should advance. No one dared to do this on account of his stature and fierce appearance. Then the Gaul began to laugh at them and to stick out his tongue. Instantly Titus Manlius, who was of aristocratic birth, was offended that such an insult should be cast at his country and that from so great an army no one should advance. He, as I say, advanced and would not suffer Roman virtue to be disgraced by a Gaul. Armed with a foot-soldier's shield and a Spanish sword he confronted the Gaul. [*They fight on a bridge.*] Manlius, relying on his spirit more than on his skill, struck shield against shield and knocked the Gaul off balance. [*The fight continues, during which Manlius stabs the Gaul and knocks him to the ground.*] He cut off his head, he tore off the torque and he placed it, covered with blood, on his own neck.

(Aulus Gellius, Attic Nights *9.13.7–19)*

Then a Gaul of enormous size advanced . . . and in as loud a voice as possible cried, "Let him whom Rome regards as her bravest man advance and fight, that the outcome of our combat may reveal which of our nations is best in war." For a long time the young aristocrats were silent: they were ashamed to decline the contest but nor were they willing to volunteer for so extreme a peril. Then Titus Manlius, the son of Lucius . . . left his station and went before his commander. "Without your permission, General," he said, "I would never leave my assigned post, not even if I knew that I could deliver a sure victory. If you allow me, I desire to show that creature dancing so fiercely before the standards of our enemy that I am born of the family that cast a column of Gauls from the Tarpeian Rock." The commander answered: "Success attend your courage, Titus Manlius, and your faithfulness to your father and your fatherland." His friends armed the young man. He took up the shield of a foot-soldier, buckled on a Spanish sword useful for close fighting. So armed and adorned, they led him before the Gaul, who was stupidly delighted and who – for it seemed best to the ancients to record this – stuck out his tongue in derision. [*They fight. The Gaul is huge whereas*] the other was of average size for a soldier. . . . He did not sing, nor did he dance about flourishing his weapons uselessly. Instead his heart was filled with courage and silent anger. He concentrated all his ferocity into winning the contest. [*Their combat is described at technical length: it is mostly a matter of swordplay. The Gaul is stabbed and collapses.*] The fallen body was left intact, suffering no other despoliation than the removal of a single torque, which, spattered with blood, Manlius placed around his own neck.

(Livy, History of Rome *7.9.8–10.12)*

Now it is not impossible for a modern historian wanting to recover this event to elect to provide a narrative account. But his version would be punctuated by qualifying expressions making clear the speculative nature of his retelling. He might inform his reader that we can be reasonably certain Manlius was dwarfed by his opponent owing to our knowledge of the physicality of the two groups. He might point out that it was the practice of Roman soldiers never to remove themselves from their station without permission from a commanding officer and on that basis suggest one way to fill in the gap between the Gaul's challenge and Manlius' combat. In this instance he might go on to remind his reader that this same Manlius, when consul in 340 BC, put his own son to death when the latter left the ranks without permission in order to repeat his father's achievement in a victorious single combat – a fact that might allow us to surmise a high degree of (grim) scrupulosity on Manlius' part here. And, finally, he might consider the likelihood that, in displaying his aggression, the Gaul stuck out his tongue: the image was known to the Romans from European shields.[12] All of this research and reconstruction, however, is more likely to come, in a modern account, in a shape something like the one given it here and not as separate narrative elements in a story. The modern historian is obliged to distinguish indubitable fact from plausible reconstruction. As one can see instantly from the parallel accounts above, ancient writers, relying entirely on the effect of their narrative, are disinclined to lessen its effect by drawing attention to its provisional quality. Quadrigarius and Livy alike put forward their versions as fully factual, including, in the case of Livy, a report of the actual words used on that day by Manlius and by his commander.

It is worth noticing how extensively Livy has transformed the narration of Quadrigarius. Livy's version is longer and far more detailed. It incorporates good Roman military practice and, in his rendering of the combat itself, Livy strives to replicate the techniques taught to the legions of his own day, and in that sense at least is somewhat more realistic than Quadrigarius' account. Livy is clearly more comfortable than his predecessor in divining the internal reactions of the participants: his young Romans feel shame as well as terror in response to the Gaul's challenge. Livy has also reduced Quadrigarius' Gaul, whose courage in that version is matched by his martial technique, into a Goliath-like fool, who never really stood a chance against Manlius' superior talent and Roman discipline. In this way, their contest really does reflect, as the Gaul claims at the beginning of the tale, the national character of the two races – at least from the Roman perspective. In Quadrigarius, Manlius' natural (aristocratic) capacity makes him a winner – and he is not too shy or delicate to decapitate his enemy or to don as a trophy a torque dripping with blood. Livy's Manlius, by contrast, is conspicuously moderate in victory. The two versions of the tale, then, are radically different – in style and in content. Livy's divergence from Quadrigarius will owe itself not to independent research into the demeanor or the personality of Manlius, but instead to his different vision of the nature of genuine Roman heroism.

In the preface to his great history, Livy observes that there are two justifications for composing history: either one has better evidence and can provide a more authentic account than one's predecessors, or one can simply tell the story better. Livy's revision of Quadrigarius does not pretend to adduce new data. Instead, it invents new particulars in order to lend a new significance to an ancient event. It is obvious that Livy regarded certain features of Quadrigarius' account as immutable facts: the challenge, Manlius' response, the nature of his armor, the winning of the torque, and Manlius' appellation as Torquatus – and the reality of the Gaul's sticking out his tongue, a specific that Livy feels compelled to record although he plainly finds the detail undignified. Around these data, however, as we have seen, Livy crafts an episode very different from Quadrigarius' version – and for some it will have been more entertaining, owing to its greater stylistic complexity, its vivid effect, and its more realistic combat. Livy's explicit moralizing, almost operatic in its prominence, also suited Roman tastes – as did his nationalist chauvinism. Livy, and presumably his readers, knew what was essential to this episode and what degree of coloring constituted a legitimate expression of the historian's talent and point of view. But this ancient habit of confounding genuine historical material with speculative reconstruction as well as with entertaining particulars can be perplexing for modern students of ancient historiography and, one suspects, often led to confusion among the Romans themselves, especially in matters dealing with their earliest history.

Matters were naturally improved in better-documented periods when there were competing accounts, which were themselves based on eyewitness testimony. Controversy could pursue an author who untethered himself from an accurate account of recent events. For instance, the historian Asinius Pollio, a loyal follower of Julius Caesar, was not too shy, when composing his own account of the period recorded in Caesar's own writings, to insist that Caesar's commentaries were composed carelessly and with a somewhat dim allegiance to the truth.[13] Still, even in the matter of contemporary Roman history, the imperative to dazzle and delight the reader did not fade.

Here Cicero provides the best example. His personal standards of historical truthfulness were high. Unlike poetry, Cicero insisted, history requires truth.[14] "Who does not know," he writes elsewhere, "that the first law of history is never to dare to record any falsehood, or that the second law of history is never to fail to record anything true" (*On Oratory* 2.62). Yet when it came to telling the story of his own career – his brilliant consulship in 63 BC when he uncovered and suppressed the conspiracy of Catiline aimed at overthrowing the government of Rome, after which, in reprisal for the extreme and illegal means to which he stretched in order to stop the Catilinarians, he was driven into exile only to return to Rome in triumph – Cicero was all too willing go for effect even at the expense of strict accuracy. In a letter he wrote to the Senator and historian Lucius Lucceius, who Cicero hoped would compose a monograph on his consulship and its aftermath, he appeals to Lucceius by emphasizing the sheer pleasure his story will give to Lucceius' readers: if properly written up, Cicero's varying fortunes – his successes, his undeserved sufferings, the ultimate and just happy ending – will prove both exciting and delectating (*Letters to Friends* 5.12.4). Cicero will provide the necessary data (5.12.10), Lucceius the stylistic elaboration. The total effect will be best, Cicero states baldly, if Lucceius will lay aside the laws of history in his case (5.12.3). What Cicero desired seems much closer to a modern and flattering docudrama than what we should call a genuine historical account of his career. Lucceius, it should be observed, said no. Perhaps the laws of history meant more to him than, in this instance, they did to Cicero. In any case, one can see in the example of Cicero the recurring tension between the normative expectations of the best brand of historiography and the Romans' routine habits of historical composition and consumption.

Cicero's hoped-for monograph never appeared. However, his contemporary, the historian Sallust, did compose an account of Catiline's conspiracy, one in which Cicero played a less than central role. Sallust's telling of the story concentrated instead on the moral failure of the late Roman Republic, a collapse embodied by the depraved patrician Catiline, his decadent allies, and their reckless and desperate resolve to seize power. Moralizing on this order frequently shunts aside actual events and eliminates anything like an economic or social explanation for the political perturbations that resulted in Catiline's conspiracy. This becomes most clear in Sallust's treatment of the year that elapsed between Catiline's failure in the elections in 64 BC and his repeated failure in 63 BC, the centerpiece of which is his portrayal of Sempronia, a woman of noble rank who was loosely associated with the conspiracy. The exact identity of this woman remains unclear to us and in any case Sallust provides few specifics. Nevertheless, this virtual cipher is depicted as the female counterpart to Catiline himself: she is well born and talented but so perverted that she is, by Roman standards, totally repugnant:

> In birth and in beauty, in her husband also and children, she was abundantly favored by fortune. She was well read in Greek and Latin literature. She was able to play the lyre and to dance – but more skillfully than is appropriate for a respectable woman. And she had many other accomplishments that minister to lasciviousness. There was nothing she held so cheap as her modesty and chastity. You could not easily tell whether she was less sparing of her money or her reputation. Her desires were so ardent that she approached men more often than she was approached by them. Even before the conspiracy she had frequently broken her word, repudiated her debts, and been privy to murder. . . . Nevertheless, she was a woman of no mean endowments: she could write poetry, tell a joke, and use language that was modest or tender or wanton as the situation required it. In sum, she possessed a high degree of wit and charm.[15]

Now in Sallust's account of the conspiracy, and so far as we know from other sources, Sempronia played no real part in the action. But she fills up a good deal of space in Sallust's account because, harridan and harlot that she is made out to be, she simultaneously registers the author's horror at the depths to which the Roman aristocracy had sunk, stimulates the reader's disgust (not least by effeminizing the conspiracy and its participants), and, finally, charges the text with an irresistible and sexy electricity. Atia plays a similar function in the series *Rome*.

It will by now be clear how extensively the methods and expectations of ancient writers of history diverge from their modern descendants. This is not to say that modern historians do not exercise their historical imaginations in their attempts to understand past events and to suggest how best to fill in the gaps in their record. And it must be admitted that in certain instances, contemporary historians have embraced techniques of exposition that seem more at home in antiquity than in modern scholarly (or even journalistic) exposition. In 1999 Edmund Morris, a Pulitzer Prize-winning author, published his biographical study of Ronald Reagan, *Dutch: A Memoir of Ronald Reagan*, in which the American President's life is recalled by a fictionalized narrator (not the only fictional character in the book) whose various personal encounters with Reagan are entirely untrue. Morris' blending of truth and fiction is generally regarded as well written, but it cannot be avoided that the fabricated elements of the work remain undistinguished from the authentic ones. In an interview with Terrence Smith, Morris described his account of Reagan as a "movie" and insisted that "the story I tell is true and good; I know that my intentions as a biographer are honorable."[16] Morris, it is patent, would have been quite at home in the company of his ancient predecessors.

No one should leave this chapter believing that the ancient record is fiction, even if bits of it were undoubtedly sensationalized by discursive strategies that are not unlike the techniques employed in contemporary docudramas or historical filmmaking. Standards of accuracy varied, and it remains the responsibility of modern students of the past to disentangle invention from reality in the ancient record. Still, in all cases, ancient historians (much like Edmund Morris) believed their intentions were honorable and each of them recognized the importance of truthfulness, however various their grasps of the concept. While ancient writers and modern screenwriters may differ in the truth-claims of their compositions, in their striving after gripping and entertaining effects, they often fall very close to one another. It was not enough in antiquity simply to record the facts of the past: the Romans sought to make their history at once grand and gratifying. In a similar way, and no doubt with an identical purpose, the creators of the series *Rome* offer an impressive, and impressively authentic, retelling of Roman history.

NOTES

1   Ancient historiography remains a controversial subject. Recent and important contributions (from varying perspectives) include: Fornara (1983), Woodman (1988), Brunt (1993), Wiseman (1993), Kraus and Woodman (1997), Mellor (1999), Bosworth (2003), and Marincola (2003). A comprehensive treatment of ancient historiography is provided by Marincola (2007).
2   All translations of ancient texts in this chapter are my own.
3   *Fragmente der griechischen Historiker* 76, F1.
4   Polybius, *Histories* 2.56.7.
5   Polybius, *Histories* 2.16.13; 3.47.6; 3.48.8; 15.36.1.
6   Polybius, *Histories* 2.56.3.
7   The term was coined by television personality Stephen Colbert on the premiere of his show, *The Colbert Report*, on October 17, 2005.
8   Cicero, *Brutus* 228.
9   Cicero, *On Oratory* 2.54; see also *On Law* 1.6.
10   Seneca, *Natural Questions* 7.16.1.
11   A notoriously unreliable source: see Cicero, *Brutus* 62.

12   See Cicero, *On Oratory* 2.266; Pliny, *Natural History* 35.25.

13   Suetonius, *Life of Julius Caesar* 56.4.

14   Cicero, *On Law* 1.5.

15   Sallust, *The Catilinarian War* 25.

16   *PBS Online NewsHour*, "Reading Reagan," October 4, 1999 (www.pbs.org/ newshour).

3

What I Learned as an Historical Consultant for *Rome*

Kristina Milnor

Truth be told, I was never an historical consultant for HBO-BBC's *Rome*. Certainly, during the fall and winter of 2003–2004, I met a number of times with various people involved in the production: first with the then co-executive producer Stan Wlodkowski, subsequently with (among others) writer and executive producer Bruno Heller, executive director Anne Thomopoulos, and director Michael Apted. At these meetings, we had wide-ranging conversations about the production and its relationship to the "reality" of ancient Roman life. I received copies of the scripts for the first two episodes and gave my opinion on their historicity; I toured the production facilities, including set, costume shop, and prop rooms; I even had the opportunity to witness some early filming, although by then my relationship to the show had become simply that of spectator to spectacle, and I was emphatically not asked for my opinion on what I saw. As I will note below, there are a few significant differences between the preliminary scripts as I received them and the episodes which were finally aired, differences which do correspond to some concerns that I raised at the meetings mentioned above. But whether the changes were the result of my comments, altered requirements of the production, or the influence of the BBC-endorsed and paid-for historical consultant Jonathan Stamp – brought on after my departure – I cannot say. What I can say is that my name does not appear anywhere in the credits for the show, that, after Mr. Stamp's arrival, the producers abruptly terminated contact with me, and that – most critically, since after all this is the language which the entertainment industry speaks – I never received a dime in payment for the work which I put into the production.

Not that I'm bitter. In all honesty, when in the fall of 2003 I received the call from Cinecittà asking me to come out to the set of *Rome* for an interview, I wasn't terribly interested in the job. I was in Italy for an entirely different purpose: to be a fellow at the American Academy and to do the research for my second book, on Pompeian graffiti, which project I thought would be critical to my bid for tenure. I didn't have a lot of time to spare for HBO or the BBC. More to the point, I don't especially like movies, and although I have highly elaborated addictions to certain television programs, I watch them to be entertained pure and simple. I don't – or, I suppose I should say, didn't – much care how they get made; my interest in them was utilitarian, and my knowledge of the vast industry which lies behind their creation was rudimentary at best. In hindsight, I realize that this puts me much on the level of the entertainment professionals whom I would subsequently meet at Cinecittà. That is, *they* didn't know or care much about *my* industry – what we might call "the history biz" – either, and my generally utilitarian sense of what their products did for me was reflected in their purely utilitarian sense of what my products should do for them. Of their tools, traditions, tricks, and trade I knew nothing; in my arrogance I honestly didn't realize the extent to which the reverse would also be true.

Given this, it is ironically appropriate that our first conversation was about language. They had contacted me, they said, because they were looking for someone who spoke Ubuan.[1] "Ubuan?" I asked. "Yes," replied the assistant to the executive producers. "The first part of the series takes place in Gaul and we're looking for someone to translate the lines which the natives speak." "Ah," I said. "So . . . Ubuan would be the language they spoke in ancient Gaul." A pause. "Well, yes." "Ah. And this was a written language, was it?" Another pause. "We don't need anything written. Just some translations for speaking." "Ah. Well, but, the thing is, I'm not sure that we know much Ubuan." (Those of you who are academics can probably recognize the scholarly "we," which I admit is often the last refuge of the scoundrel. It turns out to have been fair in this case, though, since I am assured by certain linguists of my acquaintance that we have no record that "Ubuan" even existed as a language, let alone having any evidence of what it looked like.) "Oh, well, it's okay if you don't know it. But maybe you could suggest some people that we might contact?" "Well, but that's my point. I'm not sure *anybody* knows Ubuan." "Oh, OK. Well, how about a good English–Ubuan dictionary? Can you recommend one?"

I admit that, at this point, my interest had been piqued. The sheer irony of a production which, on the one hand, wished to reproduce authentically a lost ancient provincial dialect and, on the other, rather thought that there were enough English–Ubuan dictionaries in the world to be classed into "good" ones and "bad" ones – well, I was charmed. I broke the news to the producers' assistant that, unfortunately, neither love nor money would provide *Rome* with an English–Ubuan dictionary, but that, yes, certainly, I would be happy to travel out to Cinecittà to meet with Stan Wlodkowski and discuss what other services I might be able to render to the show.

That first meeting at the set was actually quite enjoyable. Stan had fallen in love with Pompeii and we spent some time discussing my research and the role which graffiti played in the ancient cityscape. He was clearly very excited about and proud of the production. He informed me that not only was this on track to be the most expensive series ever made in the history of television, but that the ancient environments which had been constructed for the production at Cinecittà – the Forum, the Subura, parts of several different villas – made this the largest working set in the world, "larger," he concluded proudly, "than the set for *Troy*." Even at the time, I remember thinking that it was peculiarly appropriate that the production for a show about Rome and the Romans should fetishize size, cost, and relative status (relative to Troy, no less).

But I was also, I admit, a little bit seduced – not just by the glamour of it all, but by the imaginative project. I have been known to compare our work as researchers into ancient culture to the experience of flying in a plane over a nighttime landscape: we see below a vast sea of black punctuated by points of light, sometimes tiny and alone, sometimes stretched out in a long line, sometimes clustered together in a large, undifferentiated mass. Our task is to imagine both what those points of light represent – a city? a road? an industrial complex? – and what lies between them, what human endeavor exists below, real and important but cloaked in darkness and thus invisible to those searching the ground from so far above. What we as scholars do, I would argue, is deeply creative – especially true of us classical scholars, as a result of, to torture the metaphor, the height at which we are flying and some unfortunate intervening weather patterns (the Middle Ages?) which further obstruct our view of the ground. In this sense, though, we ought to find in the creators of historical dramas our natural allies, since we both work with our imaginations to try to fill in the gaps in our knowledge about the ancient world.[2] Indeed, I sometimes think that the conflicts between the history biz and the entertainment industry have more to do with our similarities than our differences, like siblings close in age who squabble over a mutually desirable toy.

On the other hand, my time on the set of *Rome* revealed to me some important distinctions between "them" and "us." The first was illustrated in a subsequent meeting which I had with Stan and the other executive producers of the show. At a certain point, as I remember it, Anne Thomopoulos leaned forward and said: "Can I ask you a different sort of question? I've been wondering about it a lot and I think it's important. Did the Romans really love their children?" Now, coming as it did in the middle of a discussion focused on nitty-gritty details (sets, costumes, plot progress), this was a question striking both for its difference from what had gone before and for its originality. In truth, I think this is quite an interesting issue, and I responded that, while I thought there might be some kind of biological imperative to love children, in a society where (for instance) infant mortality was high parents might well have a different relationship to children than they do in the modern West. Anne looked at me blankly. "So . . . they really didn't love them, right? How can we show that on screen?" I think it was my turn to look blank. I responded cautiously that I wasn't sure I'd said the Romans didn't love their children, but rather that they may have understood that love to have different parameters than it does in the modern day – as might be illustrated on screen (I supposed) in the practice of infant exposure. Anne looked horrified. "Oh, no, we couldn't do that. We don't want to make them look *evil*."

Had Anne been one of my students, and this a different context, we might have had a conversation about the word "evil" and its relationship to love and family in both modern and ancient worlds. But what strikes me now, looking back on this exchange, is the way in which it revealed the boundaries of the *Rome* production's desire to embrace and represent historical difference. Notice I do not say "historical authenticity": whether the Romans engaged in infant exposure and to what degree has been the subject of a centuries-long debate among scholars,[3] and the producers of *Rome* were not the first group to find in the practice an uncomfortable limit case in discussing the morality of Roman culture. But the actual historicity of the custom was not the point; even if we had unimpeachable evidence for it, as an idea it was considered simply too bizarre, too alienating, for a modern audience to buy. The producers of *Rome* wanted Romans who were different, but not too different; unusual, but not frightening; strange, titillating, even sometimes disgusting, but not "evil."

The reasons for this are, of course, clear. Anne's objection to representing infant exposure was not that it wasn't a historical fact – that the Romans actually *were* evil – but that it would make them *look* evil to some hypothetically judgmental and family-oriented viewer. Whether she was right or not, I can't say – which is, when you get right down to it, the point. I don't know anything about that hypothetical viewer or what vision of Rome he or she is willing to accept. I don't have to worry about whether I'm making ancient peoples look evil or not. I don't have a marketing department for my Romans; I don't need one. I spend my time wondering, worrying even, about how different I can get them to be, about how far I can rid myself of my modern expectations and desires in order to embrace as fully as possible the (sometimes literally) incredible weirdness of ancient culture. In other words, the more evil the better in my book. Would I like it if more people were willing to buy, literally buy, my version of the Romans? Of course. But that is not and cannot be my primary concern, which is why, ultimately, the history biz and the entertainment industry are worlds apart. Both of us, it is true, are in the business of asking interesting questions about the ancient world. It's just that, sometimes, maybe a lot of times, *they* can't afford the interesting answers.

Now, for the record, it has been pointed out to me that I am being deeply disingenuous here. "You think we don't have customers?" a colleague recently asked me. "What do you call our students? You think we're not 'selling' them an image of Rome?" This is a fair point, although I will say that I am allergically resistant to marketplace analogies for pedagogy. But it is certainly true that I tell stories about the Romans to my classes every day, and the more bizarre and "evil" they are, the more the 18- to 22-year-olds I teach seem to like them. This is, perhaps, a happy congruence of interest, and we might say that the only thing which therefore distinguishes me from the makers of *Rome* is that my audience is smaller and more clearly defined. On the other hand, because of the power differential between me and my students, I don't have to give them what they think they want, but rather what I think they should have. This means that I can, and often do, tell them widely diverging stories about the Romans, in order to show how different pieces of evidence may be interpreted in different ways to create different visions of the ancient world. I do this because I am not teaching stories. I am teaching classical studies. Whereas for the entertainment industry, history and the process of historical investigation will always and inevitably be supporting players to drama, in my world that hierarchy is reversed: a compelling narrative may be the outcome, but it is the means of getting there with which I want my students to walk away.

This is not, let me hasten to add, a particular criticism of movies or television programs like *Rome*. They have to cut out the process and leap to the product, that is, to show history as a set of established facts rather than a series of interpretations. After all, it is quite literally the background against which their dramas progress, and for that reason must be constructed as stable and certain. But I would argue that this means that we in the history biz are appropriately wary of the products of the entertainment industry, not for snobby, "they-didn't-get-it-right" reasons, but because of our fundamental methodological differences. As I said above, we can see those differences not so much in the questions we ask but in the answers we are willing to entertain. Yet it is critical to understand that, as a history biz professional, I don't want interesting answers because of sheer perversity. I want interesting answers because I am in the business of generating more interesting questions – a product which goes on producing *ad infinitum*, far beyond me and my small needs and desires, as close to immortality as I expect I will ever get.

In this sense, I feel rather sorry for the entertainment professionals whose creativity is constrained by the tyranny of the marketplace. But lest we become too overwrought with emotion here, let me report my memory of one more exchange which I had with Bruno Heller, writer and executive producer, during the same meeting described above. We were discussing religion, which occupies an important if odd place in the Roman world constructed by the production. I had noted that there were a couple of scenes in the script for the first episode, then called "The Stolen Eagles," which worried me. Bruno immediately thought I was referring to the scene of *taurobolium*, in which Atia prays to the Magna Mater in an underground chamber as she is drenched with the blood of a bull sacrificed above her head. He leapt to his own defense. "There's ancient evidence for that," he said. "The Romans really did that." "Um, okay," I said, thinking that I was not going to get into the nature of that evidence, a late fourth-century Christian polemicist who also had a particular version of Roman paganism he wanted his audience to buy.[4] "No, actually, I meant the scenes at the beginning of the episode. You know how it shows Pompey's wedding to Julia and also her funeral? And, um, both ceremonies take place *inside a temple*?" He looked at me. "Yes?" "Well, here's the thing. Pagan temples weren't like Christian churches. You really didn't hold private ceremonies in them. Weddings were held at home, and funerals were generally a procession followed by cremation outside the city walls. I'm pretty sure bringing a dead body into a temple would have been thought to pollute it – the temple, that is, not the body." He looked at me again, for a little while. Then he smiled, with his teeth but not his eyes. "Ah," he said. "That's very interesting. But you see – we already have the temple."

After that, there wasn't much to be said, although I will note that if you watch what became Episode 01, "The Stolen Eagle," you will not see a funeral, and what appears to be the end of a wedding ceremony between Pompey and Cornelia takes place inside the former's house. As I said at the beginning, I don't know why this is true but it *could* be for the sake of historical accuracy. But before we become too impressed, let's take a moment to note that the *taurobolium* (in all of its fourth-century polemical Christian glory) made the cut – and that, if the *Rome* production had really been serious about historical accuracy, they could have brought in a consultant *before* they constructed the set. But I realized that, for them, authenticity was in the impressive details, the titillating finishing touches, like having the Gauls speak Ubuan or staging funny ceremonies underground by torchlight. They simply couldn't conceptualize the extent to which the Romans were *really* different, not extravagantly but everyday different, different in how they smelled, they way they walked, why they laughed or got angry with the children, what they said to the shopkeeper when they went in to buy a loaf of bread. These things don't make spectacular television but they are the stuff of history, and the stuff, I would argue, that can never be realized on screen. They're also the reason I got into the history biz. So, while I'm not sorry for the time I spent on the set of the HBO-BBC series, I'm also not sorry it ended when it did. I like my Rome better than theirs.

NOTES

1   Note that this was subsequently, and correctly, changed to "Ubian" in the final version of the show. Email messages I exchanged with members of the production team, however, clearly refer to "Ubuan," although to be fair one message I still have from February 18, 2004, runs "we are still looking for an Ubuan (sp?) translator . . ."

2   A point well made by Coleman (2004).

3   On which, see Harris (1994).

4   Prudentius, *Crowns of Martyrdom* 10.1006–1085. On the practice, and the problems with using Prudentius as evidence for it, see Borgeaud (1996), 156–168.

4

Rome's Opening Titles: Triumph, Spectacle, and Desire

Holly Haynes

From its earliest representations in cinema, the ideal of ancient Rome is synonymous with spectacle. If Rome is one of the grandest signifiers of the category "Empire," it does so by being a stunning visual display – usually of death and excess. Most film or television representations of ancient Rome perform this spectacle in the gladiatorial game, the orgy (or some more decorous version thereof), and the military triumph. Spectacle is intimately linked to the arousal of the viewer's desire. This seems obvious: a quick comparison of the revenues of the action film versus the foreign "art" film demonstrates that people will pay more money for something that is more visually and immediately exciting. Film and television producers have successfully sold the idea that ancient Rome was all about visual display; therefore ancient Rome has become a very valuable commodity to the entertainment media.

History as Spectacle

The visual richness and diversity of HBO-BBC's *Rome* certainly plays on the desire for spectacle. But in addition to the variety and detail of the representation of the Roman Republic's demise, another show is staged. Paradoxically, for *Rome*'s top note is the spectacle of the exotic, excessive, and unfamiliar, its underpinning is that of realism. One of the central themes in the commentary that accompanies the episodes of the first season on DVD is the realism of the program, which expresses itself as the ordinary or everyday. But this "realism" is of course itself a show, a construct that serves the larger purpose of marketing the series. *Rome* taps its audience's desire for the past not only as an exotic other, but also as something tangible, believable, and recognizable.

To win viewers, the representation of the past must be something with which viewers can identify; hence the enormous effort expended in representing details of everyday life. Indeed the myth of what constitutes ancient Rome – the fantasy that is embodied in the spectacle – only functions against the backdrop of the everyday. It is the combination of the familiar and exotic, not the exotic alone, that the series creators know we will tune in for. The producers therefore strive to simulate life in ancient Rome at the time of Julius Caesar's death, and to show that they are not simulating. Ultimately, the secret of *Rome*'s success is that it generates through the visual pleasure of the spectacle the viewers' desire for the opposite: the real or everyday. The spectacle of *Rome* draws viewers, but what creates a bond of identification with what is represented is the attention to common detail. The nature of the spectacle of *Rome*, together with the success the series enjoys, raises the question of how and why spectacle works. *Rome* engages in a paradoxical operation of showing and simultaneously hiding; evoking and at the same time obscuring from viewers the contradictory nature of their desire.

Rome's oxymoronic dynamic signals itself immediately in the program's opening titles, of which one of the main artists of A52, the creative team behind the titles, says: "There's a lot there that creatively sets the stage for the series."[1] The animated images employed in these titles are colorful and arresting: the Pompeian mosaic of a skull framed by mason's tools, through whose eye-socket the camera takes you into the world of the narrative; a man's head that explodes in a gush of cartoon red, birthing a naked female figure; a 3D Medusa head with her snakes projecting outward from the flat surface on which she is depicted. Two different visual spaces coexist in the opening titles: the cartoon is the backdrop to the "real," or live-action, in which people come and go in everyday street scenes. This combination captures the essence of the episodes proper, in which the exotic spectacle of costume and setting transports viewers into the realm of the other and different, while such plotlines as Vorenus' problems with his wife, and the careful attention to physical detail, convey the sense of the familiar and everyday.

The animated graffiti confirm a stereotypical ideal – a "cartoon" – of ancient Rome, which in the psychology of the average viewer occupies a place just about as close to myth as it does to history. Historically, Julius Caesar did suffer a bloody demise, but the blood in the opening titles comes from an exploding head – a mythological reference to the birth of Athena. "Blood" is an important signifier in the story of this period of history, but the opening titles illustrate its second-nature existence: its reification not as actual, historical blood but as the fantasy of blood. This is history recast as myth, history as the exotic other. Conversely, the live-action shows mundane *tableaux* of ordinary looking people trudging along streets that are unremarkable except for the moving graffiti along their walls, which the live-action characters of course do not see. The live-action encapsulates the aspect of the series that is familiar and identifiable to viewers: despite the fact that the costumes and details of the scenery look nothing like what most viewers wear or see, they *signify* "everyday."

Rome captures details of interior and exterior spaces, costumes, and activities that contribute as much to a construction of contemporary reality, in the sense of what is familiar or everyday, as to an ancient Roman one. Despite the detail for which it strives, the show adheres to two popular stereotypes for what constitutes "Roman": a debauched upper class who provide titillation and shock value, and a sympathetic, hard-working lower echelon who embody "values" we recognize.[2] These stereotypes are signaled in the opening titles' combination of animation and live-action. The latter signals the "real" in the guise of the everyday – the little guy with whom we can identify.[3] The animation, by contrast, represents the exotic. But the animation, too, contributes to the fantasy of the everyday, in that graffiti provides a tangible sign of ordinary people engaging in the ordinary activity of scribbling on a wall. It is an activity with which an ordinary person today can identify, and it therefore bears the stamp of the real. In a double move, the graffiti in the title sequence both provides "hard" evidence of ancient Rome and thereby gratifies our desire for the "real," and through the animation and the orientalizing music – minor-key and seductive at the same time as menacing – represents the fascinating other that arouses our desire.

Although the DVD commentary to the episodes reiterates *Rome*'s realism by referring to its historicism and accuracy, arguably the most historically accurate aspect of the whole series are the opening titles. They capture a dynamic between viewer and spectacle similar to one that was exploited by the Roman triumphal celebration, one of the grandest exhibitions of the foreign and familiar known to us from Roman history. In the triumph, there was a display of paintings depicting the Roman general's feats in battle and placards (*tituli*) naming places, events, and people. These paintings and *tituli* secured viewers' attention by playing to their desire for the other, evoked by exoticized representations of the conquered, and simultaneously appealing to their desire to identify with what was familiar and Roman. In *Rome's* opening titles a similar evocation of contradictory desires occurs, and thus the titles provide a reading of the function of the Roman triumph.

One of the major points of contact between the titles and Roman triumphal painting and *tituli*, and the one that prompts this evocation of desire, is the recognition that making history involves spectacle. *Rome's* creators share with the triumphant general of the Roman Republic the understanding that history, cast as spectacle – the spectacle of what is absent, past, irrecoverable – is a potent catalyst for desire. The triumph fills in for the past event and cements feelings of solidarity and support for the regime that achieved it. The triumph "makes history" in the sense that it constructs a fantasy in which all members of the public can share and which propagates Rome's power and success.

In the commentary to Episode 10, "Triumph," the historical consultant, Jonathan Stamp, calls attention to the role fantasy plays in the Roman triumph, but with a provocative elision between the historical triumph Julius Caesar celebrated after conquering Pompey and the representation of that triumph in the episode. He comments upon the director's choice to use a small child in a point-of-view shot at the beginning of Caesar's triumphal march: "The director wanted that sense of wonderment for the first view of the Forum . . . the sheer shock of it, the sheer fantasy of it." It is unclear whether Stamp means that the director wanted to recreate the actual, historical "sense of wonderment" and "sheer fantasy" that he conjectures Roman citizens might feel as they watched the triumph, or that what the director wants is to elicit contemporary viewers' wonderment and fantasy. Thus he reproduces the elision of reality and fantasy that occurs in the opening titles in the interchange between live-action and animation, and that also occurs in the Roman triumph's use of paintings and *tituli*. In his analysis of the director's choices in shooting the triumph for the series, Stamp illustrates the double movement of "reality," in the recognizable and sympathetic form of the small child, and fantasy that is key to both the Roman triumph's and *Rome's* success.

Similar to the way paintings and *tituli* show how the Roman triumph "makes" history, the opening titles show the "making" of *Rome*. They betray what the spectacular nature of the series hides: that what viewers ultimately desire is not the lavishness of the costumes or sets, nor the "great" characters like Caesar, Antony, or Octavian, but rather the revelation of what is perceived as real. This "real" is embodied in the lowlier characters of Vorenus and Pullo – they, not Caesar or the other historical figures, provide the focal point of the series. It also pops up in every episode in the form of the "newsreader," who mediates between the historical events that have become the stuff of legend in the contemporary popular imaginary and the "little guys" who go about their business in the Forum. Like *Rome*'s opening titles and the paintings and *tituli* of the triumphal celebration, the character of the newsreader embodies the dynamic of desire that the spectacle must evoke in viewers in order to guarantee that they will buy what the purveyor of the spectacle is selling, which in the case of both the triumphing general and the series is a combination of entertainment and political ideology.

Although a television network's choices of programming hardly stack up against a Roman general's conquest of a foreign nation, nevertheless those choices have been significant in shaping public taste. In turn, viewer response displays a significant political dimension as television delivers both entertainment and news. Just as the Roman public depended largely upon what it saw in the spectacle of the triumph to gain an idea of the war fought in its name, what we see and understand about current events is shaped by a network's decisions about what will garner the highest ratings and by what is made available by government and military sources. The decisions both of the general orchestrating the triumph and of television networks become a, if not the, public reality of events.[4] Like the triumphing general, television "makes history" by making events available to a large audience through spectacle. Audience appeal, in the form of a visual aesthetic, is therefore in both cases a conduit for the making or reproduction of history.

In the course of the spectacle, then, the real in the form of the contingent, historical event takes on a second-nature existence as a signifier in an ideological narrative – a mythic recasting of the original event – which is in turn received as "reality." In this "reality," contingent events assume significance far beyond that of their actual circumstance, fueling social and political fantasies that may be largely unconscious, and even contradictory to expressed aims, objectives, and ideals. Thus an uneven relationship obtains between the real and the myth. The myth eats up the real, but the disappearance of the real evokes our desire for it and paradoxically sustains our interest in the myth, which, as pure structure, holds no interest without the detail of the real. Desire is displaced into myth, represented by spectacle: ultimately, however, our desire is not for the spectacle but what we feel to be beyond it.

In the case of the television series *Rome*, the spectacle reflects contemporary American fantasies of the other and the power of television to make them real. The ubiquity of television – its presence in all rooms of the household, in airport lounges, student centers, on the exteriors of buildings – lends it the status of a kind of mechanical third interlocutor in every dialogue.[5] The Roman triumph, a single event, did not penetrate daily public life on the scale that television does today, but in its manipulation of the visual as a means to focus public attention and support, it played on public fantasy in ways that are comparable to the contemporary television show.

The Roman Triumph

The immense pageantry of the Roman triumphal celebration, awarded during the Republican era to generals who had won a signal military victory over important foreign enemies, played a significant role in shaping and transmitting key cultural and political values. A Roman general coming home from a foreign war not only wanted to tout his own achievements, he also needed to justify the length and expense of the campaign and to seek election to office.[6] The triumph, a long procession through the streets of Rome that paraded all the spoils of war, effectively communicated the consolidation of Rome's hegemony. It gave the average Roman a chance, through viewing the spectacle, to glory vicariously in Rome's imperialism. As is the case with contemporary media, generals went to great lengths to secure the viewer's attention and pleasure: the whole scenario would have been extremely colorful and lively, from the general's purple and gold clothing to the four-horse chariot which he drove and the throngs of captives and loot that followed behind.[7]

An important aspect of the Roman triumph were paintings commissioned by the general to depict scenes from the battles and suggest to the public the geography of the foreign locales in which they were fought. These were carried in the procession along with *tituli*, placards that identified what the paintings represented. Given the unlikelihood that most people in the crowd would be able to see what was written on the *tituli*, or if they could, to read it, the mere presence of text itself has an important function. In discussing the image–text relationship in the context of advertising, Roland Barthes suggests that the function of the text is to pin down the meaning of the image, whose meaning is otherwise "floating" and "polysemous."[8] In the case of both the *tituli* and the opening titles of the series, the text is less important for its actual content – who really pays attention to opening credits after they announce the names of the first couple of stars? – than for its function as a guarantee of effort and quality. The *tituli* lend the actions and characters depicted on the paintings concreteness; as Barthes puts it, they allow viewers "to focus not simply [their] gaze but also [their] understanding." Similarly, when viewers watch the opening titles, they *see* the actors' names but are already *imagining* the characters they play, while the credits in general signify the concrete efforts expended in the creation of the show.

The spectacular visual natures of both the triumph and *Rome* series, as encapsulated by the opening titles, respond to the desire for the exotic side by side with the familiar. In the case of the triumph, this constituted the display of captured foreigners and enormous amounts of loot together with the solidarity it elicited from the whole city gathered together to watch; in *Rome*, it is the presentation of an ancient past whose external trappings and mores are excitingly different from our own, and yet whose characters often think, speak, and react as we do. Ultimately, the viewer–spectacle relationship in both cases embodies the struggle of the self to define its identity against an other. The immediacy of the spectacle encourages identification through the arousal of emotion, excitement, and desire.[9]

A spectacle such as a triumph excites the spectator's senses, both triggering and satisfying the desire to participate in the display, and ultimately, to identify with the success of the recipient of this kind of glory and honor.[10] The historian Appian records the response of the crowd to the triumphal paintings displayed by Julius Caesar in his triumph of 46 BC, after his victory in the Civil Wars:

> People groaned when they saw the picture of Lucius Scipio, the general-in-chief, wounded in the breast by his own hand, casting himself into the sea, and Petreius committing self-destruction at the banquet, and Cato torn open by himself like a wild beast. They applauded the deaths of Achillas and Pothinus, and laughed at the flight of Pharnaces.[11]

The Romans were acutely aware of the political power that could be gained by generating and harnessing these emotions through spectacle.[12] Therefore, the visual played a major role in Roman social and political relations, and triumphing generals had a big stake in how their success was viewed – literally, in the sense that like the spectacle of the triumph itself, a good painting, which commemorated his *gloria*, could ensure public approbation and support. Glory was a cornerstone of Roman Republican ideology and its acquisition was directly linked to political success.[13] The medium of the triumph therefore incorporated the returning general's

particular individual success into the public imaginary narrative of what
Rome stood for and what it meant to be Roman.

Beyond the details of actual events, triumphal paintings represent history
in the making. They awaken viewers' desire to participate in that making;
and the act of commemoration held important ideological significance for
a Roman audience. The triumphing general's political success is closely
linked with evoking the desire of this audience.[14] The series *Rome* also
needs our vote, and like triumphant generals seeking continued political
support, through an intense visual experience it both shapes and reflects a
broader system of political and cultural beliefs. To be successful, both
television production and Roman triumphs necessitate tapping into a
society's view of itself in such a way as to generate pleasure with what it
sees – an awakening of its desire. HBO-BBC's formula bases itself on two
key elements: the representation of an exotic social group, such as the
power-brokers of the late Roman Republic, and the "realistic" representation of that exotic element.

In *Rome*, much effort has been spent on providing a detailed and satisfying answer to the question: "What was it really like?" A vital component
in the transformation of the concrete, historical event to the realm of the
"reality" that makes it available to the public consciousness and imagination is the fiction of immediacy. In order for the show – in the sense both
of spectacle and television – to win the approval of its audience, it must
stimulate belief in the availability of the historical moment. A consistent
theme of the directors' commentaries on *Rome* is its historicity, that is, its
faithful adherence to the reality of the ancient Roman past. In his commentary on Episode 09, the director, Jeremy Podeswa, discusses the historicity of the interior of Atia's house as a backdrop to the action, which
shows Caesar at dinner with Atia's family: "Historicity makes it so much
richer and more textured." Again in the context of a street scene that forms
the background to Vorenus' heroic championing of a shopkeeper beleaguered by thugs, Podeswa stresses that "so much of the show is really in
the background" and that the realism of the background action is important "[so] that you believe the texture of what you see around you . . . what
this series really does is create a sense that you are in ancient Rome, that
it feels real, contemporary, not bound in the dustbin of history."

Podeswa's use of the terms "historicity," "history," and "real" are worth
unpacking. "Historicity" apparently means the reproduction of material
details such as paintings on the walls of a house. Podeswa gestures in the
direction of describing its effects, but in fact his statement is vague: what
is "it" that historicity makes "richer and more textured"? How and why

does attention to historical detail enrich or texturize anything? That the director's point is obscure is significant, since the lack of reality – the absence of the historical moment that is filled in by the proliferation of details – must be obscured from viewers in order to maximize their enjoyment of the show. And their enjoyment paradoxically comes from the creation of a belief that what they see is history. The belief stands in for history, which by itself, without the texture and richness provided by the spectacular visuals of the show, is a "dustbin."[15]

"Really" therefore expresses on the one hand a desire for factual information: the story is more satisfying if we can be assured that a record of "hard" evidence – the tangible traces discovered by archaeology; the written record – documents the practices we see represented. "Really" also signifies the desire for verisimilitude: "hard" evidence notwithstanding, these practices must be represented within the boundaries of what convention tells us is believable, or further, bearable. It is in this sense that a television show moves beyond simply reinforcing something we already know – a preexisting reality to which we demand the show correspond – to shape a perspective of what counts as reality.

Seeing and Not-Seeing

As Peter Holliday suggests, triumphal paintings had an important social and political function: "The Roman governing class commissioned historical paintings to inform a specifically Roman audience of its achievements, to educate that audience about its policies, and thus to persuade that audience to adopt its views and follow a particular course of action. It used historical paintings to implement ideology."[16] After the triumph, the paintings and *tituli* would be publicly displayed, often in a building constructed from the proceeds of the war or a temple of the god to whom the general had dedicated the victory. They furnished a visual record of the event that would reinforce and perpetuate for future generations the ideology it represented. But in the context of the triumph itself, the average viewer would probably not have been able to recognize the details of triumphal paintings and *tituli* clearly. What, then, was the point of carrying them in the procession at all?

On the one hand, the *tituli* call attention to the veracity of what the paintings represent; they announce to viewers "this really happened." Paradoxically, however, the importance of the paintings and *tituli* together derives just as much from what is *not* seen. Just as the content of the *tituli*'s text is less significant than its mere presence, there is something important about the very existence of the visual in this context, regardless of the apprehension of the details of its content. Indeed the fact that the details of the paintings and the text of the *tituli* do escape viewers becomes a crucial element in the paintings' overall success in hooking them. The more viewers *see*, the more immediate their experience, but the less they *recognize*, the more space is left for their own reconstructions of it. The visual nature of the painting triggers desire, but its channeling requires the absence of the painting, which can be filled in by what we might call the logic of the viewer's desire: the narrative that supplies the cognitive links between viewer and image. The success of the painting therefore lies not in the transparency of its details but in their obfuscation: the *not-seeing* is the key to the overall effect.

A large part of the attraction of the series *Rome* is its same-but-different quality: the illusion that we're seeing the "real thing," except in a much more interesting setting than the ones we actually inhabit. However, the exoticism must be overlooked as quickly as it is recognized. It acts as a trigger for our desire, whose final goal is the show's realism; that is, in the end, the "realism" that reflects and confirms a twenty-first-century fantasy of self and other. It is this "realism," and not exoticism, that gives this show traction in the public's imaginary register. *Rome*'s success is the product of its invention of a particularly compelling "realism," one that accommodates both history and fiction.

It is significant, then, that in *Rome*'s opening titles, exoticism appears as the background of realism. The individuals that populate the street scenes of the live-action footage take no notice of the animated world on the walls, and for the most part the reverse is true too – with one important exception. A she-wolf and a goat, depicted one behind the other on the receding arches of a colonnade, peer out as if they are observing the activities of the live-action world. Their gaze is deeply knowing, even a bit sly; behind them, on a third arch, a figure with a shield appears to kick a fallen foe. The images of the animals were the ones that stayed with me after I first watched the titles, and their effect derives from this cross-over gaze: they are the eyes of our desire, looking back momentarily at us. What is the source of this desire? It is the scene of domination that appears as the hasty sketch behind – almost, but not quite, impossible to discern.

The animated graffiti in this opening sequence includes some text along with the images. The text flashes by quickly: sometimes the words are abbreviated or the phrases nonsensical, so that for the most part the text signifies "Roman letters," or "exotic, unreadable ancient language." Again, however, there is a notable exception: a phallic figure appears together with the word ARMA ("weapons," in senses both martial and sexual).[17] Both image and text are very clear; in this moment nothing else competes for our attention. Both signify domination, but the sexual dimension of the image makes clear the connection with desire. The juxtaposition in an instant illuminates the short-circuit that exists between desire and domination – one the dialectical twin of the other.

A great part of *Rome*'s effectiveness is its ability simultaneously to gratify our desire for the spectacle of domination and to veil it from us. The series creators, like triumphant generals, understand that we need both to see and not see; the visual is a stimulus that paradoxically requires a blindness in order to work. It is a property of the successful visual stimulus to mediate between the two contradictory registers: to hide at the same time as appear to reveal wholly. The viewers' desire cannot be successfully tapped unless identification takes place, and the process of identification is one of fantasy. *Rome* stages this process in the narrative of each episode, and signals it to the viewers in the opening titles.

NOTES

1   See A52's press release at www.darnellworks.com/a52/nr0088.htm.

2   These stereotypes abound in the Hollywood sword-and-sandals epics, and are well exhibited in Stanley Kubrick's *Spartacus* (1960), in which the upper class is associated with luxury and deviant sexuality (Laurence Olivier's Crassus propositioning Tony Curtis), and the lower class with Kirk Douglas' Spartacus, played as a populist leader who embodies the cohesion of family and social groups; see Futrell (2001). On Hollywood stereotypes of ancient Rome, see Wyke (1997); Cyrino (2005).

3   On contemporary attitudes toward ancient Romans as projections of self and other, see Joshel, Malamud, and Wyke (2001), 6–11.

4   See Luhmann (2000) on realism as constructed by the media; see also Bourdieu (1999).

5   For the cultural impact of television, see Morley (1995).

6   Holliday (2002), 22.

7   For descriptions of triumphs by ancient authors, see Appian, *The Punic Wars* 8.66; Plutarch, *Life of Aemilius Paulus* 34; Florus, *Epitome* 1.13.26–27.

8   Barthes (1977), 38–39.

9   See Mulvey (1989) on the pleasure of cinematic voyeurism: "Among other things, the position of the spectators in the cinema is blatantly one of repression of their exhibitionism and projection of the repressed desire onto the

performer" (17). This formula works well to describe the appeal of the triumph.

10   On the empathetic response that images have the power to evoke, see Freedberg (1989), 41–53; on the type of identifications and interactions produced by visual stimuli, see Olin (1996).

11   Appian, *The Civil Wars* 2.101.

12   See Wiedemann (1992) on the connections that were conjured in the public imagination through the spectacles of gladiatorial combats and beast hunts in the arena: "Domination over animals is thus parallel to, and can be used to symbolise, social domination" (62). That is, showing the public a spectacle that involved a clear winner and loser whips up its enthusiasm for and identification with the power and dominance of the winner.

13   Finley (1983), 129; Nicolet (1980), 89.

14   How the triumph plays to different social groups would be a study by itself. However, the fundamental point is that the triumph would have to create enough appeal among all groups in order to be a viable means of propagating the fantasy of Rome's glory. It is significant that under Augustus and the inception of imperial government, when triumphs began no longer to be awarded except to the *princeps*, a major method of communication became the grandeur of the visual in the form of architectural display and the proliferation of theater and arena spectacles.

15   On the importance of a realistic effect even within the fantasy of the animated graffiti in the opening titles, note the remarks of the editor of A52, the team that created them: "From the beginning, we envisioned a palette that used the richest, most vibrant colors possible, so my next step was to begin grading all the scenes to match our aesthetic, and then to begin integrating the CG graffiti into the walls. To make those elements look real – while also making them stand out – we used a combination of techniques, combining color correction and compositing . . . and adding grain and details from the walls" (see note 1).

16   Holliday (1997), 130.

17   See Adams (1982), 16–17, 21, 224.

5

The Fog of War:
The Army in *Rome*

Lee L. Brice

Popular misconceptions of how the Roman army functioned are largely the result of a Hollywood-induced "Fog of War." The image that viewers commonly take away from most films, television series, and documentaries set in the Roman world is that the career of Roman soldiers was a series of large-scale battles punctuated by severe punishments. Such an impression is fundamentally flawed and needs a corrective. The thesis argued here is that *Rome* provides viewers with a film production that successfully illustrates many aspects of military life in the Roman world. Although its very nature as filmed entertainment makes it a fictionalization of history, in its treatment of major issues *Rome* remains true to the atmosphere of the period with which it is concerned – the Civil Wars at the end of the Republic.[1] After briefly placing *Rome* in a cinematic context, the following discussion demonstrates the thesis by examining two facets of military life – pitched battles and camp life – based on the historical record and showing how those aspects are treated in the series.

The Roman Army in Film

The Roman army has often appeared on film and in television series but seldom in a manner that might be described as informative of soldiers' lives. Feature films and television series set in the ancient Roman world invariably include the army, but usually as part of their *mise en scène*. One of the best examples of the use of the army as background scenery occurs in *The Fall of the Roman Empire* (1964), where the opening half of the film is set in Marcus Aurelius' stark northern fortress. In *Quo Vadis* (1951), the army is less a part of the set than a useful prop for communicating tone. Similarly, in *Gladiator* (2000), the army opens as a tool for ensuring freedom, which is then sublimated to a more totalitarian purpose under Commodus' rule.[2] In these cases where the army is part of the *mise en scène*, to paraphrase military historian Michael Howard, it is easy to "lose sight of what armies are for."[3]

While the Roman army can play many roles in film production, it is occasionally employed on screen as an army. Some films set in ancient Rome, including *Scipio l'Africano* (1937), *Ben-Hur* (1925 and 1959), *Hannibal* (1960), *Spartacus* (1960), *Cleopatra* (1934 and 1963), and *The Fall of the Roman Empire*, emphasize the combat function of the Roman military (army or navy) to the exclusion of nearly all else. Even in these productions, where the military is shown as a fighting force, its appearance can hardly be described as particularly accurate or informative of soldiers' lives. These films should not be criticized for failing to achieve all that some historians crave; most films and television series avoid the mundane details that make up the bulk of military life because they are not as dramatic as battles, and the artistic requirements necessary to achieve detailed, historical accuracy are expensive.

Trying to capture the genuine experience of the individual soldier has recently become more popular in Hollywood and is showing up in various films. Ken Burns's use of soldiers' diaries gives his miniseries *The Civil War* (1990) a personal feel.[4] Films of the "historical" genre including *Braveheart* (1995), *Saving Private Ryan* (1998), *The Patriot* (2000), *Gladiator*, and *Master and Commander: The Far Side of the World* (2003) are among recent works that appeared to some viewers to have achieved a level of accuracy in depicting soldiers' experience because they employed extreme violence. While military life could be violent, it was not often so; there is more to a plausible historical presentation than large quantities of blood and lost limbs. The impulse to find extreme, onscreen violence synonymous with historical reality will not go away (e.g., *Apocalypto*, 2006), nor has the violence actually achieved any higher level of accuracy in the depiction of soldiers' lives than older films.

It appears that the ultimate venue for a plausible presentation of soldiers' lives lies in series made for television. The sets for these productions are on screen for far longer than a typical feature film set and can therefore stand up to extended scrutiny. The BBC series *Sharpe's Rifles* (1993) and most recently the HBO series *Band of Brothers* (2001) have attained varying levels of success in presenting aspects of military life in the Napoleonic and

World War II periods, respectively. Both these series are dramatic productions in which particular soldiers and officers are the subjects. *Rome* continues this trend of presenting soldiers' lives more realistically than older films. The predominance of the military in *Rome* is not surprising since it reflects the importance of genuine military activities during the late Republic; it is also consistent with series creator Bruno Heller's choice of two soldiers in Julius Caesar's army – Lucius Vorenus, a centurion, and Titus Pullo, a legionary – as protagonists. As a result, viewers are treated to military life on a scale not previously seen.

Sound and Fury: Pitched Battles

The magnitude and significance of pitched battles like those seen in the films *Spartacus* and *Gladiator* capture the imagination and sell films and books, but as the ancient sources make clear, for most soldiers the experience of such large engagements was limited and personal. In its portrayal of ancient combat, the production team for *Rome* has succeeded in presenting a more plausible construction of military life than previous efforts into the soldiers' experience and involvement in combat. The series captures the irregularity of battle as well as its personal scale while also reflecting recent research into Roman military tactics.

Roman sources confirm that the pattern of military life included limited combat in relation to time in service. Caesar, who according to Pliny the Elder (*Natural History* 7.92) had fifty-one pitched battles, fought considerably more battles than any other Roman commander. Yet in his active military career of more than fifteen years, his battle time averages out to fewer than four such engagements a year. Soldiers fighting in campaigns under other commanders, including Marius, Sulla, and Pompey, spent even less time in pitched battles. Most of the fighting a soldier saw during his career consisted of skirmishing, raids, detachments, garrison duty, and sieges, some of which became larger engagements. Battles, however, seem more common than they actually were because of the attention they receive in the ancient sources.

The decision of *Rome*'s producers to omit extensive battles (especially the famous ones) in favor of briefer engagements or indirect references bracketed by military preparations and recovery is much more true to the realities of military duty. Out of the twelve episodes in Season One, only two battles appear on screen and the main protagonists participate in only one of those. Instead, Vorenus and Pullo engage in a variety of military

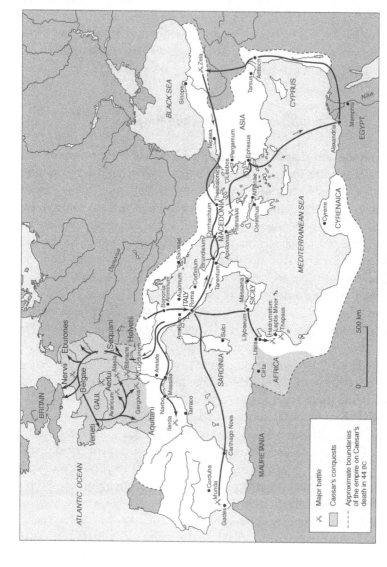

Figure 2 Caesar's military conquests. Source: Le Glay, M. (2005). *A History of Rome*. Oxford: Blackwell Publishing.

tasks including reconnaissance, bodyguard, detachment duty, transport, marching, drill, garrison, and battle. Their participation in a second battle is indicated only when Vorenus tells the story of Thapsus to his children in Episode 09, but the action of battle is omitted. The protagonists miss the only other pitched battle shown on screen, Pharsalus, in Episode 07. The limited appearance of pitched battles in *Rome* as opposed to other military duties effectively conveys soldiers' typical relationship with pitched battle. It is worth noting that had the series been based on any other period in Roman history, there would have been even fewer pitched battles in relation to soldiers' other military activities.

Historically, men participating in battles seldom experience them in a way that bears any resemblance to their descriptions by ancient authors. Soldiers do not see a battle as a whole so much as they experience with all of their senses only that part in which they are involved.[5] This limited experience is the personal scale of combat. In the case of much pre-gunpowder warfare, and Roman infantry fighting in particular with its reliance on the short sword, the soldier experiences each combatant closely enough to smell him and get spattered with sweat and blood. The din of shouting and screaming by combatants on both sides as well as the clashing of swords and shields was sufficiently close and loud to drown out much other noise, including orders. Dust thrown up by so many men and horses gets in the eyes and ears and under armor adding to the discomfort, further circumscribing the soldiers' focus. In these circumstances – the Fog of War – soldiers often have no definite idea how things are going outside their own field of view.[6] Nearly every battle narrative for which any detailed evidence survives includes such scenarios.[7] These experiences make up the personal scale of battle common to the individual soldier's experience. Such genuine experiences seldom transfer well to the big screen.

Some series viewers may have been disappointed not to see big productions of battles like Pharsalus in the style of *Gladiator* or *Alexander* (2004), but their omission is appropriate. Rather than attempt the expensive effort of creating a huge pitched battle sequence, *Rome* emphasizes the personal experience of battle beginning with the opening episode, where the viewer finds Vorenus and his men covered with sweat and blood at the siege of Alesia in Gaul. They are focused on the task at hand: combat. The battle is loud, confusing, and frenetic. The sharp point of the battle is at the front line of shields, while the soldiers further back try to maintain order among the ranks. Thus the scene communicates a personal scale appropriate to soldiers' battle experience, setting the tone of the series. The use of hand-held cameras, close-ups with limited depth of field, key low-angle shots, and judicious editing further emphasizes the limited scope of the combatants' vision. The camerawork also obscures the number of men actually fighting in the scene, thus allowing the production to save considerable expense without sacrificing drama and effectiveness.

The limited way in which the production team presents the battle of Pharsalus is consistent with the earlier scene at Alesia. Confused close-up images of combat change rapidly as silhouetted soldiers strive, swords and shields clash, an unidentifiable standard falls, random soldiers lie dead and wounded, and blood flows in a stream, all in a red fog. Again, camerawork and choppy editing contribute to the confusion. The soundtrack with its shouting, crying, metallic cacophony, and percussion-dominated music affirms the confusion and the inability of the actor to know more than his immediate surroundings. Even the identity of the cheering side is not immediately clear. Only when Caesar is on screen is the outcome obvious. The choice to shoot the battle this way may have been driven as much by budgetary requirements as by a desire to convey historical realism, but it is nonetheless affecting. These scenes will not satisfy those who wish to see large battles, but they provide a more appropriate framing of the action.

Finally, another aspect of pitched battles that the series imagines is Roman combat tactics. The actual manner in which the Roman army fought is still incompletely understood, but the series makes an attempt at presenting a plausible reconstruction. Ancient sources including the historian Livy and the military writer Vegetius report that legionaries sought to maintain the orderly ranks of shields along the front line and stab between and over their shields while using the shields offensively. Furthermore, it was typical to array men on the battle line in columns with some depth.[8] How the orderly line and the columns interacted during battle is poorly understood. Questions typically examined include whether the columns functioned as replacements for men who fell; in other words, did fresh men step in to replace tired men? Did the men behind hold the front-line men in place by pushing against their backs, or did their presence intimidate the enemy and simply keep the men in front from fleeing? Historians investigating the Roman army have tried, based on ancient sources and material culture, to create models for explaining how combat tactics worked. While historian Adrian Goldsworthy's suggestion that battle was punctuated by breaks for recovery provides a solution to some problems concerning the replacement of men on the battle line, a definitive reconstruction of Roman battle remains elusive.[9]

As Jonathan Stamp, the historical consultant for *Rome*, acknowledges in the DVD commentary, the battle reconstruction in the series is based on "the latest geeky research."[10] The fact that Vorenus and his men are covered in blood and sweat even before the enemy assault suggests that the viewer should imagine that the episode opens in the middle of battle and the ranks have just had a short break from fighting, in the manner that Goldsworthy suggests. The sword and shield tactics employed by the Roman reenactors evoke ancient descriptions. The ranks are orderly, and the way in which Vorenus is able to maintain and recover the situation when Pullo breaks ranks is a good illustration of the discipline for which the Roman army was renowned. The method of replacing the soldiers by having them step through gaps between the columns provides a visualization of how such a process might have worked. While it may not be the definitive reconstruction, the scene is valuable because it provides viewers with a sense of how complicated Roman tactics could be and of the importance of discipline and drill to success. The version of combat presented in Episode 01 is the most plausible scenario captured on screen to date and demonstrates that reenactments consistent with historical research and experimental archaeology are possible without losing their dramatic appeal.

Beyond the Battle: Camp Life

The presentation of life in military camps (*castra*) is limited in *Rome*, but the atmosphere of discipline, training, ceremony, sickness, and boredom is evocative of historical realities. Camp life in the Roman army was a mixture of tedium and toil under potentially harsh and crowded conditions. Historically, when the army was stationary it built *castra* with ditch and stockade. The camp was laid out in a standardized arrangement of blocks – including roads, tent rows, and other facilities – centered on the *principia* or commander's headquarters, near which was his living quarters (*praetorium*) and the tribunal platform from which he would review troops, deliver orders, and harangue the men (Polybius, *Histories* 6.26.10–34.6). The headquarters also served as the storage for the standards and for the voluminous records kept by the legion. The men slept in groups of eight, called *contubernia*, in tents of sewn leather. The size of the camp also provided space for training and drilling as well as cooking and chores. Under such close conditions with limited sanitation, disease was an ever-present threat of which the Romans were well aware. Fresh water and well-placed latrines were part of the facilities, and the camp was moved when necessary to reduce the chances of contagion (Vegetius, *Military Matters* 3.2). The camp provided a regular environment safe from enemies and kept the legions contained and out of trouble.[11]

Rome effectively captures the spirit and many of the nuances of life in Roman *castra* in various ways. The camps in which the action occurs are organized and inhabited in a manner consistent with descriptions in the ancient sources. The gates, roads, headquarters, tribunal, and tent rows are where one would expect to find them. The command tent in each camp is properly imposing as the hub of activity. Smoke, noise, cries and shouting, dirt, and the ever-present elements convey the constant assault on the senses and the grubby environment. The presence of wounded men is a reminder of mortality, as are the tribunes' reports to Caesar listing the number of men who have died of disease. The small fires, stacked weapons, drying laundry, wash basins, animals, and other small details of material culture reflect an unexpected attention to detail that creates an air of authenticity. The horses in small corrals and a stray dog suggest the presence of animals that were a necessary component of the camp. Through the use of close-ups, low angle shots, hand-held cameras, and limited wide angle shots, the director suggests rather than shows the size of Caesar's camp. Only on departure is its full size revealed to the viewer. There are some decorative issues with which some viewers will quibble, but the overall presentation successfully reflects an unexpectedly detailed reconstruction.[12]

The very nature of military service meant that most soldiers spent far more of their career engaged in camp life than on a battlefield. Since pitched battles typically occurred during the warmer campaign season, half the year could be spent in camp during the worst weather. Even during the usual campaign season, there was much maneuvering before and between battles and camps had to be built for the night. As demonstrated by Caesar's campaign against Pompey, waiting for battle strained logistics and forced the men to subsist on a root called *cara* (Caesar, *The Civil War* 3.48). Once the battle was completed soldiers returned to camp nightly to rest and recover. Sieges were much more common than battles; these took time to resolve and soldiers spent much of the campaigns in spread-out fortifications that functioned like regular camps. Caesar's siege operations in and associated with Alesia lasted the better part of a year.[13]

Proportionally, the amount of screen time *Rome*'s actors spend in camp is much greater than the time they spend in battle. Forts or camps in which action occurs appear in eight of the first ten episodes, while battles occur in only two of them. This arrangement reflects the "hurry-up-and-wait" reality of military life. The tension of waiting for battle and surviving on thin rations is illustrated in Episode 07 where weary and dirty soldiers cook field rats for food, thus conveying the same logistical difficulties Caesar faced before Pharsalus in 48 BC. Caesar's men may not actually have roasted rodents, but the use of rats as a prop is effective and makes more visual impact on screen than the *cara* root Caesar mentions in his memoirs. Clearly, life in the camp was the norm while battles were the aberration.

This camp-based pattern of "make work" activity meant that boredom was a potential problem that could lead to indiscipline, but various ways of mitigating boredom were developed. Military duties needed to be exercised daily. In addition to guard duty, training, and drilling, there were various unpopular chores to occupy soldiers' time including foraging, digging wells, and maintaining the camp. These tasks were often tedious, hence their unpopularity with the troops. The historian Tacitus (*Annals* 1.35.1–2) reports that in the early Empire soldiers seeking to avoid such tasks could bribe centurions to get out of them; this situation may have prevailed in the late Republic too. Training, drilling, and the regimentation of daily routine (Vegetius, *Military Matters* 1.1, 8–27, 2.23–24, 3.4) were all facets of military discipline aimed at turning men into soldiers and making them obedient to orders, efficiently aggressive and steadfast in battle, and orderly in camp – the behavioral expectations in the Roman military. Moreover, such discipline not only kept the soldiers active and exercised in such a way as to maintain unit cohesion, it also served to minimize opportunities for troublemakers to incite trouble.[14] The nature of the military as a society and the camp as a confined space within which that society functioned provided a level of social pressure on soldiers to conform to institutional norms of behavior.[15]

The duties in which soldiers and officers in *Rome* engage reflect various aspects of life in the *castra*. Viewers see soldiers returning from foraging for food and firewood, standing guard duty, marching drills, training, cleaning and repairing equipment, making reports, talking in groups, resting, playing games, cooking, assisting the wounded, attending assembly, and preparing for battle. The importance of the legionary standards is reflected in their treatment in camp and their storage. Soldiers appear in various states of cleanliness and uniform as they go through their daily routines. As expected, much of camp life was mundane and unexciting.

Rome also effectively illustrates the role of officers in camp. Caesar and Pompey hear reports, have their slaves maintain their treasuries and files, read and write missives, and hold councils with their officers (*consilia*) in the headquarters tent. As expected, both Pompey and Caesar are shown in their respective tents talking about the battle to come, planning the campaigns, and receiving visitors. Caesar's acceptance of Vercingetorix's surrender in Episode 01 and his speech calling for war in Episode 02 evoke the theatricality officers could employ while in camp. In addition to illustrating his role in training, Vorenus' shouting at soldiers while overseeing the whipping of Pullo in the first episode is redolent with ceremony and theater. Elsewhere, centurions are shouting and gesticulating in ways that evoke training and drilling in the camp. The status of the different grades of officers is repeatedly emphasized through costume, set, and gestures which are consistent with historical expectations and true to the atmosphere of camp life.

In addition to the various in-camp tasks, it was common for soldiers to be assigned to an officer or serve in detachments (*vexillationes*). Like most ancient institutions, the Roman army was extremely conservative. Instead of creating many new units, commanders tended to use legionaries and allied soldiers to fill all sorts of functions through detachments. Such assignments would include tasks like bridge building, garrison duty, reconnaissance, escorts, communications, and policing. Caesar used his regular legionaries, not a specialized unit, to build his bridges and lay out his roads. In this way the legion remained a flexible institution that commanders could adapt as the need arose.

There were also some specialized and allied units with most legions. Artisans responsible for fabricating and repairing equipment formed one group of specialists in every legion, and musicians formed another. Although musicians could play at ceremonial occasions, they were more important for their role in contributing to battle preparation and in signaling maneuvers (Caesar, *The Gallic War* 7.47; Tacitus, *Annals* 1.68.3). In the late Republic, some specialists were drawn regularly from among the allies. Caesar's army included allies from Crete, Numidia, the Balearic islands, Gaul, and Germany. Italian cavalry seems to have diminished in importance by the mid-first century and Romans drew their cavalry from allies, particularly Spanish, Gallic, German, and Numidian allies. Caesar drew heavily on Gallic and German allies for his cavalry units and even used Germans as his bodyguards.[16] As is apparent, specialized and allied units were common elements of camp life in the late Republic while detachments still dominated soldiers' careers.

In its use of detachments *Rome* again succeeds in illustrating a neglected aspect of military life. After Caesar's eagle is stolen, Antony makes reference to a detachment of men responsible for crucifixions and then sends Vorenus and Pullo on a detachment to recover the standard. Later, Caesar sends them to Egypt to recover Cleopatra. Specialists appear in the form of musicians and archers who are active in camp. The archers never engage in anything more active than celebration, but the musicians play their historical role at ceremonies and on the march.[17] Caesar's historical reliance on allied troops is illustrated by the presence of the Ubian cavalry he sends out to scout toward Rome and which later accompanies him to Greece. The rough costumes of these riders and their mounts may cause some to grumble, but they appropriately suggest the otherness of these Germanic fighters as well as the way these peoples used their appearance to intimidate opponents.[18] Taken as a whole, the presentation of specialists and allies is consistent with other aspects of the production in illustrating issues with which the military had to contend and some of the solutions that developed over time.

Maintenance of good discipline was a constant concern. Officers focused on daily duties designed to instill and maintain a high standard of conduct. Training and drill ensured not only unit effectiveness, but also cohesion; consequently, these and other chores were supposed to be maintained throughout the year.[19] Despite the measures taken against it and the traditional reputation of the Roman army, there were still incidents of unrest among soldiers. The most common form of unrest – desertion – was a constant problem, but more serious incidents including indiscipline, insubordination, and mutiny also occurred. During the period covered by Season One of *Rome*, Caesar suffered two serious mutinies (49 and 47 BC), and various minor incidents and mutinous moods, as did Pompey and other subordinate generals on both sides.[20] Any violations of discipline were subject to punishment. Capital punishment was the most serious penalty for military crimes and applied to a wide variety of offenses. Lesser and more common penalties included whipping, beating, humiliation, demotion, incarceration, and dishonorable discharge.[21] Such punishments were carried out in public and served both the religious function of expiating the guilt of the larger unit and as simple deterrence. The public nature of enforcing discipline also provided officers with a chance to employ theatricality in winning favor among the troops.[22]

Repeated references in *Rome* to desertion, unrest, dissent, and insubordination in the ranks as well as celebration, elation, and punishment offer a more realistic portrayal of the range of moods within the Roman military than the traditionally popular idea of a uniform, machine-like discipline in Caesar's army.[23] As the series begins, Pullo engages in insubordination by breaking ranks in battle and then strikes his centurion, Vorenus. Later he calls Vorenus rude names. As expected, Pullo pays for his indiscipline with a public flogging and confinement. The public flogging may not have appeared as brutal as it would have been in reality (or even in other films), but it is not difficult to imagine the pain and humiliation such punishment inflicted. As already noted, Vorenus' listing of the penalties (regardless of whether this list is correct or complete) is intended as ceremony and training. The scene also communicates to the audience the daily reality of potential violence in the Roman army much more effectively than, for example, the scene of decimation in *The Fall of the Roman Empire*. The presence of other men in the camp jail or guard-house illustrates that indiscipline in the series is a ubiquitous problem, just as it was in ancient Roman armies. Desertion is the more common form of indiscipline in *Rome*. The tribunes' "roll call" reports in Episodes 01 and 02 illustrate the regularity and extent of this issue, a constant dilemma for all Roman commanders. After the Civil War has begun, both sides suffer from desertions and defections. When Pompey is in flight following Phar-salus, many of his soldiers desert. Even after the war, Pullo engages in or contemplates desertion before finally receiving discharge.

As for dissent in the ranks, there are various references in the script to mutinous moods on both sides. Six episodes (01, 02, 04–07) contain refer-ences to Caesar's men being unhappy, bored, or restless in camp. There are nearly as many allusions to Pompey's men being in a similar frame of mind (Episodes 02, 04–06). Pompey's raw recruits are undisciplined and his officers in charge of them are insubordinate, as they all flee when Caesar's cavalry shows up in Episode 03, again illustrating the necessity and effectiveness of Roman discipline. Following the battle of Thapsus (Episode 09) the remaining Pompeian officers and men are depressed and have lost their morale. Soldiers from both sides show their discontent in various ways, including griping openly in camp and acting out against civilians. The cause of discontent for both sides is reportedly inaction. The societal instability of the Civil War appears to be a contributing factor, as it was in the period 49–46 BC. The unsettled military mood depicted in *Rome* is a valuable reminder that Roman military discipline was imperfect when compared with the Fog of War that many films, television series, documentaries, and popular books have disseminated.

Brutality was not the only way of maintaining order in camp. Officers recognized that rewards were also an effective tool for maintaining dis-cipline and morale. Rewards ranged from promotions and pay raises to torques and arm bands. Commanders often made sure they could see their troops during battle, not only to be able to direct them, but also to see actions meriting recognition. After combat, awards were handed out in a public ceremony in which the commander had a chance to engage in theatricality and rhetorical display designed to lift the general morale and status of the soldiers. The appearance of such awards on military funerary reliefs suggests their real importance to soldiers.[24] Since centurions suffered such high rates of mortality as a result of leading from the front line, there were always opportunities for promotion after a battle. Promotion always brought with it increased pay, but more importantly rise in status and prestige, both within the military and to a lesser extent in society at large.[25] Promotion was, therefore, an effective reward for some men.

Rome illustrates how rewards and promotions were important elements of life in the *castra*. As the battle at Alesia opens, Vorenus' uniform displays various awards for bravery, which were presented only by his commander and were highly valued by soldiers and officers for the lasting prestige they conferred. After the recovery of the eagle in Episode 01, Vorenus is moreover promoted to top centurion (*Primus Pilus*, "First Spear"). Such a promotion would have resulted in an increase in pay, but more importantly a rise in status and prestige; this provides a reminder to his comrades and to the viewers that it was historically possible for a man to rise in rank based on merit.[26] His increased status in the series is reflected in the way he is treated in camp and the opportunities that later open to him.

Other historical rewards included booty and bounties. Soldiers relied on plunder for resources to supplement their income and improve their standard of living. The opportunity to sack cities and plunder the dead offered strong incentives for being successful in combat. Booty included not only precious metals, but also slaves. The draw of plunder was occasionally too strong. For example, Caesar sometimes had to restrain his men from plundering when it might detract from the war effort.[27] Given the limited annual pay soldiers received (225 *denarii* in three installments) and the inconsistent availability of plunder, cash bounties for continued service could also be a strong incentive. At Brundisium in 49 BC, Caesar promised his men 5,000 *denarii* if they would follow him. Little surprise then that in his commentaries Caesar worries about the availability of cash throughout his campaigns, and in Spain (49 BC) the financial strain led to an outbreak of military unrest. He finally paid the sum following his quadruple triumph in 46 BC.[28] Sulla, Marius, Pompey, and Caesar all relied on bonuses and plunder as incentives for service and loyalty during civil war. The use of bounties would grow so common after 49 BC that the historian Appian characterized the armies of the late Republic as little more than mercenaries (*The Civil Wars* 5.17). In sum, the combination of rewards and punishments was an effective and an omnipresent characteristic of military life.[29]

The importance of plunder and bounties is effectively illustrated in the series. As viewers first encounter the figure of Caesar, his men are in the midst of sacking Alesia, thus illustrating its importance for Caesar and the plot. A character in the guardhouse observes that they have two days to plunder the city, thus providing the modern audience a sense of the scale involved. Still confined in the guardhouse, Pullo's reaction to the news makes clear that in this case missing the opportunity to plunder was actually a greater punishment than flogging since such penalties hit soldiers economically. Caesar's men also demonstrate the importance of the booty by the zeal with which they are seen handling captives and bargaining for prices. When Vorenus returns to Rome, he demonstrates the typical significance of the Gallic booty. The purse he empties for his wife contains an odd assortment of gold teeth, coins, body parts, and jewelry; however, he refers to the slaves he has acquired in war as his entire investment, equal to the enormous sum of 10,000 *denarii*. As Vorenus makes it clear that the sum is enough to pay off his building and provide additional resources for his future business, the audience can grasp the significance of the sum in Roman society as well as the importance of booty as an incentive for the man in the army.

Viewers may like to think of the modern world as the one with a fixation on the expense of military endeavors and the need to have money on hand, but through its emphasis on money *Rome* remains true to the financial atmosphere of the military during the Civil War. In Episode 02, Caesar calls an assembly and in a thoroughly theatrical display awards Pullo a bounty of 500 *denarii* (more than two years' pay) for his support when Antony was attacked in Rome by Pompey's men. The publicly awarded cash augments the rhetoric of the moment and seals the soldiers' support in the time of crisis. Thus Caesar illustrates a typical Roman pattern of using praise, honor, and cash to inspire his soldiers. Because of its importance in swaying loyalty, money remains a key element of the series. Pompey has his men steal cash from the treasury, but the subsequent loss of that money drives the plot, as both sides contend for it. Caesar and Pompey both worry about having enough money available to secure the loyalty of their soldiers, realizing that rhetoric alone is insufficient to motivate everyone. The topic emerges again before and after the battle of Pharsalus when the Pompeian commanders discuss the need to levy funds and the difficulty in doing so. In Episode 11, Caesar calms discontented veterans with bribes. The acquisition of funding for the military appears as a concern in nearly every episode. Thus, *Rome* effectively illustrates the close connection in the Roman world between money and military success during the Civil War.

For most observers, the Roman army, like so many military institutions that appear in the popular media, is shrouded in a fog. Its historical presence and importance are undeniable, but the details are poorly understood. The HBO-BBC series *Rome*, as it turns out, is an antidote to the Fog of War. *Rome* suggests that Roman military life was made up of more than battles and leaders, and in doing so meets historical expectations. Ancient sources corroborate that military life was one of tedious assignments and drills punctuated occasionally by harsh discipline and adrenaline-filled battles. Mundane aspects of military life may carry less drama than battles and assassinations, but it is not possible to understand the way any military works without paying attention to those lives.

Rome also suggests what is artistically possible in the creation of "historical" films. It demonstrates that it is possible to communicate a level of historical veracity without focusing excessively on combat or on extreme violence. That is not to conclude that *Rome* is perfect. As with any fictionalization of history, it has its errors of commission and omission. There may be details of all types with which different viewers will quibble, but if taken as a whole there is little point in quibbling – the production succeeds. Indeed, *Rome* proves that aspects of daily military life can be illuminated without sacrificing adventure, humor, depth, and drama.

Rome is valuable because it illustrates that the life of a Roman soldier, and by extension any Roman, is much more interesting and complicated as a topic than the usual presentations of the Roman military as a disciplined monolithic unit suggest. Other aspects of military life, including the use of soldiers as political thugs, brigands, and mercenaries, and the difficulty of adjusting to civilian life appear in the series, but these topics must await future opportunities for discussion. *Rome* is most important, however, because it provides an effective visual tool with which to encourage popular consideration not only of Roman military life and the place of the military in society, but also of ancient history as a whole.

NOTES

1 Sorlin (2001), 28, 38–41; Rosenstone (2001), 60; Guynn (2006), 15.
2 Winkler (2001), 51–55; Pomeroy (2004).
3 Quoted in Keegan (1976), 28.
4 Burns (1996), 179.
5 Keegan (1976), 61–73; Goldsworthy (1996), 248–282; Daly (2002), 156–202.
6 Thucydides, *The Peloponnesian War* 7.44.1; Cicero, *Letters to Friends* 10.30; Tacitus, *Annals* 1.65.4; *Histories* 1.35–44, 3.22–25.

7   Goldsworthy (1996), 1–11; Daly (2002), 156–201.

8   Livy, *History of Rome* 21.57, 22.4–5, 25.21, 30.34; Frontinus, *Stratagems* 2.3.22; Vegetius, *Military Matters* 1.26, 2.17, 3.15, 19.

9   Goldsworthy (1996), 176–180, 206–223; Sabin (2000), 10–17; Daly (2002), 59–63.

10 Jonathan Stamp, DVD commentary to Episode 01.

11 Davies (1989), 33–52, 209–231.

12 The bright red camp banners with their black and gold eagle symbols have more connection with twentieth-century iconography than with Julius Caesar, but are an effective element of the silent dialogue between the producers and the audience, communicating symbols and themes which any historically aware viewer will interpret. The banners suggest that Caesar is moving toward tyranny and totalitarianism, regardless of his protests to the contrary. See Winkler (2001), 51–55; Pomeroy (2004).

13 Goldsworthy (2006), 315–342.

14 Davies (1989), 3–70; Horsmann (1991), 109–186, esp. 164–186; Goldsworthy (1996), 251–252, 279–282; Brice (2003), 58–59, 151–155, 168–171.

15 MacMullen (1984), 440–456; Lendon (1997), 243–252.

16 Caesar, *The Gallic War* 1.15, 2.7, 10, 20, 24, 6.29, 7.4, 34, 8.10, 30; *The Civil War* 1.41. Speidel (1994), 12–15; Goldsworthy (1996), 68–73, 183–188.

17 In a poetic choice, Bruno Heller named the leader of Caesar's musicians "Gracchus," thus echoing the name of the famous late second-century popular magistrates and continuing a Roman cinematic tradition of employing Gracchus as a character name.

18 Quibbling over particular items of military equipment and especially the use of stirrups matters little to the presentation since this does not detract from their overall impact.

19 Davies (1989), 41–55; Goldsworthy (1996), 250–259.

20 For numerous citations see Chrissanthos (1999), 70–84, and Brice (2003), 82–85.

21 Polybius, *Histories* 6.37, 6.38.2, 11.29; Livy, *History of Rome* 2.49, 59, 8.7–8, 36; Caesar, *The African War* 19.3; Appian, *The Civil Wars* 2.94, 3.43, 79; Frontinus, *Stratagems* 1.9.4, 4.1. Brice (2003), 58–61. Crucifixion was extremely rare as a penalty for citizens.

22 Caesar, *The Gallic War* 1.20; Appian, *The Civil Wars* 2.92–93; Plutarch, *Life of Julius Caesar* 70; Tacitus, *Annals* 1.26–30, 34–35, 42–44. Goldsworthy (1996), 145–149.

23 For examples of the old view see Keppie (1998) and Gilliver (1999). For a corrective see Goldsworthy (1996), Brice (2003), and Lendon (2005), 172–315.

24 Polybius, *Histories* 6.22, 39; Caesar, *The Gallic War* 1.52, 7.27; *The Civil War* 3.49; Valerius Maximus, *Memorable Deeds and Sayings* 8.14.5. Maxfield (1981); Horsmann (1991); Goldsworthy (1996), 276–279; Keppie (2003).

25 Dobson (1974), 393–395; Goldsworthy (2006), 193–195. I tend to agree with Goldsworthy (2006), 193, that centurions were low-grade officers, not non-commissioned officers as has been traditionally thought. Recent work completed on centurions has focused exclusively on the post during the Principate, and cannot apply to the situation in the Republic.

26 Maxfield (1981).

27 Caesar, *The Gallic War* 2.24, 33, 5.19, 6.34, 7.45; *The Civil War* 1.21, 2.12; *The African War* 3. Harris (1979), 102–104; Goldsworthy (1996), 259–262.

28 Caesar, *The Civil War* 1.39; Appian, *The Civil Wars* 2.41, 47, 101–102; Plutarch, *Life of Julius Caesar* 37, 55; Cassius Dio, *Roman History* 41.26, 43.19–23; Suetonius, *Life of Julius Caesar* 69. For numerous citations see Chrissanthos (1999), 70–84.

29 Harris (1979), 102–104; Maxfield (1981); Horsmann (1991); Goldsworthy (1996), 145–149, 162–163, 259–262, 276–279.

6

Caesar's Soldiers: The *Pietas* of Vorenus and Pullo

Brian Cooke

Not long after viewing the first episode of *Rome*, I was pleasantly surprised to find myself dusting off copies of Julius Caesar's *Commentaries* and Vergil's *Aeneid* that I had not touched since I'd last taught the classics years ago. Week by week, as I enjoyed watching the trials and adventures of Lucius Vorenus and Titus Pullo, I was equally delighted to note how well the series develops these characters as reasonably authentic Roman soldiers and citizens. Looking back at ancient history through the experiences of these heroes, this chapter focuses on several significant military and political themes that Vorenus and Pullo exemplify in fact and in fiction. More specifically, this chapter explores the dynamics of soldiering, citizenship, *pietas*, and politics in the late Republic.[1]

Although the HBO-BBC series portrays Lucius Vorenus as an "honorable and pragmatic centurion" and Titus Pullo as an "arrogant, rebellious legionnaire," Julius Caesar actually describes these two soldiers in *The Gallic War* as "high-ranking centurions" who were "close to reaching senior rank" (*The Gallic War* 5.44).[2] In 53 BC, just before the storyline of *Rome* begins, Caesar reports how the real Vorenus and Pullo helped liberate one of his legions when it was besieged and at risk of annihilation in northernmost Gaul. Encircled and entrapped by the Nervii, the most warlike of Gallic tribes, Caesar's legion withstood seven days of fierce attack before mounting a daring counter-offensive led by centurions Vorenus and Pullo. In this decisive battle, the Romans first withdrew one cohort to lure the Nervii to an unfavorable position.[3] But while "fighting at the defences was at its height," Caesar reports that Pullo led a bold counter-attack with Vorenus close behind him. "They killed several Gauls and both returned safely within the defences to great acclaim. Thus fortune played with them both in their rivalry and struggle, so that despite their enmity each helped and saved the other, and it was impossible to decide which should be considered braver of the two" (*The Gallic War* 5.44).

Unlike many high-ranking Roman officers who were professional politicians with little military experience, centurions were professional officers who earned their rank through courage, skill, and victory in war. There were approximately sixty centurions in each legion, and competition among these officers was fierce for recognition as *Primus Pilus* or First Spear. This contest both for honor and for military rank is the most likely cause of the tension between Vorenus and Pullo as described by Caesar: "There was always a dispute going on between them as to which had precedence over the other, and every year, they clashed in fierce rivalry over the most important posts" (*The Gallic War* 5.44). Reasonably well educated and capable of earning a living in a peacetime trade, centurions were invaluable to their commanders who relied heavily on their loyalty, bravery, and military counsel in war.

Although Caesar suggests a preference for the real Pullo, the series *Rome* favors Vorenus as the senior centurion whose family fought in Magnesia and Zama and whose father once rode with Sulla. In this role as *Primus Pilus*, Vorenus is consistently portrayed as a trusted ally, close confidant, and staunch defender of both Caesar and Antony. "I need you, Vorenus," says Antony. "There's no better man in the legion. None more respected by the men" (Episode 04). A strong and pious man of Roman virtue, Vorenus is a war-hardened yet peace-seeking soldier who evokes comparison with Aeneas, the reluctant hero and preordained founder of Rome.[4] Just as Vergil sings the story of Aeneas, the series portrays Vorenus as a dutiful warrior and troubled patriot who struggles to reconcile his allegiance to the Republic with his devotion to gods, friends, and fatherland. This tension among diverse loyalties creates a riveting storyline that illustrates the complex concept of *pietas* that is a hallmark of Roman character and politics.

The series *Rome*, by contrast, presents Pullo as a poor and ordinary yet brave and endearing legionary. "Me," says Pullo, "I have simpler tastes. Kill my enemy. Take their gold. Enjoy their women. That's it" (Episode 01). Son of a northern Italian slave, Pullo is the consummate legionary, a professional soldier who is fierce in war, loyal to his commander, and fearless when armed with short sword (*gladius*), large shield (*scutum*), and javelin (*pilum*). Barely literate and poorly prepared for peacetime employment, soldiers like Pullo were attracted to service by a small yet predictable wage

Figure 3   Brothers in arms: Pullo (Ray Stevenson) and Vorenus (Kevin McKidd). Photograph from *Rome*^{SM} courtesy of HBO®. *Rome*^{SM} and HBO® are service marks of Home Box Office, Inc.

and the potential for glory in war, plunder in victory, and a grant of rural land in northern Italy or southern France upon retirement. As Mascius' later appeal to Vorenus for property illustrates, the promise of land after retirement from service was an especially powerful motivation. "Our brothers need more than just money," says Mascius. "Money runs out one day. Then, what do they do? Take up a trade maybe? Unlikely! We want land in Italy" (Episode 11).

Roman soldiers knew their prospects for survival, victory, and lifetime income were closely connected with their commander's military genius. Each Roman legion had a unique history that was closely linked to the military and political ambitions of its commanding generals. This allegiance both to legion and to commanding officer was especially true for the Twelfth and Thirteenth Legions, which were newly organized in 58 BC by Caesar and deployed specifically for victory in the Gallic campaigns. This deep reciprocal devotion between Caesar and his army is corroborated by the Roman biographer Suetonius: "Caesar loved his men dearly . . . He always addressed them not as 'My Soldiers' but as 'Comrades' which put them into a better humor; and he equipped them splendidly. The silver and gold inlay of their weapons improved their appearance on parade and made them more careful not to get disarmed in battle . . . Sometimes, if a victory had been complete enough, he relieved the troops of all military duties and let them carry on as wildly as they pleased. One of his boasts was: 'My soldiers fight just as well when they are stinking of perfume'" (*Life of Julius Caesar* 67).[5]

A Roman soldier's life and livelihood depended on the superiority of his weapons and the strength of the lines he formed with his fellow legionaries. This emphasis on military organization and group discipline becomes immediately apparent in the series' opening scenes when Pullo is punished for breaking ranks and fighting independently. Those soldiers whose individual actions threatened the performance and well-being of the entire legion were subject to severe punishment at the discretion of the senior centurion. "Legionary Titus Pullo is a hero of the Thirteenth Legion, but look at him now!" commands Vorenus. "Justice knows every man's number. He has committed a terrible sacrilege and he will pay for it with his life. As will every man who breaks with the law. Brawlers and drunkards will be flogged. Thieves will be strangled. Deserters will be crucified" (Episode 01).

While Vorenus and Pullo were real soldiers, it is not clear if they were historically members of the Thirteenth Legion. It is certain, however, the real Caesar rallied the real Thirteenth while at winter quarters in Ravenna before crossing the Rubicon and initiating civil war in January 49 BC. As told in his *Commentaries*, Caesar "exhorted them to defend against his enemies the reputation and standing of the man under whose generalship they had for nine years played their part for Rome with outstanding success, won a large number of battles, and pacified the whole of Gaul and Germany" (*The Civil War* 1.7).[6] As told by the series *Rome*, Caesar says: "Our beloved Republic is in the hands of mad men. This is a dark day and I stand at a fork in the road. I can abide by the law, surrender my arms to the Senate and watch the Republic fall to tyranny and chaos. Or I can go home with my sword in my hand and run those maniacs to the Tarpeian rock!" (Episode 02). In yet another version of this historic event, Suetonius reports that Caesar interpreted a trumpet-playing apparition sitting on the Rubicon riverbank as a favorable omen.[7] "Let us accept this as a sign from the Gods," Caesar exclaimed. "*Alea iacta est.* The die is cast."

Rome's dramatization of the Rubicon crossing and the early Civil War campaign is consistent with Caesar's own reports of his lightly contested advance into Italy. Rather than waiting to assemble more legions, Caesar and the Thirteenth marched southward along the Adriatic coast to occupy

Ariminum, Ancona, Auximum, and Sulmo where the Thirteenth Legion under the command of Mark Antony was greeted by "cheering soldiers and townsfolk alike" (*The Civil War* 1.7–18). Within two months, Pompey and his soldiers had retreated to Greece via Brundisium and Caesar had secured control of Italy. This swift victory was puzzling to Vorenus who had expected a stiffer defense of his beloved Republic. "It makes no sense. We should have been stopped by now. Why is Rome not defended? Soldiers of the Republic do not run. So it must be a stratagem or a trick. If Mars were watching, he would not allow such a disgrace" (Episode 03). Pompey, of course, believed this strategic retreat would lead to victory in a war of attrition that ultimately would exhaust Caesar's legions. To his credit, Pompey also wanted to avoid unnecessary war on Italian soil between Roman legions.

After securing control of Italy, Caesar returned to Rome in March 49 BC to legitimize his authority. Upon his arrival, Caesar called a meeting of the Senate and "encouraged and requested them to take responsibility for the state and administer it jointly with himself. But he said that if they were frightened and ran away, he would not shirk the task and would administer the state by himself" (*The Civil War* 1.32). Caesar, however, knew it was imprudent to govern in Italy while Pompey's legions remained as yet unconquered in Spain, Africa, and Greece. After only three days in Rome, Caesar redirected his attention first toward Spain, where he defeated the strongest Pompeian fighting forces, and then toward Africa, where he routed his Roman enemy but struggled with a local Numidian army under the command of King Juba. By year-end, Caesar had consolidated control of Italy and Gaul and returned to Rome where "in his capacity as dictator" he held elections that named him consul for the year 48 BC (*The Civil War* 3.1).

Once "reelected," Caesar did not delay. After only eleven days in Rome, he hurried to Brundisium, eager to cross the Adriatic to confront Pompey himself at last and end the war. As Pompey had predicted, however, Caesar began to experience significant logistical problems that undermined his preference for fighting swift, decisive military campaigns. Nearly invincible on land when at full strength, Caesar's legions were becoming weary, sick, and short-handed after nearly ten years of fighting. They also lacked sufficient ships to transport the army across the short yet dangerous strait to Greece.[8] Although Caesar crossed the Adriatic safely with seven legions on January 4, 48 BC, he was badly outnumbered and in need of further reinforcement.[9] "Now the cat barks at the dog and Pompey is chasing me," says Caesar in a message to Antony. "I can outmaneuver him for a while but not forever. I ask you to bring the Thirteenth here as speedily as you are able" (Episode 06). In the ensuing months, a Pompeian naval blockade obstructed Caesar's efforts to transport essential reinforcements until a wicked spring gale devastated Pompey's fleet while sparing most of Caesar's ships.[10]

The stage was now set in August for a decisive battle at Pharsalus where Caesar's veteran legions squared off against a Pompeian army that was superior in numbers but far less loyal and disciplined. When the signal to commence fighting was given, Caesar reports a reenlisted centurion named Crastinus rallied his legion with a speech worthy of Vorenus: "'Follow me, you men who are in my company and give your general the aid you have promised. This is the only battle left; once it is over, he will regain his position and we our freedom.' And looking at Caesar he said, 'I shall do things today, general, that you will thank me for, whether I live or die'" (*The Civil War* 3.91).

Although Crastinus was one of "thirty strong brave centurions" who died that day,[11] Caesar's legions crushed the enemy in a rout that Pompey Magnus quite accurately recounts for Vorenus in the "Pharsalus" episode of *Rome*: "It didn't seem possible to lose. The battlefield was on a plain by a river. At the foot of some low hills. My men held their ground well. So I sent my horses to his right flank. Only the cowards were repulsed by a single cohort of reserves. Turned and fled. Two hundred horses crashed directly into my left flank, rolled up my line like a carpet. Put the whole damn army to flight. That's how Pompey Magnus is defeated. That's how the Republic died" (Episode 07).

Not long after his victory at Pharsalus, Caesar followed Pompey to Egypt "to prevent him from again being able to gather other forces and renew war" (*The Civil War* 3.102). Upon arriving at Alexandria in October, Caesar was immediately immersed in a dispute between Ptolemy XIII and his sister Cleopatra over succession to the Egyptian throne.[12] Hoping to forge an alliance with Caesar, Ptolemy ordered Pompey beheaded. But Caesar chastised Ptolemy for this action and aligned himself with Cleopatra. "Shame on the house of Ptolemy for such barbarity," says Caesar. "He was a consul of Rome . . . quartered like some low thief. Shame!" (Episode 08).

While Caesar lingered in Egypt, Pompey's former legions regrouped in Syria and North Africa. Now reawakened in August 47 BC after months of indulgence with Cleopatra, Caesar soon reestablished his military domination of the eastern Mediterranean in a short, fierce battle at Zela.[13] In his *Commentaries*, Caesar reports he "was quite overjoyed at such a victory, although he had been victorious in so many battles. He had brought a major war to an astonishingly rapid end, and recollection of his sudden danger made his easy victory under difficult circumstances all the sweeter."[14] In later years, Caesar described this triumph with just three words: "*Veni, vidi, vici*" or "I came, I saw, I conquered."[15]

In January 46 BC, Caesar turned his attention to Africa where his last formidable opponents, a group of die-hard Senators that included Cato, had again joined forces with King Juba. As was his custom, Caesar led from the front ranks, arriving first in Sicily where he "pitched his tent right by the shore . . . to ensure that everyone was ready whatever the day and the hour" to cross to Africa when the weather became more favorable.[16] Once in Africa, Caesar summoned the seasoned Thirteenth and Fourteenth Legions for reinforcement. When these veteran armies arrived without incident, Caesar reports his "spirits were lifted" (*The African War* 34). Soon after, Caesar deployed the Thirteenth Legion strategically in the center at the town of Uzitta[17] and on the left flank in his decisive victory at Thapsus. In these battles where he depended more heavily than usual on new recruits, Caesar encouraged the untested soldiers to "emulate the courage of his veterans and to covet the fame, status, and reputation of the latter which they would themselves enjoy once victory was theirs" (*The African War* 81).

At the conclusion of the African campaign in April 46, Caesar returned to Rome where he hosted four grand triumphs to celebrate his Gallic, Alexandrian, Pontic, and African victories. Undefeated in war, Caesar now faced his biggest challenge yet, restoring peace after years of civil discord and internecine violence. In this political campaign, veteran officers like Vorenus, who had proven their loyalty in battle, became invaluable as dutiful magistrates and civil servants. "My name is Lucius Vorenus, veteran of the Thirteenth Legion. I bring you good news," Vorenus says in his first postwar campaign speech. "Caesar has put an end to patrician tyranny and will ensure that the common people be heard. Tomorrow, Caesar holds a triumph, a symbol of his love for the people of Rome. Five days of feasting and games as appreciation for the trust and support the people of Rome have given him. I would not be standing here on Caesar's slate if I did not know that he has only the Romans' best interest at heart. With tomorrow's triumph, a new era begins, for all Aventine, for all Rome" (Episode 10).

Although the transition from soldier to citizen was easier for military officers who were given political appointments and endowed with opportunities for recurring income, it was extremely difficult, if not impossible, for common soldiers like Pullo who chose not to reenlist and were little prepared for any vocation other than war. "You can't march with us," a former colleague says to Pullo when he tries to rejoin the Thirteenth for its triumph. "You've left the legion, haven't you? You've signed yourself out. It's enlisted men only in the triumph. You're a civilian. If you want to sign up for a few more years that's a different story. You can march with us till your feet are nubs. I don't make the rules. I follow them. It's enlisted men only, don't push it. Now, walk on then, citizen!" (Episode 10).

With few possibilities for alternative employment, former soldiers like Vorenus and Pullo hired themselves out as strong men and bodyguards, work that was well suited to their military experience and temperament. Although Vorenus' labors were legitimized by political association with Caesar, while Pullo's work was discredited by criminal affiliation with Erastes Fulmen, the two soldiers ultimately were employed in the same craft that rewarded them for their fighting skills and their personal loyalty to a wealthy and powerful patron. Vorenus may have exchanged a soldier's tunic for a Senator's toga, but fundamentally he was a career soldier whose greatest allegiance was to his commanding officer.

Viewing the HBO-BBC series from a twenty-first-century perspective that is characterized by fierce, conflicting, and increasingly violent beliefs about nationalism, patriotism, and religious identity, it is likely contemporary viewers will relate to Vorenus' struggle to prioritize his diverse obligations to Rome, to Caesar, to the gods, and to his family and friends. This apparent conflict, however, was far less relevant in the late Republic than it is today. Surely, Roman honor or *pietas* was defined by three factors: faith in the gods who ordain the course of history; pride in Rome as a triumphant expression of manifest destiny; and deep personal devotion to family and friends. But loyalty to a close network of immediate and extended family superseded all other obligations. This is why Vorenus' decision to defy Republican law and defend Pullo in the arena (Episode 11) is such a quintessentially Roman act. It also explains why Caesar praises his loyal centurion's selfless devotion to Pullo, his comrade and brother-in-arms (Episode 12):

> Well now, Vorenus, what am I to do with you? Defying my express orders, you dared interfere with a legally sanctioned execution – an act of gross criminality and disobedience. By right I could have you thrown off the Tarpeian rock. But the people, simple souls, have made great heroes of you and Pullo. If I were to punish you the people would be made extremely angry. I do not wish to make the people angry, ergo I can not punish you. If I can not punish you, I must reward you, else I seem weak. Listen to this now, Cicero. By popular acclaim, I shall name Lucius Vorenus a Senator of Rome. Will you speak for your people in the Senate? . . . You shall make an excellent Senator. For the first few weeks, you will stay close by me. Know the drill?

NOTES

1 On Caesar and the Roman military, see generally Gilliver, Goldsworthy, and Whitby (2005); Fuller (1965).
2 Translations of *The Gallic War* are by Hammond (1998).
3 Caesar, *The Gallic War* 5.42–43.
4 On the concept of Roman honor, see Barton (2001); on *pietas* in Vergil, see Garrison (1992).
5 Translations of Suetonius are by Graves (1982).
6 Translations of *The Civil War* are by Carter (1998).
7 Suetonius, *Life of Julius Caesar* 32.
8 Caesar, *The Civil War* 3.2.
9 Caesar, *The Civil War* 3.6–8.
10 Caesar, *The Civil War* 3.25–27.
11 Caesar, *The Civil War* 3.99.
12 Caesar, *The Civil War* 3.106–107.
13 Caesar, *The Alexandrian War* 65–78.
14 Caesar, *The Alexandrian War* 77; translation by Carter (1998).
15 Suetonius, *Life of Julius Caesar* 37. On the Zela campaign, see Gilliver, Goldsworthy, and Whitby (2005), 149.
16 Caesar, *The African War* 1; translation by Carter (1998).
17 Caesar, *The African War* 60.

7

Becoming Augustus: The Education of Octavian

Barbara Weiden Boyd

Who exactly was Augustus? We have many sources of information to turn to for an answer, and yet the man remains elusive. His name, like most names of elite Romans, is highly informative about his familial connections: he was born Gaius Octavius, son of C. [=Gaius] Octavius and Atia, niece of C. Julius Caesar; once adopted in his uncle's will, he became C. Julius Caesar Octavianus; once settled with reasonable security – as much security as any leader of the Roman state is likely to have felt for hundreds of years – he was universally known as C. Julius Caesar divi filius [son of the deified] Augustus, and so led the state for over forty years.[1] The shift in nomenclature – from Octavius to Octavian (as he is called in *Rome*, anachronistically but in keeping with modern scholarly practice) to Augustus – marks a number of important cultural shifts, both for the man and for the *res publica Romana*: as he moves from one family to another, and so from relative obscurity to the struggle for acceptance as his adoptive father's rightful heir to uncontested political ascendancy, the Roman world too undergoes a paradigm shift, leaving behind its republican identity and, after thirteen years of crisis, assuming its new status as what we commonly call imperial Rome.

In fact, this character's three identities – Octavius/Octavian/Augustus – can be used, at least when considered with an eye to the historical record, as shorthand labels for three contiguous historical periods: the life of Octavius, born in 63 BC, runs parallel to the rise of the so-called first triumvirate, its eventual dissolution in civil war, and the dictatorship of Julius Caesar, and ends abruptly with Caesar's assassination; the life of Octavian, "born" in 44 BC, runs parallel to his adoption in Caesar's will, his positioning as

Caesar's heir and, after some skirmishing, as Mark Antony's partner in administering the state, its armies, and its provinces in the second triumvirate (a threesome in name only after Lepidus' forced seclusion in 36 BC), and ends dramatically on or shortly after January 13, 27 BC, when at the urging of L. Munatius Plancus (Suetonius, *Life of Augustus* 7)[2] the new *princeps* assumes the honorific Augustus;[3] and the life of Augustus, "born" together with the *res publica restituta*, runs parallel to the age – a period marked by distinctive styles of social and political organization, classicizing and monumental art and architecture, literary sophistication, and peace – that bears his name, drawing to a close with his death in AD 14.

This very abundance of information either derivable from or closely associated with the names of Octavius/Octavian/Augustus is, however, deceptive, as it does not take us very far at all in our search for an answer to the question with which we began: who was Augustus, exactly? It is easy enough to identify him by name(s), family connections, and historical circumstance, as I have just demonstrated in summary fashion; to clarify his familial associations, his political achievements, and even his symbolic power. Indeed, all these qualities are important elements in the social and political construction of Augustus' identity as an historic personage; but they are far less helpful with what we might call his psychological construction, that is, a category of identification (and self-identification) that is premised on how the character, education, and experiences of a child shape the future adult. Our richest ancient sources for the early years (Suetonius, Nicolaus of Damascus, Cassius Dio) offer us overdetermined "backward glances" to the time before the youth's testamentary adoption by Julius Caesar; the hagiographic tendencies they all display are counterbalanced only by the opposite extreme in Tacitus' *Annals*. And of course the words of Augustus himself in the *Res Gestae* (*Achievements*), autobiographical though they indeed are, are no less oblique and artful for all their immediacy. How was Augustus raised? How educated? And how did these formative experiences affect him? What was he like, not just physically but emotionally, intellectually, interpersonally? How did his childhood and adolescence shape the man he would become? What made him tick?

For reasons of convenience – and so as to avoid unnecessary confusion – I shall refer throughout to the historic personage whose portrayal in *Rome* is the topic of this chapter as "Octavi(an)us" or "Augustus," and to the HBO-BBC character himself as "Octavian." The distinction, however, is not based simply on a desire for historical correctness (indeed, were I so motivated, I would insist that we call the adolescent portrayed in *Rome*'s first season "Octavius," and would challenge what might be considered an entirely unnecessary and therefore flagrant inaccuracy in the script), but in order to emphasize the presence of two different fictions in the minds of my readers, and to clarify my own focus on the way in which these two fictions inform each other. In other words, how does the Octavian seen on our television screen presage Augustus, both the historical personage and the fictional character that he will become in the putative future season(s) of *Rome*? And how do our ideas about Augustus, based on what we know about him from a variety of ancient sources, enable us to understand, appreciate, squirm at, or even sympathize with the fictional Octavian?

Readers seeking a catalogue of historical inaccuracies in *Rome*'s depiction of the adolescent who would be Augustus will therefore be disappointed by the following discussion; while I shall point to at least a few of these inaccuracies in this chapter, my primary purpose is to explore some of the ways in which the series constructs a *Bildungsroman* of sorts for the future *princeps*, and so provides a realistic portrait of the psychological person whose existence is almost entirely obscured in the historical record. Other chapters in this volume look at characters whose existence is either almost entirely fictional (e.g., Titus Pullo and Lucius Vorenus) or who, though of impeccable historical credentials, are, as a result of chance, authorial bias, or cultural ideology, characterless *tabulae rasae*, barely mentioned or ignored in the historical record (e.g., virtually all the women, slaves, and foreigners). Augustus, however, is hardly a *tabula rasa*; rather, he might conveniently be compared instead to a palimpsest, a writing surface that has been written on and scraped clean repeatedly, so that its original surface has been not only effaced but also substantially replaced through later acts of inscription. In his brilliant analysis of the Augustan era, the Roman historian Ronald Syme commented that it was "[n]ot for nothing that the ruler of Rome made use of a signet-ring with a sphinx engraved."[4] The portrait of the man that Syme himself proceeds to construct in his influential study of the end of the Republic and Augustus' rise to power is a product of a complex mixture of acute and learned *Wissenschaft* and historically and culturally determined assumptions about the nature of empire and of human nature itself.[5] The construction of a dramatically plausible Octavian, therefore, poses particular challenges and is of unusual if not unique importance to the success of the historical fiction that is *Rome*. In this chapter, I wish to focus on how a convincing construction of Octavian's identity emerges from a series of scenes and interactions that, while almost entirely fictional, allow us willingly to suspend scholarly disbelief at the occasionally very elastic definition of history visible in *Rome*, and so validate the power of the series to convey to multiple audiences the means to, and meaning of, power in the Roman world. In so doing, I shall turn to the written evidence that we do have, incomplete and skewed though it is, for those details that provide a reasonable starting point. Readers will, I hope, soon see that the fictions of ancient historiography and those of Hollywood (or Cinecittà) work together to create an Octavius/Octavian/Augustus who is both believable and comprehensible.

Octavian Viewing

Mos maiorum, or ancestral custom, is a (if not the) fundamental premise in the construction of Roman identity, whether our goal is to understand the complex systems of patronage, social mobility, and interfamilial networking which shaped the Roman state over hundreds of years, or the text of a single poem by Catullus, a single freedman's funerary monument, or the decoration of a single *lararium* (household shrine) in Pompeii. As the very term suggests, *mos maiorum* was transmitted from one generation to the next. The lessons to be learned from the examples of one's ancestors and elders were shaped by Roman historical memory, and Roman history in turn determined the character of Rome's future.

Rome's construction of the young Octavian as a student of Roman history and politics, classical literature, and contemporary *mores* therefore takes center stage in Season One. We frequently see the young Octavian sitting at a desk, presumably studying, or in the garden reading. His political instincts are already well developed when we first meet him: when his mother proposes (Episode 01) to send him to Caesar with her gift, Octavian expresses doubt that his great-uncle will return to Rome anytime soon: "The Senate's hostility will prevent him. Legally speaking, it is not . . ." Atia's annoyed refusal to listen does not compromise the accuracy of Octavian's comment. I shall comment below on a number of occasions in which Octavian's precociousness impresses his listeners; the scene in Episode 02, in which Octavian observes from the shadows as Mark Antony explains to Pompey, Cato, Cicero, and others that Caesar wants them to extend his command so that he will have legal immunity, shows us how Octavian's political astuteness was acquired in the first place. Again, his presence at the epileptic seizure of Caesar (Episode 04) follows his observation of Caesar's calculating offer of a truce to Quintus Pompey. Octavian emerges from the shadows to question the tactical logic of this offer, only to stop in mid-sentence when Caesar begins to writhe.

The single most influential figure in the construction of Octavian's character and intelligence, however, is his mother, who repeatedly asserts the superiority of experience to bookish learning. In Episode 06, Atia's insistence that Octavian acquire sexual experience takes her reluctant son away from his studies: "You *will* penetrate someone today, or I'll burn your wretched books in the courtyard. Off with you!" After Octavian has had intercourse, however, Atia sends him away from Rome to pursue his studies at the safe distance of Mediolanum. His performance of masculinity thus insulates him, as it were, from what she perceives as the feminizing dangers of bookishness. I shall return below to consider other dimensions of Octavian's sexual initiation.

A further development of this pattern of interaction between mother and son occurs in Episode 09, when the triumphant Caesar is dining with Atia and her family and friends. Caesar now asks the newly mature youth, just back from Mediolanum and with the shadow of a mustache on his upper lip, what he would do if he were Caesar. Octavian offers astute advice about public works projects and the appointment of new Senators. In response, Caesar decides to appoint Octavian a *pontifex*, or priest of the state religion. Atia can hardly contain her delight at the honor thus brought to her son and family; but Octavian answers that he would prefer to devote his time to his poetry. Atia dismisses the idea; but when Caesar agrees that poetry can wait, Octavian yields.

On first consideration, Octavian thus might be thought to be acquiescing to his mother's will and abandoning literature. Shortly thereafter, however, Octavian's interest in poetry reasserts itself, when, bored with the study of prodigies, he offers to read poetry to his sister. She for her part (and at the instigation of Servilia) is eager to learn what she can from him about Caesar's mysterious condition. As they sit together – in a directorial gesture to both Dante's Paolo and Francesca and several of Lawrence Alma-Tadema's Victorian depictions of poets and lovers[6] – he reads aloud Catullus' sparrow poem (Poem 2). His seduction by Octavia all but inevitably ensues shortly thereafter, as the life-lessons forced upon him by his mother and his own poetry-infused maturity merge, making him no longer simply an observer of but a participant in the sweep of Roman history. The youth whose first appearance in the series *Rome* is as a passive viewer of Atia as she bathes takes control of his manhood in Episode 09 and stands poised, as Season One ends, to assert his authority over his family, Caesar's legacy, and the Republic itself.

Viewing Octavian

Suetonius reports that Octavius' natural father, by all accounts destined to win the consulship, died suddenly upon his return from a successful pro-praetorship in Macedonia; his son was 4 at the time (*Life of Augustus* 3–4, 8). Octavius' mother Atia was sometime thereafter remarried, to Lucius Marcius Philippus; Suetonius notes that, as Octavius' stepfather, Marcius Philippus joined Atia in attempting to discourage the youth from returning to Rome upon the assassination of Caesar (*Augustus* 8; see also Dio 45.3–4). Lacking detail as it does, the historical record nonetheless firmly identifies an adult male as head of the household in which the boy was raised through much of his childhood. In *Rome*, on the other hand, a father-figure of any sort is conspicuously absent from Octavian's family circle. The absence of Marcius Philippus from the script is just one of many ways in which the *dramatis personae* of this historical fiction, as in most historical dramas that make their way to the large or small screens, are reduced to an essential minimum; not even most ancient historians would lament the absence of this shadowy stepfather. But the void created by his absence has significant implications not only for the depiction of a sexually promiscuous Atia it allows (not at all the model mother seen in Tacitus, *Dialogue* 28.4–5), but also for the environment thus created for her children: without a *paterfa-milias*, the household of Atia is politically vulnerable and so well aware, at times painfully so, of the importance of maintaining good relations with actual or potential patron(s). Atia's dependence upon the favor of her uncle Julius Caesar in turn establishes a rationale not only for her hostility to Servilia but also for an event for which the audience must wait until Season Two, the adoption of Octavi(an)us in Caesar's will – an event that, without an adequate "back story," it would otherwise be difficult to make comprehensible to a non-specialist audience. Taken to what is perhaps its greatest extreme in Atia's abortive attempt to marry Octavia to Pompey after Julia's death (Episode 01), this foregrounding of the Julian bond also allows Atia to push young Octavian into what is his first major action in the series (Episode 01), his fictional journey to Gaul, to which adventure I shall return below.

First, however, I want to draw attention to several important conse-quences of the absence of a father-figure for the construction of Octavian's character, consequences which can only be understood in light of what we know about the role played by family dynamics in the formation of Roman identity, particularly the identity of a Roman man. Without a father or stepfather on the scene, Octavian is raised in the company of women; it is only natural to wonder how, in a culture obsessed with maintaining a polarized and hierarchical sex/gender system, this fatherless family could adequately provide for the construction of Octavian's identity as *vir*, a Roman man.[7] Several features of the fictional narrative created by *Rome's* writers supply the answers.

In such a system, it is crucial that a boy be instructed in the culture and *mores* of men by men, especially older elites who have achieved success in the competitive arena of Roman public life. Atia acknowledges a concern for Octavian's proper maturation into his role as eventual *paterfamilias* when, in Episode 04, she insists that her son eat the testicles of a freshly butchered goat to ensure his masculinity: "You've been developing a distinctly feminine *anima*, and I do not like it."[8] Shortly thereafter (Episode 05), Atia entrusts her son to the tutelage of the legionary Pullo, who has been enlisted by her to train her son in the "masculine arts": war, sex, and hunting (or as Atia puts it, "How to fight and copulate and skin animals and so forth"). Subsequently, we see two brief scenes of Pullo and Octavian with wooden shields and swords, engaged in mock swordplay. In the first, Octavian gives up in exhaustion and complains that he has "no soldiery" in him; later (Episode 06), Octavian's technique can be seen to have improved markedly: he trounces Pullo, and pretends to finish the tutor off with his wooden sword. This accomplishment suggests a basic competency on the boy's part in the skills of war.[9]

Now an unlikely twosome in spite (or because) of the social gulf that separates them, Pullo and Octavian proceed to the "hunt" at the close of Episode 05, when they stalk, torture, and eventually kill Evander, the ill-starred lover of Niobe, after extracting Niobe's secret from him. While Pullo provides both the premise for this episode and the physical strength required to execute it, it is the boy Octavian who directs Pullo's actions and declares the episode finished and never to be spoken of again. Thus reasserting his superior status, Octavian in effect becomes the teacher, and Pullo the student. The third of Atia's charges to Pullo, Octavian's sexual initiation, completes the series of lessons in the climactic Episode 06. At the behest of Atia, Pullo escorts his hesitant charge to an appropriate brothel (itself apparently serving only elites: Pullo is firmly put in his place by the madam-manager, when she observes that the likes of him need not even think about being serviced there). The fulfillment of this sexual rite of passage is then celebrated at home and marked by the gift of a new toga from Atia (a gesture to the *toga virilis*, or toga of manhood),[10] as Octavian's inclination toward normative sexual behavior is assured and his virility confirmed by his performance of the archetypal act of masculine aggression.

Before turning to look at how Octavian learns in other ways throughout the series how to be a Roman *vir*, I want to focus on several other implications of Octavian's incipient performance of manhood. The brothels depicted on several occasions in the series are vivid recreations of the *lupanaria* known from both physical remains (especially in Pompeii) and literary references to them.[11] Returning to Rome (Episode 02), Vorenus advises Pullo that the brothels in the Subura are cleaner than those located elsewhere; this piece of information both acknowledges the availability of commodified sex in Rome and anticipates the lack of privacy that characterizes the brothel we soon see. The social differences between Vorenus (respectable, married, Roman) and Pullo (an "Ubian," and so Roman in name only, without family, property, or other tokens of a stable place in the social hierarchy) also provide a nice background against which to view the very different type of brothel visited by Octavian in Episode 06: not simply clean, but expensive, discriminating, and discreet.[12] Octavian is there introduced to the available prostitutes by their manager, who offers brief but suggestive commentary on the physical characteristics of each. The boy stands silent through three such previews, evincing little interest in the prostitutes on offer (including several women of a variety of ages, sizes, and ethnicities, and at least one youth). He then quickly announces his choice: a red-haired girl who appears to be little older than he is. Octavian's lack of interest in the youth on display is of course a gesture toward normative heterosexual behavior in ancient Rome; it also firmly establishes Octavian's masculine identity as aggressive penetrator, while setting up an implicit contrast with the deviant/desperate same-sex intrigue of Servilia and Octavia.[13]

Octavian's choice of prostitute and the mode of intercourse he wishes to engage in also support this characterization. He does not opt for one of the more exotic women, preferring instead a girl who, at least in appearance, might be Roman (and who has a faint resemblance to his older sister Octavia). In fact, she is foreign, and can speak only enough Latin to communicate with her customers; her heavy accent places her origins in what we would nowadays identify as Eastern Europe or Southern Russia.[14] The name she has been given by her employer, Egeria, is therefore highly ironic: while she has no idea where she came from ("Rome take me very young"), she bears the name of the divine nymph who counseled Numa Pompilius, the second king of Rome (Livy, *History of Rome* 1.21.3). Octavian expresses satisfaction with her origins, as he realizes that she is a representative of the peoples conquered by Rome; his sexual penetration of her thus mirrors Rome's expansionist penetration of and dominance over much of Europe and the East, even as her symbolic name foreshadows his own future as the head of the Roman state. Octavian's wish to penetrate the girl from the rear, meanwhile, seems a natural result of his unromantic and preternaturally businesslike disposition; while his attitude toward the entire episode is not quite one of disgust, neither does he deign to exhibit any pleasure.[15] He thus holds tightly onto his precarious dignity in a situation that is for numerous reasons incongruous, and Egeria's evaluation of his performance – "like bull" – is at once a humorous comment on Octavian's childish physique and an acknowledgment of the power relationship that exists between man and woman, free and slave, Roman and barbarian, dominator and dominated.

The accomplishment of this three-step process of maturation and masculinization is a requisite for Octavian's inevitably increasing importance to the plot. In addition to looking forward to Season Two, however, this series of events also looks back to Octavian's opening gambit in Episode 01. I refer to the episode in Gaul, when Octavian is escorted by a bodyguard selected by his mother to deliver a fine horse to Caesar in his camp after the latter's victory over Vercingetorix (52 bc). This entirely fictional event[16] is useful not only in introducing Caesar and establishing for the general audience his relationship to Atia, but also in bringing the young Octavian into plausible contact with Vorenus and Pullo. This plotline is, however, risky for the characterization of the young Octavian, who thus appears from the outset of the series to be an effectively defenseless victim of both his mother's scheming and the Gallic raiders who attack his traveling party, kill all his bodyguards, and take him into humiliating captivity. The problematic character of this episode is established by an exchange immediately before the attack. Octavian has shown signs of physical exhaustion, so the chief bodyguard extends his arm to Octavian to reassure him that the journey will soon be over.

BODYGUARD: Master Octavian ... [*reaches out to the boy as he begins to slump on his horse*] Visio is only a few more miles.
OCTAVIAN: Don't touch me without permission. [*sternly*] Water.

The irony of the boy's childish imperiousness is brought out moments later, as Octavian, already something of a mama's boy, is symbolically emasculated, his physical defenselessness exposed. Unable to protect himself, he falls into the hands of barbarians. Only the *deus ex machina* embodied in Vorenus and Pullo can free him from his captors and provide him with a safe escort to Caesar.

The conversation that ensues between Octavian and his saviors is indicative of both the boy's physical vulnerability and the psychological bravado he knows he must display in order to regain his dignity:

> OCTAVIAN: Listen to me. I order you to release me this instant. . . . I'm no slave. I'm Gaius Octavian of the Julii. Great-nephew of Caesar.
> PULLO: Gaius who?
> OCTAVIAN: I am a Roman citizen of noble birth, and I order you to cut these ropes.
> PULLO: Say please.
> OCTAVIAN: [*after a pause*] Please.

Pullo's treatment of Octavian in this scene, cheeky and playful, sets the stage for the comradeship they will establish later in the series; it also looks ahead to the delicate negotiation of interpersonal boundaries that will both link the two in a modernist *foedus amicitiae* (alliance) and ensure the maintenance of an impermeable social separation between them. Octavian's order to be treated as a noble, while ludicrous on the emotional level – after all, he says this to the two men who have saved him after his manhandling by the Gauls – is an assertion of both his social status and his emerging manhood, characterized equally in Roman culture by impenetrability.[17] Octavian then proceeds to demonstrate the aggressiveness of his assertion by taking a large piece of wood from his captors' wagon and using it to bludgeon one of the Gauls. The response of Vorenus and Pullo, who observe his desire for blood and do not touch the adolescent, gives implicit assent to his aggressive assertion of impenetrability, as the two men recognize that he is both Roman and of higher status than they. Thus differentiated from Octavian, they are also shown to be fundamentally different from Octavian's barbarian captors, who are unable or unwilling to observe the niceties of status boundaries in the Roman world.

The plotline involving the loss of Caesar's eagle and its eventual recovery, together with the recovery of Octavian, is important in several other ways for establishing the role and character of the future *princeps*. The linking of Octavian and eagle has an obvious symbolic value: as the bird of Jupiter, the eagle is frequently associated in Roman thought with supreme power and divine dispensation. In Livy (*History of Rome* 1.34.8) we find the story of the eagle that seizes the cap of Tarquinius Priscus as he is about to enter Rome and assume its kingship; moments later the bird drops from the sky and replaces the cap on Tarquinius' head. In his comment on this prodigy, Ogilvie (1965) compares one of the many events listed by Suetonius as signaling from conception onward the imminent ascendancy of Augustus: once when the young Octavi(an)us was snacking on a piece of bread, an eagle suddenly snatched the bread, flew up into the air, and then dropped down again to place the bread back in the child's hand (*Life of Augustus* 94; see also Dio 45.2).[18] The restoration of the eagle to Caesar thus constitutes, at least for his men if not for him, an omen heralding Caesar's divinely sanctioned authority; the fact that the young Octavian arrives in Caesar's camp escorting not only his mother's gift but also this symbol of military might associates the boy with his great-uncle's promising political future and simultaneously hints at his own even more promising future. Finally, the recovery of the standard by Vorenus and Pullo also allows the young Octavian to exhibit his precocious understanding of Roman political maneuvering: while Vorenus and Pullo take the loss of the standard and its ensuing recovery at face value as indicative of the endangered honor of the general and his legions, Octavian quickly dismisses their interpretation of the standard's importance and explains that the standard has no symbolic value for Caesar; rather, its theft is something that the general can exploit to his own advantage.[19]

OCTAVIAN: Caesar wouldn't pull a hair for his eagle. You're on a fool's errand.

VORENUS: If Caesar didn't care about his eagle, why did he send us to find it?

OCTAVIAN: It would look strange if he made no efforts. Actually, losing the eagle is useful to Caesar.

Octavian thus displays an intellectual maturity that will prepare him to assume the role of a Roman man along with his *toga virilis*.

Through the sequence of episodes in which Octavian appears, *Rome* emphasizes a political awareness in Octavian that sets him apart from his female relatives, establishes his preparedness to assume the role of *paterfamilias*, and distinguishes him from men of lower social status. In narrative terms, we participate in the construction of an exceptional political identity *ab ovo*. The youngster's sophisticated understanding of how the Senators, Pompey, Antony, and Caesar interact also functions as a prequel to the role he will play in Season Two, when amid political uncertainties the 18-year-old Octavian will have to decide how to position himself as heir to his murdered great-uncle (now adoptive father), how to negotiate an alliance with Caesar's longtime friend and colleague Antony, and how to avenge Caesar's death.[20] Each of these processes will require a combination of luck and political astuteness: the young Octavian of Season One demonstrates throughout the series both his readiness for such challenges and the divine dispensation that will make him *princeps*.

NOTES

1 Syme (1939), 112–113, noting that the name which marked him as an adoptee, Octavianus, was one that he "preferred to drop"; it is likely that when given the opportunity he chose instead to use C. Iulius C. f. [Gai filius, i.e., son of Gaius] Caesar. I emphasize that the relative security of Augustus' Principate asserted here was indeed relative: we know of several challenges to his authority, particularly in the first decade. See Raaflaub and Samons (1990) for specifics.

2 All references to ancient sources are to standard editions of their work: Livy's *History of Rome*; Suetonius' *Life of Augustus*; Tacitus' *Annals* and *Dialogue concerning the Orators*; Cassius Dio's *Roman History*; Augustus' own *Res Gestae*, or *Achievements*; and Nicolaus of Damascus' *Life of Augustus*.

3 On the momentous events of January 13–16, 27 BC, see Lacey (1974).

4 Syme (1939), 113.

5 For a recent assessment of Syme's achievement and legacy, see Wallace-Hadrill (1997).

6 Particularly suggestive are Alma-Tadema's *Lesbia Weeping over a Sparrow* (1866; private collection) and *Venantius Fortunatus Reading His Poems to Radegonda VI* (1862; Dordrechts Museum).

7 Skinner (1997) provides an up-to-date synthesis of the Roman sex/gender system.

8 Atia's use of the word *anima* is a nice touch, gesturing both to the Latin spoken by her historical counterpart and to the Jungian appropriation of the term.

9 McDonnell (2006), 181–185, discusses the importance of education in the arts of war to the relationship between elite father and son. In *Rome*, Pullo's social inferiority to Octavian ensures that he cannot assume, however awkwardly, the role of surrogate father.

10 McDonnell (2006) notes that, during the Republican period, the rite of passage symbolized by the *toga virilis* "occurred when the *paterfamilias* deemed the youth mature enough to fight in the army" (177).

11 McGinn (2004) provides an authoritative discussion of the evidence for prostitution in the Roman world, and the many problems surrounding it: chapter 2, on the economics of venal sex, is a particularly useful introduction to the subject. At 232–239, McGinn describes what is perhaps the best-known Roman *lupanar*, in Pompeii.

12 McGinn (2004), 226–228, compares the decorative scheme of the House of Jupiter and Ganymede in Ostia with the titillating splendor of a modern Nevada brothel.

13 *Rome* acknowledges ambivalent Roman attitudes to same-sex intercourse among men, especially elites, in Episode 05: in the aftermath of Caesar's epileptic seizure, Atia, having heard gossip from her slaves who misinterpreted Octavian's part in the episode, compliments her son on his conquest: "Let's see Servilia compete with a soft young boy like you. What power we shall yield." Her comment may also allude to a well-known slander against Caesar wielded by his political enemies, that as a young man he had been a lover of King Nicomedes of Bithynia (Suetonius, *Life of Augustus* 2, 49).

14 The writers of *Rome* comment here on how little things have changed in 2,000 years: in the wake of the demise of the USSR and the opening of the West to the East, and vice versa, Italy has become a center for the trafficking of prostitutes, both voluntary and involuntary, from several formerly Eastern bloc countries.

15 The position he selects is one that we have seen before, and in a situation where it implies subordination: his sister Octavia knelt on hands and knees for Pompey in Episode 01. Though we may be tempted to view Octavian as something of a prig in this episode, his sexual formation in *Rome* is far more realistic than that described by Nicolaus, who comments enthusiastically on the young Octavius' year-long abstention from sex and the resulting enhancement of both his voice and his physical strength (*Fragmente der Griechischen Historiker* 90, F129).

16 Perhaps loosely based on an event we hear of as occurring somewhat later (46 BC) in Nicolaus (*Fragmente der Griechischen Historiker* 90, F127.21–22): left behind in Rome because of illness, Octavius valiantly and with few attendants followed Caesar to Spain some months later, only to arrive after the completion of the war there.

17 See Walters (1997), 33–35, on the ambivalent position of the freeborn male youth who has not yet reached adulthood; Santoro L'Hoir (1992), 12–28, on the use of the Latin terms *vir* versus *homo*.

18 Note also the eagle prodigy thought to be a portent of Tiberius' succession described at length by Bowersock (1984), 180–181.

19 The episode involving the standard also complements the recurring importance of standards in Augustus' political career: the loss of Crassus' standards to the Parthians in 53 BC was much lamented by the Romans; their retrieval in 20 BC and subsequent housing in the temple of Mars Ultor provided Augustus with a useful distraction from the original motive for the temple's construction, vowed at Philippi as a symbol of vengeance over the assassins of Caesar. Their retrieval is also celebrated, and so associated with the cosmic harmony brought to the world by Augustus, on the cuirass worn by the *princeps* in the (most likely posthumous) portrait of the Prima Porta Augustus.

20 Toher (2004) offers the most recent assessment of the character and actions of Octavian in the months immediately following Caesar's assassination.

8

"Not Some Cheap Murder": Caesar's Assassination

Alison Futrell

The assassination of Julius Caesar serves as a watershed moment in the metanarrative of Western history.[1] For Romans, this was the disruption of a far-reaching agenda in which Caesar was actively engaged, his significant reform not just of the workings of Roman political authority, but of a range of institutions and features of Roman life. Even in its abbreviated run, Caesar's impact profoundly affected Rome and her empire; the assessment of that impact was far from unified.[2] Caesar as icon transcended the survival of the Roman Empire to become a lens through which the Roman legacy was understood, but more importantly a universal figure of regal power, one of the Great Rulers of the World, as the West constructed it.[3] The assassination of this emblematic figure was imbued with great significance, beyond the political. Generations of artists and intellectuals extracted meaning from the inherently dramatic (and fairly standardized) details of the event that survived in the primary tradition, meaning that connected Caesar's death and the means by which it was accomplished to larger elements of the human experience. Recent television serials, including *Xena: Warrior Princess*, ABC's *Empire*, and the HBO-BBC series *Rome*, follow in this tradition by depoliticizing the assassination, using both story arc and cinematic technique to reveal the metaphoric weight of the death of Caesar.

The Ancient Script

The surviving ancient narratives describing the death of Caesar display a remarkable consistency of detail, relaying a pattern of events that may ultimately be based on an "official" version of what happened released sometime after the assassination.[4] Key catalysts for action against Caesar at this particular time are selected, catalysts that suggested immediate danger to the conspirators. These included Antony's offer of a crown to Caesar at the festival of the Lupercalia early in 44,[5] Caesar's deposition of C. Epidius Marullus and L. Caesetius Flavus, tribunes of the plebs, who had removed crowns from the statues of Caesar,[6] and an interaction with a group of Senators that lent itself to interpretation as a gross example of arrogance on the dictator's part.[7] All sources point to specific actions by Caesar that tempted fate, as it were.

Clear indications of the hand of fate itself are likewise noted in the ancient text. Warnings of the assassination of various types were given, from eerie religious omens, to Calpurnia's nightmare, to written admonitions left unread or gone astray.[8] Indeed, Caesar was delayed at home on the fateful day, seemingly ready to heed the many portents and call off the Senate meeting, but after some hesitation he made his way there.[9] Once he reached the gathering, further delay and the physical isolation of the dictator took place.[10] The ancient tradition notes phases in the assassination process, such as the crowding of conspirators in proximity to Caesar, as if ready to press petitions on him, the initiation of the attack by Cimber and Casca, Caesar's response to the assault and the final interaction with Brutus.[11] They likewise note the generally horrified reaction of those present to this astonishing situation, an indicator that the assassins had apparently misread the mood of the city in their plan to reclaim the liberty of Rome by killing the tyrant.

Shakespeare's Assassins

Modern representations of the assassination are influenced by Shakespeare's *Julius Caesar*, historically one of the more popular of his works for stage performance, in no small part because of its susceptibility to reinterpretation in order to reflect contemporary events.[12] Editing of material, redistribution of speeches, relocation of setting, all have been habitually used to direct the audience's understanding of the political relevance of the play. In the twentieth century, it became prevailing practice to place *Julius Caesar* in a modern setting to emphasize its "timeless" message about power.[13] The specifics of that "timeless" message, however, are debatable, slippery. Eighteenth- and nineteenth-century productions focused on the character of Brutus as chief protagonist, interpreting the play as a warning against corrupting ambition, with Caesar's contagious tyranny as a clear danger to freedom and democracy.[14] Twentieth-century productions have been more ambiguous in dealing with the political issues raised, as directors have more broadly distributed cynical and manipulative character tones among the speaking parts, offering at the same time more charismatic and sympathetic Caesars, often comparing the assassination of Caesar with the mob's accidental slaughter of Cinna the poet as more or less equally disruptive and immoral actions. The political stance of the play is thus more ambivalent and the audience is not necessarily expected to empathize with any of the increasingly gray characters.

The assassination is the climax of Shakespeare's piece; the staging of its presentation serves as a commentary on the "real" motives of the conspirators and the true nature of their relationships with each other, with Caesar, and with power.[15] In the Royal Shakespeare Company's 1991 version, for example, the dictator became a "natural animal" in this scene, sort of a bellowing bull in a china closet, dangerous and wounded, drawing a dagger of his own in self-defense, lurching from one assassin to the next until he encountered Brutus. Caesar's final interaction with Brutus is always a charged moment, the placement of Caesar's lines ("Et tu, Brute? Then fall Caesar") relative to stage action arranged to reveal character, past, and intent. At the 1997 Pennsylvania Shakespeare Festival, for example, Caesar ceased all struggle when he faced Brutus, asked his familiar question, and then flung himself on Brutus' knife, sacrificing himself, it is implied, to Brutus' political ideals. The encounter frequently serves as an emotional turning point, Caesar's realization of the futility of further struggle, even equanimity or forgiveness achieved by staging the encounter as a sort of hug-and-stab. *How* the assassins stab Caesar also is made to carry meaning: when and how they reveal their weapons, and whether they assault Caesar from behind, hinting at cowardice and deceit, belying the lofty claims of courage and the greater good articulated elsewhere by the conspirators. The choice to make the assassination awkward or clumsy, an act of "butchery by men inexperienced in killing,"[16] likewise has an effect, suggesting the absence of real political or military acuity on the part of the assassins, their lack of foresight in the shifting currents of political crisis.[17]

Visual elements, such as the collapse of monumental statues or red lighting creeping across the stage, point to social destruction and pervasive bloodshed to come. In a Paris production, Caesar's murder was given strong Christian overtones with the use of key symbols, including a yellow neon cross on stage, weeping women cleaning the corpse's feet with their hair, and the accompaniment of choral religious music.[18] A 1986 Florida version, retitled *Julio César*, placed the action in Cuba. A Santera's prophecy of doom introduced the sequence, and César, the bearded, cigar-smoking dictator, fell at the foot of a statue made of sugar cane, hacked to pieces by machete-wielding figures in shadow. The generally anti-Castro sentiment of the local audience led to a standing ovation in this case.[19] For a 1998 Canadian production the slowly falling dictator pulled down a series of fluttering burgundy banners from above, creating, visually, rivers of textile blood to "drown" the actor and flow across the stage.[20] The perceived presence of blood has an emotional impact, of course; here is an effort to "cinematize" staged performances of *Julius Caesar* in accordance with shifting audience expectations.

Modern audiences are more accustomed to the narrative conventions of film and television than they are to those of the stage. Graphic violence has become a *lingua franca* in the past thirty years or so, often perceived as a necessary component in achieving an emotional impact on jaded modern viewers. Heightened attention to the details of violent action, made possible with special film effects and editing, is now interpreted as "real" in the common visual vernacular.[21]

There have been relatively few revivals of the Shakespeare play in the media of film or television. Producers have chosen to expand their treatment of the death of Caesar beyond the tight focus of the play, in film most often contextualizing the assassination within his relationship with Cleopatra. In recent years, however, Caesar has mostly appeared on television, the more intimate cousin of the film medium. The serial nature of television allows greater time for the development of relationships in narrative. The fact that those narratives enter our homes, our living rooms, our bedrooms, shifts our connection to the medium toward a more personal level. Although the techniques of storytelling have been largely taken over from film conventions, the pacing is quite different. Caesar's assassination is enriched with a long, slow, personalized buildup.

Brutus: Beware the Ides of March

One of the most extensive televised setups for the assassination was in the syndicated series *Xena: Warrior Princess* (hereafter *X:WP*), in which Caesar, as the embodiment of Rome, is made the prime mover behind Xena's hero quest.[22] Caesar/Rome is Xena's nemesis, the source of chaos, oppression, and corruption that is to blame for "the land in turmoil" that "cried out for a hero" (title voiceover). The assassination of Caesar parallels, inverts, and is causally linked to the crucifixion of Xena at the end of Season Four.

Crucifixion is a fundamental motif in the Roman arc of the series, a symbol carrying multiple meanings from its Christian prominence. It refers most obviously to sacrifice and apotheosis, to atonement, and also to imperialist oppression and god-killing sacrilege, the latter meanings especially prominent in films about ancient Rome. Ten years prior to the narrative action of the series, Xena, then a restless leader of a band of sea-rovers, encountered and kidnapped a young Julius Caesar. Intrigued by his confidence and ambition, Xena offered Caesar partnership, her strength to be allied with his in conquest. Caesar agreed, only to betray and crucify Xena and her followers. Xena's (first) crucifixion and its subsequent downward spiral into evil is a fundamental part of the character's back story.

The evil Xena's efforts to conquer and control an ever-widening territory serve as almost a parody of the Roman Imperial Mission, one that lays bare the ethical implications and human costs of empire. That she does so in reaction to trauma at Rome's hands is fundamental to understanding the importance of the Roman theme in *X:WP*. Xena's evil period is characterized by her effort to become her key tormenter, the Roman Empire in a broad sense and Julius Caesar on a personal level. The "real" motivations underlying her negative actions, articulated as self-hatred, a crippled soul, embracing death in life, mirror, it is implied, the "truth" behind the grandiose plans of Xena's evil twin, Julius Caesar.

Xena's crucifixion likewise launched Caesar's quest, envisioned by him as a divinely sanctioned project of fate; "destiny" has selected him to rule the world as part of an all-encompassing great plan.[23] Caesar's eerie conviction that the fates preserve him for this grand achievement is key to its fulfillment: Caesar is fearless, willing to take great risks because of his belief that nothing can really impede his destiny. Xena's crucifixion is meant to send a message to Caesar's rivals, to mark him as someone more impressive than the typical Roman politician. The use, here and elsewhere, of crucifixion as "a message" and an emblem of authority indicates the direction of Caesar's dream: his opponents can expect a humiliating death at the hands of a calculatingly brutal warlord.

Caesar's own interpretation of his mission reflects the "authorized," traditional assessment of historical Rome, presenting a counternarrative to the general anti-imperial stance of the series.[24] Caesar sees his role not as merely the acquisition of power; any "thug with an army" can have power. Driven by patriotic duty to "achieve the impossible," Caesar fights for peace and prosperity in a Rome riven by civil unrest.[25] He is "the only hope to restore the democracy of the Republic."[26] Indeed, Caesar has been the undeserving victim of Xena, his discarded "Thracian whore"; Brutus alludes to a multitude of wrongs inflicted on Caesar by Xena, who is allegedly blinded by an irrational hatred. The Caesarian "spin" on the relationship presents each as obsessed by the other, constantly thinking of the other, constantly seeking to destroy the other, to the detriment of those around them.[27] The opposing drives at work in this relationship are intriguingly depicted in a dream/nightmare/oracular vision of Caesar's in the "Ides of March" episode. Replacing Calpurnia's dream in the primary narratives, this scene horrifically combines desire, union, ecstasy, hatred, and fear as Xena joins Caesar in his bed, clutching a climactic knife in her hand.[28]

Betrayal and treachery run throughout the Roman arc in *X:WP*, starting with Xena's initial betrayal and crucifixion by Caesar but continuing with multiple mutual betrayals by members of Rome's ruling elite. Brutus' betrayal is given a different interpretation in the *X:WP* narrative, however; Caesar is characterized as the traitor, not the "honorable" Brutus. Caesar's betrayal of Xena was but the first of many, as friend after friend has fallen at his behest. Caesar has likewise betrayed his ideals; Brutus comes to realize that the redemption of Rome for which Caesar labored was an illusion, and that Caesar's goals are a danger to the homeland. It is Brutus, not Caesar, who is told to "Beware the Ides of March," for on that day the Republic he loves will be killed by the rising dictator, with Brutus himself set to be assassinated shortly afterward. The exposure of Caesar as traitor, as an anti-hero, is the key factor in the disruption of the Roman narrative: Brutus and the Senators, previously frozen by deceit or incapacity into inaction, rise to murder Caesar.

Xena's hero quest is also sanctified, quite literally, by a wealth of Christian resonances that come together in the "Ides of March" episode. Caesar's assassination is bound up in the plans of Satan, who wants to preserve Caesar as leader of Satan's worldly empire. To do so, he must lure Xena away from her energetic efforts to save the world. The temptation of Xena fails, at great personal cost to Xena and her companion Gabrielle. Both make the hard choice to turn from their spiritual paths, sacrificing their own goals for the sake of friendship, a priority that leads to their crucifixion, which has been a repeated visual motif, a "vision" of destiny, throughout the fourth season. This represents the fulfillment of "destiny" on a number of levels. Xena's first crucifixion launched the Roman narrative, by providing Caesar with ideological and financial ammunition for his conquest/vision. Her second crucifixion is explicitly linked to Caesar's failure, as Xena's crucifixion and Caesar's assassination represent a blow against karmic regression for humanity, sacrifice necessary to the greater good.

The event itself is depicted in a series of tight, fast intercuts between the assassination of Julius Caesar and the crucifixion of Xena; each parallels and inverts the other in meaning. Caesar in the Xenaverse dies because of his selfish megalomania, while Xena dies as an act of selflessness. While the series makes clear that each death has a cosmic impact, the immediate cause is not political or religious, but rather to do with friendship. Caesar is willing to sacrifice loved ones to achieve his ends, to betray Brutus as he has betrayed Crassus, Pompey, and Xena. Xena is crucified because she gave up her own interests, her hero's quest, and her chosen path, to save Gabrielle, her loved one: she chooses the "way of friendship." Cinematically, the two actions parallel each other. The scene is cut so that Xena seems to feel the stabs and Caesar reels from the blows of the hammer. The music soundtrack of strings and percussion punctuates the blows and reactions. The shots throughout are mostly close-ups of body parts, stabbing, nailing, and the faces of Xena, Caesar, and Gabrielle, a choice that enhances the intimacy of the sequence, giving it a "you are there" proximity. The encounter between Brutus and Caesar is a revelation of Caesar's hostility, at last, as he snarls his question through a mouthful of blood. Brutus stabs him face-on, a declaration of his own hostility. Here we find no hug-and-stab, no epiphany of love abiding though wronged. An overhead shot of the circling Senate reveals the corpse of Caesar, the camera pulling back as the colors start to cool (through the miracle of digital grading), bleeding into the blues of the crucifixion scene, where the Roman soldiers are leaving the corpse of Xena in a Calvary-esque landscape of cold and death. Lest we fear for the fate of the world, the episode/season ends with the post-mortem transcendence of Xena and Gabrielle, as they rise toward the heavens, accompanied by a chorus of angelic voices.

A Cheap Assassination?

Aired as a summer ratings draw in 2005, ABC's *Empire* was described by one reviewer as the Wal-Mart version of a Roman spectacle.[29] Lifting motifs, shots, and dialogue themes from the (much better) films *Gladiator* (2000) and *Spartacus* (1960), the miniseries tried to capture public taste for idealistic Roman gladiators, but was generally acknowledged by critics as insipid, flaccid, not even campy enough to be amusing. Created by

Thomas Wheeler, *Empire* purports to dramatize the "coming of age" of Octavian in the years following the death of Caesar, as he faces unlikely dangers and intrigues, training for Roman leadership at the side of his older buddy and mentor, the gladiator Tyrannus.

The first episode established the basic premises of the series around the assassination of Caesar and was by far the strongest part of the piece.[30] From the opening scenes, the signs of Roman leadership are conflated with gladiatorial action, as shots of Caesar's triumphant return to Rome are intercut with a sequence of Tyrannus arming for combat. Key dialogues take place in the stands of the arena, where Caesar first reveals his intent to redistribute land from the hands of the wealthy few to the people of Rome as a whole. Caesar is thus a radical populist for ABC, his agenda given more emotional weight in a midnight meeting between the dictator and Tyrannus, the best of gladiators, the people's hero. The two of them stroll in the wheat fields near Rome, as all gladiators must do when they dream their poignant dreams, and Tyrannus confesses that he hopes one day his son will be free.[31] Caesar then articulates his own personal drive: all he's ever done has been on behalf of the people, for whom he conquered the world, fighting for ten years, only to return to the city to see the Senators growing ever more wealthy and the people deprived of the land and treasures rightfully theirs. Caesar intends to fix that situation. Anticipating fierce opposition from the Senate, Caesar will need a warrior by his side, someone good with a sword who will speak truth to power. Caesar has chosen Tyrannus for this task, as this beloved gladiator represents the best qualities of the Roman character: strength, courage, and honor. In exchange for a few weeks' work with Caesar (for surely only a few weeks will be required to enact political and social leveling in the Roman world), Tyrannus and his son will live free, in a world without chains. As the heroes come to their agreement, violins swell in the background, punctuated by the pounding of patriotic timpani.

Empire displays little political nuancing: the Senators are selfish with their power, jealous of their privilege, while Caesar spouts sentimental platitudes about freedom and the people. The gross generalities in which Caesar expresses his agenda tilt his beneficent authority toward paternalism, a stance made clearer in the representation of the assassination. Nods are made toward the traditional "script" of the event: there are omens (a young Vestal reports a bucket of blood and sick goats), there are unheeded warnings from friends and loved ones to avoid the Senate. There is the physical isolation of Caesar incorporated into the sneaky plans of the conspirators; here, instead of Antony, it is Tyrannus who must be sidelined.

The assassins arrange the kidnapping of Tyrannus' helpless little boy: to hammer home what sinister terrorists the Senatorial conspirators are, the act break lingers on pathetic images of the pretty young wife, frantically searching for her son in a crowded street.

As in *X:WP*, the assassination itself is intercut, to link and compare it to the gladiator Tyrannus' back-alley fight with the thugs who have stolen his small son. In terms of screen time, the cuts are weighted heavily toward Tyrannus' battle against the kidnappers, a choice made perhaps to enhance the action quotient of the piece. The fact that the fight sequence is dimly lit, however, makes the action hard to follow, even difficult, at times, to distinguish hero from evil minions. The viewer's emotions are thus less engaged, which, in turn, affects the impact of the assassination sequence, despite the liberal use of cinematic techniques meant to ratchet up the pathos in the murder of the dictator-father. The assassination cuts are filmed in slow motion, which typically functions to heighten the emotional impact of the action; wordless sung female vocalizations are meant to enhance this effect. No crowding around Caesar takes place until the assault is well underway; Cassius, here the first actually to stab Caesar, rushes toward him from across the Senate floor, thrusting a sword (in slow motion) before him. The effect is to make the attack seem very scripted indeed, as the Senators gradually move forward to do their assigned tasks. A close-up on Brutus shows little emotion, perhaps a slight grimace as he lurches into something of a hug-and-stab, as the actors' bodies in the medium shot obscure weapon and wounding. The paternal weight is heaviest here, when Tyrannus' dispatch of the last thug is juxtaposed to Brutus' strike against "beloved Caesar." The camera cuts to Tyrannus clutching little Piso to the parental bosom, then back to Caesar in the arms of Brutus, gasping out his last words: "And you, my child . . ."[32] Fatherly love struggles desperately against agents of underhanded corruption, bereft of human feeling.

The scene plays out with an overhead shot of Senators swirling around the collapsed Caesar, followed shortly by an overhead of a seemingly dead Caesar lying amid the crimson streams of his cloak, here substituting for blood. The camera rises, as it did in the *X:WP* sequence. Returning from commercial break, however, it seems that Caesar was not yet dead, despite the cinematic positioning. He has time still to gasp out his final wishes to Tyrannus, entrusting Octavian into the hands of the simple and true-hearted gladiator; the explicit connection made here between a perceived morality of gladiators establishes the narrative justification for the rest of the miniseries and claims a meaning for Roman imperial rule.

"Cheaper than Theatre and the Blood is Real"

A big step above *Empire* in terms of production values, the HBO-BBC series *Rome* offers a vibrant, messy visualization of a key historical period, with a treatment of Roman politics the producers intended as a dramatized version of primary source material. The series emphasizes the manipulation going on behind the scenes, the "truth" of politics with its corruption, chance occurrences, and unidealized pragmatism. The series climaxes with Caesar's assassination; the long, slow build to his demise depends, however, on personal relationships. The murder is embedded in a series of betrayals and their counterparts – dramatic expressions of loyalty – that culminate in the final episode. The success of the assassination is guaranteed by Caesar's acts of personal treachery: his betrayal of his love for Servilia to his political aims and his betrayal of his friendship with Brutus, his willingness to exploit Brutus as a tool for his own purposes.

The ground is established for the assassination with the opening voiceover, which highlights class tensions as the basis for civil war, but, importantly, points to the catalyst of Pompey and Caesar's soured friendship. The motif is reiterated throughout the depiction of the war, but functions primarily as rhetoric, a means of persuasion in negotiation or as a feature of the public image built by Rome's leaders, the current neglect of which must be justified to a popular constituency.[33] The real betrayal of friendship focuses on the Junii, building much more slowly and subtly from the first episode. Caesar deliberately feeds a feckless Brutus misinformation about troop morale and Caesar's military strength in Gaul, knowing that this will be passed to Pompey casually and believed by him because it comes from the honorable Brutus, Caesar's friend. The episode focuses on Pompey's superficial deviousness – he "has the cunning of a sardine" – but the absence of trust in Brutus that Caesar displays, his blasé manipulation, points toward Caesar's fatal flaw (Episode 01).

The character of Brutus is developed as a socialite, someone disinterested in the tedium of politics. In an intriguing piece of foreshadowing, Brutus claims a preference for the "German" style of politics, where disputes are settled with a fight to the death (Episode 01). The assertion, on the one hand, stands out as a playful exaggeration, meant to shock and amuse his companions in a social setting. Brutus is not a belligerent character, far from it. The allusion carries validity, however, if it is read as an expression of Brutus' sincerity, his discomfort with layered, multiple motivations. The Germans demonstrate a straightforwardness in their political dealings that Brutus can respect.

Figure 4   The Gallic campaign: Caesar (Ciarán Hinds) rides into camp. Photograph from *Rome*^SM courtesy of HBO®. *Rome*^SM and HBO® are service marks of Home Box Office, Inc.

Caesar, interestingly, demonstrates a straightforwardness in his relationship with Servilia that she cannot tolerate. The resumption of the long-term romance between the two is overlaid with Caesar's cautiousness, something that Servilia recognizes as restraint in his commitment. His letter announcing his return is one of his "letters to friends" that speaks of his "great affection" and his "longing" for her, not his love and dedication (Episode 01). Their relationship, a threat to Atia's position as chief *matrona*, is ultimately doomed by Caesar's political priorities. In severing their romantic connection, Caesar assures her that he does this against his own "inclination," but he must privilege the well-being of the Republic. Servilia rightly reads this as, again, a refusal to articulate his feelings for her as "love" and as evidence of Caesar's habitual disregard for the personal, despite his carefully phrased acknowledgments of friendship and esteem. Caesar only displays emotion when Servilia's hurt, anger, and frustration are focused into her shriek of disbelieving outrage, "The Republic!" Reacting to her overt contempt, Caesar hits her repeatedly (Episode 05). The encounter shapes the intensification of Servilia's hatred and the growth of her plans for revenge.[34] At first, Servilia marshals the support of the gods, crafting *defixiones*, lead curse tablets, to specify the details of Caesar's (and Atia's) torment. Servilia then sows disruption and chaos among the Julii. Reeling from the repercussions of that effort, stung by her apparent failure to blight the triumphant Caesar, Servilia finally chooses to destroy Caesar politically, deploying as a tool her rival in love, the Republic.

Brutus' political choices are guided by his friendship with Caesar. Repeated expressions of loyalty for Caesar and the Julii are never pointed up as surface declarations. His decision to support the Senatorial cause is articulated purely as a choice between friendship and the compulsory support of the Republic decreed by Pompey. Even believing that "Caesar cannot win," Brutus finds it difficult to choose (Episode 03). During the Civil War, Brutus defends Caesar's offers to the leaders of the Senate, unwittingly serving Caesar's maneuverings. When surrendering after Pharsalus, however, Brutus is set back by Caesar's refusal to acknowledge the personal sacrifice Brutus has suffered. Caesar downplays this in an expression of his famed *clementia*: "We have merely quarreled a little and now are friends again" (Episode 07). Brutus is pushed into conspiracy by his mother's unrelenting pressure, her castigation of his groveling submission to Caesar, and, ultimately, by Caesar's qualified vision of friendship. Caesar easily compartmentalizes the ties of friendship, asserting the persistence of fidelity even when engaged in hostilities (Episode 10). For Brutus, the personal weighs more heavily. The fatal test of loyalty comes when Caesar's actions betray his real lack of confidence in Brutus' friendship, when he insists that Brutus, a figurehead of increasing resistance to his authority, leave Rome for the governorship of Macedonia. Brutus counters with an accusation of betrayal, charging that Caesar's continuous lack of trust in him indicates that Caesar places him in the diminished category of "personal friend," who will always be sacrificed to Caesar's political ambitions, "for the sake of the Republic" (Episode 11). In the last meeting of the conspirators, Brutus is still visibly burdened by his decision to jettison his loyalty to Caesar; his rejection of "private" scenarios of stabbing or poisoning Caesar seems to reinforce his own commitment to the visible honor of public service. "This is not some cheap murder! It is an honorable thing we do. It must be done honorably, in daylight, on the Senate floor, with our own hand . . . with my hand." The camera then focuses on Brutus' hand, as Servilia takes it, a gesture that does not read as comfort in this context.

The traditional, familiar "script" of the assassination is absent or deliberately undermined in *Rome*, further problematizing its meaning for the audience. Supernatural omens are collapsed into a single, intriguing vision of a flock of birds briefly forming a human skull in the sky (Episode 12). The omen takes place, however, in the airspace above the rustic fields owned by Vorenus, with no apparent witnesses to experience the warning;

indeed, one wonders if the warning refers to Caesar's mortality or that of
Niobe. Calpurnia's dream is shown, but its impact is minimized by the
presentation, which limits the expression of the prophecy to the private
ambience of the bedroom, pillow talk between husband and wife that
reinforces their conjugality rather than pointing toward the Ides.[35] The
horrific imagery found in the ancient sources is not clearly articulated; this
is merely the most recent of a series of nightmares troubling Calpurnia's
sleep. Caesar claims to have had such dreams all his life, but the claim is
clearly meant to dismiss their importance, rather than highlight Caesar's
connection to the forces of destiny. The "had-he-but-known" human
warnings of the assassination, which focus in the primary material on an
unread message sent by Artemidorus, here are shifted into a pre-dinner
party chat with Atia, who stresses the compulsion of Brutus by Servilia.[36]
This effectively depoliticizes the conspiracy with its emphasis on Servilia's
personal hatred; Caesar had already dismissed the ephemeral graffiti and
now fatally downplays the danger of Servilia's rage.

In *Rome*, the assassination proper is again depicted as a series of intercuts, here between the events in the Senate meeting and Vorenus' confrontation with the adulterous Niobe; in both, the claims of outraged loyalty
are muted by the high emotional cost of its restoration. Vorenus marches
through city streets, pushing aside members of the public and any obstacle
that impedes him. His rampage continues at home, where he destroys in
rage the outward symbols of contented domesticity. Niobe acknowledges
her guilt, offers a rational justification, does not defend herself or plead for
forgiveness, but commits suicide, in accordance with female exemplars of
Roman tradition.[37] Her self-murder follows upon Vorenus' taking up a
knife, a sign, perhaps, of his intent to exact severe paternal justice, of his
valorization of personal suffering on behalf of a social ideal.[38] This tragic
resolution of the private conflict is positioned after, however, the "honorable" public action of the conspirators, an action that disintegrates visually
into chaos and despair.

The peak moments of the assassination point to uncertainty and lack of
foresight among the conspirators. Cimber, the traditional initiator of the
event, lunges at Caesar ineffectually, resulting in an awkward scuffle with
the folds of Caesar's toga. "What are you waiting for? Now! Now! Now!"
Cimber's quavering call to action speaks of nerves bordering on hysteria,
further reinforced by the screaming onslaught of Casca, flushed and lunatic.
Much of the sequence is shot from Brutus' perspective, a vision of growing
horror punctuated by close-ups of Brutus' reactions. The camera uses an
overhead shot of Senatorial action swirling around the struggling Caesar,

positioned earlier in the event than those in *X:WP* and *Empire*. Here, the absence of music allows the audience to focus on the groans of Caesar, the sounds of knives entering his flesh, and the spreading miasma of blood staining the togas of the victim and the assassins, all effects meant to heighten the intimacy and realism for the viewer. The camera shifts to slow motion for the fatal sequence, as ambient music now hushes the sounds of slaughter. The "leaping trout shot," as Caesar's head appears above the level of his massed attackers, presents Caesar as a desperate animal.[39] The Senate has become a slaughterhouse, with conspirators slipping in streams of blood, Caesar collapsed and twitching in dying spasms. The encounter with Brutus dims the music, replaced by Cassius' harsh panting and the ring of Brutus' knife, retrieved from where he had earlier let it fall. Cassius must put the knife in Brutus' hand and push him from behind to accomplish the "honorable thing we do." Caesar, mortally wounded, struggles simply to focus on Brutus, kneeling, tear-streaked, to complete his public duty; in silence, the viewer hears clearly the sounds of the last stab. There is no final articulation of connection between the two, no reconciliation implied by Caesar's gesture of resignation to fate. Neither, however, is there a hug-and-stab. The camera then rises to survey the carnage. Cassius' proclamation of "Thus ever for tyrants!" is met with silence and the effort of Brutus to remove himself from the effects of his actions. He slumps next to Caesar's "throne" and screams "No!" The assassination is clumsy, brutal, an act of butchery that fails as a declaration of Roman honor. Home and State are stained with blood and there can be no real justification or resolution.

NOTES

1   This chapter is dedicated to Erich Gruen, long-time mentor and dear friend, who bears no responsibility for any remaining incongruities or eccentricities of mine. Thanks also to Mary-Kay Gamel and Sandra Joshel, who offered comments on an earlier draft.

2   See discussions of the ambivalent image of Caesar in succeeding imperial dynasties in Pelling (2002), Geiger (1975), and Hannestad (1992). Likewise, the assassins: see Rawson (1986).

3   Various meanings of Caesar's image in the modern world are discussed in Wyke (2006) and Yavetz (1983). Brutus' role in the assassination has also made him an enduring cultural icon, providing an inspiration for political activists claiming a populist bent. See Clarke (1981).

4   See Toher (2006). The meaning extracted from actions, motivation, and character of participants varies among the ancient sources.

5   The Lupercalia incident is in Nicolaus of Damascus, *Life of Augustus* 21; Velleius Paterculus, *Roman History* 56; Plutarch, *Life of Julius Caesar* 61; *Life of Antony* 12; Livy, *Summaries* 116; Suetonius, *Life of Julius Caesar* 79; Appian, *The Civil Wars* 2.109; and Cassius Dio, *Roman History* 44.11. Some authors allege Antony acted in concert with Caesar to "test the waters" about the kingship; others suggest Antony was hostile to Caesar and set him up for political failure.

6   The removal of Marullus and Flavus is in Nicolaus 20, 22; Suetonius, *Julius Caesar* 79; Livy, *Summaries* 116; Cassius Dio 44.9–10; Appian 2.108; Plutarch, *Julius Caesar* 61; and *Antony* 12. Most authors suggest Caesar violated the sacrosanctity of the tribune because he suspected them of using the incident for demagogic effect. Authors differ as to whether their fears of Caesar's regal aims were valid or not.

7   The "arrogance" exemplum is in Nicolaus 22; Livy, *Summaries* 116; Suetonius, *Julius Caesar* 78; Plutarch, *Julius Caesar* 60; Appian 2.107; and Cassius Dio 44.8. All these sources refer to Caesar's failure to stand when a group of Senators approached to announce that a new batch of honors had been voted to Caesar. There are various rationales as to whether Caesar was "really" arrogant or perhaps sick or forced by friends to commit this gesture of arrogance.

8   Suetonius, *Julius Caesar* 81 and Plutarch, *Julius Caesar* 63 tell of birds, lights in the sky, strange behavior of horses, and the soothsayer persistent in cautioning Caesar about the Ides, the latter also noted in Velleius Paterculus 57 and Cassius Dio 44.18. Nicolaus 23 adds formal auguries portending disaster; there are bad sacrifices also in Appian 2.115 and Cassius Dio 44.17, as well as Suetonius and Plutarch. Calpurnia's dream is described by all of these. Written warnings unheeded are found in Nicolaus 19; Velleius Paterculus 57; Suetonius, *Julius Caesar* 81; Plutarch, *Julius Caesar* 64–65; Appian 2.116; and Cassius Dio 44.18.

9   Nicolaus 23 connects the delay both to omens and to Caesar's health issues, the latter included in Suetonius, *Julius Caesar* 81. Plutarch, *Julius Caesar* 63–64, Appian 2.115, and Cassius Dio 44.18 also detail delay and near cancellation.

10 Antony kept away: Plutarch, *Julius Caesar* 66; *Antony* 13; *Life of Brutus* 17; Appian 2.117; Cassius Dio 44.19.

11 General similarity in Nicolaus 24; Suetonius, *Julius Caesar* 82; Plutarch, *Brutus* 17; *Julius Caesar* 66; Appian 2.117; and Cassius Dio 44.19.

12 Its prominence in school curricula is another reason for this popularity, the greater familiarity this affords helping to override the double alienation of the ancient setting and the Shakespearean English. See Derrick (1998), 133–138.

13 The most famous example is Orson Welles' 1937 production for the Mercury Theater, with its heavy use of contemporary Italian fascist symbols and dress.

Toward the end of the century, however, the play tends to be relocated to Latin America, as a "natural" home of extremist dictators for an American audience. See Anderegg (1999, 2005).

14 See Daniell (1998), 102, who notes that the character of Caesar typically verged on caricature in the eighteenth century. Spevack (2004), 32–35, notes the importance of Thomas Betterton's late seventeenth-century staging that emphasized Brutus as central character and philosopher/patriot. Both Spevack and Daniell point to a change initiated in the famous spectacular staging by Herbert Beerbohm Tree in 1898, which rearranged material to feature Antony as protagonist instead of Brutus.

15 See Munkelt (2004) and Greenwald (2005).

16 As described in a review of the 1993 production by The Other Place at Stratford-upon-Avon; see Watermeier (1994), 9.

17 The antithesis is the highly choreographed presentation. The 1995 New Jersey Shakespeare Festival staged it like a 1930s movie dance number, with Caesar working his way diagonally down Busby Berkeley-style steps, changing assassin-partners as he went. See Lukacs (1995).

18 At the 2000 Festival d'Automne; see Munkelt (2004), 63.

19 See Edel (1987).

20 See Watermeier (1999).

21 See Prince (2006).

22 The series producers have stressed their interest in offering a revisionist version of the ancient past. See R. J. Stewart's commentary for the DVD version of Episode 421.

23 Xena's funds finance Caesar's expeditions to Gaul and Britain, depicted here as imperialist conquest. Caesar's long-term goals are discussed in Episode 212.

24 See Futrell (2003).

25 Caesar's impossible goal: Episode 212. Peace for Rome: Episode 420. Resolution of civil unrest: Episode 421.

26 Episode 420. Such a restoration would indeed seem "impossible," given the hostility of Republican Romans to Greek-style democracy; see Livy, *History of Rome* 2.1.

27 "Thracian whore": Episode 605. Caesar's obsession: Episode 212; Xena's obsession: Episode 316.

28 Nightmare sequence: Episode 421.

29 Perigard (2005).

30 Gilbert (2005) notes the "real promise" at the start, which disappointingly "dumbs down" to "increasingly shallow" acting; Kronke (2005) likewise notes a relatively strong beginning that descends into "turgid melodrama."

31 Note repeated use of wheat field flashback sequences in *Gladiator*. Reference to dream of freedom for son recalls *Spartacus*. See Cyrino (2005), 89–120, 207–256; Winkler (2004); Futrell (2001).

32   A translation of "*kai su teknon*," cited by Suetonius, *Julius Caesar* 82, as Cae-
     sar's last words.

33   See references to the Pompey–Caesar relationship in Episode 01, and finally
     in Episode 05, when Pompey speaks of Caesar as a son equivalent.

34   It also parallels the later attack on Servilia in Episode 09. Both violent encoun-
     ters signal a shift in Servilia's status and her corresponding efforts to regain
     her position of influence. See Futrell (2006).

35   The tone of conjugal intimacy is enhanced by the teleplay: the scene follows
     one where Vorenus and Niobe articulate the duties and rewards of
     marriage.

36   Artemidorus is replaced here by Octavia, who pushes her mother to warn
     Caesar (in Episode 11). Also a hint at an aborted warning comes in Episode
     12, where a petitioner shrieks for "A moment of [his] time!" as Caesar leaves
     his house for the Senate.

37   A reference to the famously chaste Lucretia, whose post-rape suicide is under-
     taken despite her own "innocent" status as victim of Sextus Tarquinius' lust;
     see Livy, *History of Rome* 1.57–60.

38   Roman adultery law focused on the erring married woman as guilty threat to
     the property interests of the *paterfamilias*. Various efforts were made by
     Augustus to institutionalize what may have been informally practiced by
     individual families: the right of the husband or father to kill a wife caught *in
     flagrante*. Niobe expresses this fear in Episode 03, where she warns her daugh-
     ter that, should she betray the truth of the infant's parentage, "[Vorenus] will
     kill us all!"

39   Quote from Bruno Heller in his commentary on Episode 12.

9

Women's Politics in the Streets of *Rome*

Antony Augoustakis

"What a congeries of heroes! Such vim! I feel like Helen of Troy!" Atia exclaims when Antony arrives at her house to meet Cato and Cicero, in Episode 02. As the actress Polly Walker admits in the DVD extra feature "Friends, Romans, Countrymen," Atia "should have been the emperor . . . but unfortunately she was born a woman . . . who nevertheless channels all her energy and power into her son." In the DVD feature "When in Rome," series creator Bruno Heller calls her an anti-heroine, an arch-manipulator. In creating the characters of *Rome*, both Heller and historical consultant Jonathan Stamp have systematically avoided some of the pitfalls of copying other comparable productions, such as *I, Claudius* (1976) – granted, Siân Phillips' Livia constitutes the cinematic predecessor of Walker's Atia.[1] But the series suggests that in a male-ordered world, where women are excluded from active political life, characters like Atia have to build "networks and alliances" and thus tend to become the "shadow rulers" of Rome (as the official website claims: www.hbo.com).

In this study, by focusing on the fictional feud between Atia and Servilia (played by Lindsay Duncan)[2] as it unfolds in the twelve episodes of the series, I shall examine the affiliation between these two women and their historical counterparts. By looking closely at the dramatic events that lead to open civil war between the Junii and the Julii, it becomes evident that though in charge of the upbringing of their children, especially their sons, it is not seldom that Roman *matronae* affect their sons' decisions. The rivalry between the two noble women forms a subplot assisting the main theme of civil strife in the late Republic, a theme which leads to the climax of events, Caesar's murder by Brutus. At the same time, however, we witness a process whereby Servilia's own body is transformed into the body politic.[3] After Atia submits her to public humiliation, Servilia rises up to take vengeance both on Caesar for having spurned her love and on his manipulative niece for shaming her. She accomplishes this by turning her own son against the dictator, under the pretext of liberating the Republic just as his remote ancestor had done in 509 BC. In rewriting the highly competitive male politics of the late Roman Republic, the show aspires to underscore the importance of women as active players in securing generational succession, but at the same time the series refocuses the camera from the male protagonists of the period to the less accounted for, and historically marginalized, wives and mothers.

". . . the Most Holy and Excellent Mother":[4] Atia and Servilia in the Ancient Sources

Reconstructing Livia or Messalina does not present the same difficulty as giving flesh and voice to Atia and Servilia, to whom the scant historical record rarely attributes such a significant role as the series *Rome* does. Atia Balba Caesonia, most probably born in the late 80s, was the daughter of Julia, Caesar's sister, from her marriage to Marcus Atius Balbus from Aricia in the Alban hills, a man with close connections to Pompey (Suetonius, *Life of Augustus* 4).[5] After Atia's first marriage to Gaius Octavius, she gave birth to Octavia Minor (born around 66–65 BC) and Gaius Octavius, known as Octavian (born in 63 BC). Upon the death of her husband in 59 BC, a year later Atia married Lucius Marcius Philippus (consul in 56 BC), in contrast to her portrayal in the series as unmarried and passionately infatuated with Antony. Atia sought refuge at the temple of Vesta, together with Octavia, after Octavian's march to Rome upon his victory at Mutina, as the historian Appian informs us (*The Civil Wars* 3.91–92). Atia died between August of 43 and January of 42 BC, during her son's first consulship, and received great honors from Octavian himself (Suetonius, *Augustus* 61.2; Cassius Dio, *Roman History* 47.17.6). In Suetonius' reconstruction of the life of Augustus, a century after the emperor's death, we find the story of Atia's impregnation by Apollo (*Augustus* 94; see also Dio 45.1.2–3), unmistakably a historiographical *topos*, following the biographical traditions of Alexander the Great and Scipio Africanus, and no doubt a figment of Augustan propaganda:[6]

> I read in the books of Asclepiades of Mendes, entitled *Theologoumena*, that
> Atia, attending the sacred rites of Apollo in the middle of the night, had her

litter positioned in the temple and fell asleep, while the other matrons were also sleeping. All of a sudden, a serpent slid up to her, then quickly went away. On waking, she purified herself, as she would after sleeping with her husband. And at once there appeared on her body a mark in the image of a snake and she was never able to get rid of it, so that ever afterwards she avoided going to the public baths. Augustus was born ten months later and for this reason is believed to be the son of Apollo. It was Atia, too, who before she gave birth, dreamed that her insides were carried to the stars and spread over all the earth and the skies.[7]

It is not surprising, therefore, that in imperial literature Atia is refashioned as the originator of success in Octavian's life because of her central role in his upbringing and social education. In the historian Tacitus' *Dialogue concerning the Orators* (28), for instance, Atia is portrayed as an exemplary mother, ranked together with Cornelia, the mother of the famous Gracchi, and Aurelia, the mother of Julius Caesar himself. In the beginning of his narrative of Augustus' pedigree, however, Suetonius observes a possible low-birth provenance from Atia's side (*Augustus* 4):

> [Antony] alleges that Augustus' maternal great-grandfather came of African stock and earned his living first by keeping an oil-shop and later a bakery in Aricia. Cassius of Parma, for his part, taunts Augustus in a letter with being the grandson not only of a baker but also of a money-changer, alleging: "Your mother's dough came from the crude bakery in Aricia; a money-changer from Nerulum shaped the loaf with his filthy hands."

According to Cicero, Antony insulted Atia's origin from the Latin city of Aricia to reproach Octavian for his low birth ("the mother from Aricia," *Philippics* 3.15).[8] In his now fragmentary account of the *Life of Augustus* (*Fragmente Griechischen Historiker* F130), Nicolaus of Damascus underlines Atia's plans to promote her own son, Octavian, and to improve her family status in Rome, after the murder of Caesar.[9] Nicolaus' portrait is more closely akin to Atia's representation as an ambitious mother in *Rome*:[10]

> [Atia] said [Octavian] must show himself a man now and consider what he ought to do and put his plans in action, according to fortune and opportunity. . . . (16) His mother Atia, when she saw the glory of fortune and the extent of the Empire devolving upon her own son, rejoiced; but on the other hand knowing that the undertaking was full of fear and danger, and having seen what had happened to her uncle Caesar, she was not very enthusiastic. . . . Hence she felt many cares, now anxious when she enumerated all the dangers awaiting one striving for supreme power, and now elated when she

thought of the extent of that power and honor. Therefore she did not dare
to dissuade her son from attempting the great deed . . . but still she did not
venture to urge him on, because fortune seemed somewhat obscure. She
permitted his use of the name Caesar and in fact was the first to assent
(18).[11]

Nicolaus' Atia discerns the perils of Octavian's sudden emergence in the
political affairs in 44 BC,[12] while her fictional counterpart in *Rome* displays
a vacillating indecision between the two parties: she hastens to denounce
and forsake the Caesarian party at first, while she is equally ready to put
on the cloak of a purposeful tenaciousness that borders on heartlessness
when the outcome proves Caesar triumphant.

Servilia presents a stumbling block to Atia's strategy of political and
social ascendancy in the turbulent years of the late Republic. In *Rome*,
Servilia's passion for Caesar, coupled with the pervasive insinuation that
Brutus may have been Caesar's own son – both stories based and expanded
upon the historical evidence from Suetonius (*Life of Julius Caesar* 50), Plutarch (*Life of Brutus* 5), and Cicero's invectives ("mother of the tyranni-
cide," *Letters to Atticus* 14.21) – is transformed into indignation and hatred
that fuels her son's fateful decision in March of 44 BC. Almost twenty years
older than Atia, Servilia was born around 100 BC, the daughter of Quintus
Caepio and Livia, sister of Marcus Livius Drusus.[13] Caepio divorced Livia,
who then married Marcus Porcius Cato and bore him the famous son, Cato
the Younger, who fought Caesar at Utica in 46 BC and shortly after committed suicide.[14] Unlike Atia, who can boast of her affiliation to Caesar but
who nevertheless has only recently turned into a powerful figure and by no
means can assert entitlement to a glorious past, Servilia's strongest weapon
is her link with the noble family of the Junii.[15] On the one hand, she is the
descendant of Servilius Ahala, who in 439 BC without hesitation killed
Spurius Maelius in the Forum, thus cutting short the man's attempt at
tyranny (Plutarch, *Brutus* 1). On the other hand, her marriage to Marcus
Junius Brutus (who died in 78 BC) enables Servilia to generate a direct
relationship between the liberator of the Roman plebs in 509 BC and her
own son, Brutus, the liberator of the people in 44 BC.[16] The decision to turn
against the man with whom she shares deep love and affection is portrayed
in the series as a painful one. The most famous account of Servilia's involvement with Caesar is reported by Suetonius (*Julius Caesar* 50):

> But above all Caesar loved Servilia, the mother of Marcus Brutus, for whom,
> during his last consulship, he bought a pearl worth six million sesterces and,
> in the course of the civil war, in addition to other gifts, knocked down to

her some expensive estates which were on sale at auction at a very modest price. Indeed many were astonished at the low price and Cicero wittily remarked: "The price was higher for a third was knocked off." For it was believed that Servilia was prostituting her daughter, Tertia, to him.

The story of the pearls will be revisited in our discussion of the twelfth episode of *Rome*.[17] What constitutes an important aspect of Servilia's portrayal in *Rome*, however, is the intimate relationship and the extent of her exertion of power over Caesar, behind the scenes.[18] To be sure, love can turn into hatred very easily.

Weaving Affections

Rome is about civil war, a theme prominently reflected in both the public and the private spheres. Just as Caesar and Pompey strive to impose an end to the long-standing, bloody war that has wreaked havoc on the Republic, so too does Vorenus seek to build the broken bridges with his wife, Niobe, upon his return from war. Through the creation of various interrelations, the audience becomes privy to the complexity of affections that civil strife has brought about. At the end, when Caesar dies in the Curia (Senate House), some seize the opportunity to proclaim victory over evil and rejoice in the longed-for restoration of the Republic; at the same time, however, what Vorenus has so meticulously striven to restore – his own household – collapses in a few minutes with the suicide of Niobe. The dissolution of the body politic results in the frantic behavior of the Roman population, as they are called to take sides: domestic turmoil reflects civil mayhem.

Affection for the Caesarians or the Pompeians is transformed into a polysemous word, appropriated in the discourse of private life. In the first episode, Caesar entrusts Brutus with a letter for Servilia, who complains that he has not written often from Gaul. In his letter, Caesar uses the word "affection" and causes Servilia's dismay at the replacement of the word "love" by a close, yet not exact, synonym. At the welcoming party for Brutus, we see Brutus for the first time asserting that Servilia is nagging him on to politics; she replies that it has been the family tradition for five hundred years. After Caesar's rejection of Servilia, affection for the man turns into vengeance, which in turn is cloaked under the pretext of alleged affection for the Republic. Both Atia and Servilia claim to have in mind the interests of the Republic as they go about scheming for its downfall,

Atia by promoting Octavian and Servilia by urging Brutus to murder and chaos.

There are, however, no clear boundaries between affection for one's country and love of a more personal sort. In Episode 03, Brutus admits there is no middle ground, as he has decided to follow Pompey, although Caesar is his dear friend: "The Republic is more important than any friendship," he shouts. Servilia's decision to stay behind in Rome enrages Brutus, who attributes it to pure lust. As he kisses her hand, nevertheless we get a glimpse of the tender filial piety he feels for his mother, as they are both torn between love and country.[19]

Affection between Servilia and Caesar comes to its climax in the fourth episode, when their reunion takes place. Their love affair is reminiscent of the gentleness shared by an older couple, for example the love between Penelope and Odysseus,[20] in sharp contrast to the more youthful passion and rampant sexuality between Atia and Antony.[21] This contrast between different ages becomes an important theme in *Rome*. Intentionally, I believe, the character of Calpurnia (played by Haydn Gwynne) looks older than both Servilia and Atia, though she would have been only 18 when she married Caesar in 59 BC (she was born ca. 78 BC), since the series aims to portray Calpurnia as "dignified . . . a species of statue," as Posca describes her in Episode 04. The struggle between older and younger generations in *Rome* is evident not only in the case of Pompey and Caesar, but also in the case of Antony and Octavian, as younger men are bound to succeed their older friends, who in turn become their worst enemies. We watch a resolute Octavian come of age, a perfect match for the cunning Antony. And yet, in the case of Servilia and Caesar, we realize that Caesar seems to give himself up completely to his paramour. In Episode 05, we see Servilia playing dice with Caesar, and Caesar surrenders to her when she tells him she will not be merciful but rather require that he "pay his debts."[22] Caesar's affection for Servilia precipitates Atia's jealous reaction, when Antony declares to her that Servilia has "unmanned" Caesar. Of course, Atia summons the pretext of another affection, that of the Republic: "If he were not mewling in bed with that witch, he would be chasing down Pompey. The Republic is at stake!"

Servilia's "unbridled" passion for Caesar, however, depicted as an act of lust for the newly imposed tyrant, affects Caesar also: just as Servilia becomes the *fellatrix* and supporter of a dictator, so Caesar is denigrated on wall-graffiti with a phallus in his mouth and the inscription "*Caesar Tyrannus*" (Episode 04). In Episode 05, Calpurnia's exposure to the graffiti "*Servilia futatrix*" and "*Caesaris fellator*," commissioned by Atia, initiates Caesar's decision to break up with his mistress. Caesar's next visit to

Servilia bears no traces of their previous peaceful engagement, as he coldly informs her that they are finished. He wraps his decision in the excuse of pursuing Pompey, for the good of the state: "Be assured, it is not that I do not love you . . . I must do what is right for the Republic." Servilia's affections now have to be channeled elsewhere, as they are first transformed into rage and the production of the curse tablets, and eventually to the support of Cato's cause, the love of the Republic.[23]

In her grief and anger, Servilia now turns to an activity befitting an ideal Roman *matrona*, weaving. However, Servilia never loses her political identity: she shows mercy and forgives Atia's foul play in commissioning the offensive and denigrating graffiti by inviting Octavia (played by Kerry Condon) to a session of weaving in Episode 07, an episode that elides the details of the Battle of Pharsalus from the narrative and instead focuses on Caesar's exercise of political *clementia* ("mercy").[24] Caesar and Servilia are portrayed as two sides of the same coin, as clemency is in reality abused by both as the means to achieve their purpose: on Caesar's part it is used as a synonym for destroying freedom and decapitating the Republic. Servilia's device of weaving becomes a source of agitation for Atia: "I know she's tedious, really, weaving!" With the loom in the background, the audience sees the homosocial bond develop between the two women, Servilia and the much younger Octavia, as they begin to enjoy each other's company. When the slave Eleni announces to her mistress that Caesar has won the battle at Pharsalus but there is no news of Brutus, the homosocial bond is transformed into something stronger.

Servilia and Octavia continue their weaving session in the ninth episode, after a tense reunion between Servilia and Caesar at Atia's house.[25] Octavia worries about Servilia's painful feelings for Caesar. As Servilia admits that he still has some terrible hold over her, she enlists her young lover to get the truth about Caesar's secret affliction (the *morbus comitialis*, or epilepsy) from Octavian. Servilia's exploitation of Octavia knows no boundaries, since she does not hesitate to reveal to her that her mother, Atia, is behind her husband Glabius' death. Servilia's efforts, however, will come to an abrupt stop, when Atia discovers the truth about her daughter and her chief enemy.

Women's Bodies and the Body Politic

Taking care of a woman's body is an intrinsic aspect of everyday life in *Rome*. In Episode 04, while Atia is choosing from among her wigs,[26] Servilia expresses nervousness about her looks, because it has been eight long years since her last meeting with Caesar. Eleni, the body slave serving as *ornatrix*, allays her fears by telling her mistress that she smells like flowers, to which Servilia responds with a sarcastic question: "In bloom?"[27] Repeatedly Atia comments on Servilia's appearance, in an endless competition of beauty intimately linked with social activities, such as the politically charged soirées at Atia's house. For example, Atia tries to interest a rather indifferent Calpurnia in her gossipy assessment of Servilia's looks: "She has none of the goatishness one normally sees in women her age" (Episode 04). Later, it is no coincidence when Octavia, still reeling from the news that her mother killed her husband, turns all her loyalty toward Servilia right after she sees Atia with a seamstress trying a new dress (in Episode 09). Octavia is disgusted with the ostentatious pretensions of her class, a development which slowly isolates her as she finds refuge in the cult of the Magna Mater.

Preoccupation with one's body and its integrity becomes an important theme in the last episodes of the series, as it fuels the plot and leads to the climax of events: the murder of Caesar. Atia avenges Servilia's seduction of Octavia by orchestrating Servilia's public humiliation. In a sculptor's yard, as Servilia's *lectica* travels through the streets, Atia's henchman, Timon, ambushes the slaves escorting Servilia (Episode 09). When the litter falls to the ground, Atia's body slave, Merula, chops off Servilia's long red hair, as several men pull off her dress and whip her body with a stick. While she is stripped of her clothes, Servilia cries several times: "Keep and protect me!" The act of cutting Servilia's hair signifies something akin to her death.[28] Moreover, just as Servilia tries to protect her damaged *pudicitia* ("chastity") by covering her violated body with her torn dress, so does Caesar employ the gesture at the very end: in a last effort to guard his body from the assassins' blows and avoid further pollution, he wraps himself in his toga and covers his eyes.[29] From her symbolic death, however, as we shall see, Servilia will rise victorious at the end.

In the next episode (Episode 10), Atia pays a visit to a fragile Servilia, pretending that what happened to her, namely "a noble woman stripped naked and beaten on the streets," is "too sinister . . . horrible, horrible." Servilia promises that justice will eventually find the culprits. There is a connection between what happens to Servilia and her son's actions, as Atia makes clear. When Atia shifts the discussion to political affairs, she adds that she is afraid Brutus would try some foolish act of bravery instead of submission to Caesar, implying Servilia's own surrender to her power, now that her uncle is the master and commander of the city and of the Empire. As Atia proclaims: "Men are so silly about their honor." When she invites

Servilia to participate in Caesar's triumphal procession and games, Servilia declines with severity intact on her face. Later when Brutus visits his mother, he suggests the country might be a place that would speed up her recovery. Servilia, however, has other plans: "I rise when I have reason to do so. Don't loiter here pretending to be solicitous . . . Go to your friend's obscene display." Servilia's rejection of the triumphal "bread and games" is closely associated with her abused body, which not only is the cause of her absence but also becomes the source of her own rejuvenation and the vindication of the Republic. Just as in 509 BC Lucretia's insulted body is transformed into the crucial political "ground" for the transition from the monarchy and tyranny of the Tarquinii into the beginning of the Republic,[30] so Servilia's almost dead body is progressively resurrected to take vengeance on Caesar and in turn strip Atia of her insolent power. She lets Caesar celebrate his triumph, because her own triumph will come at the very end.

Servilia is conspicuous by her absence from the spectacle of Caesar's triumph, but she is replaced by the defiant Vercingetorix, the leader of the Gauls, whom we see captured after the Battle of Alesia in the first episode. There he is led before Caesar and is stripped naked, like Servilia, an act of ultimate humiliation and a token of his submission to the conqueror of Gaul. In Episode 10, he is executed by strangulation, sealing Caesar's victory. At the end of the episode, however, the link between Vercingetorix and Servilia is laid bare. While the body of the Gaul, rescued from a trash heap in the city, is burned by his fellow countrymen in the woods away from the city, when the uproar of the day's triumphal procession has subsided, we see Servilia that night in full splendor, having dressed up for the first time after the unhappy incident. The viewer is made to feel as if the courage of Vercingetorix were transplanted into the heart of Servilia,[31] who now recovers fully and emerges as the one person in whose hands the restoration of the Republic lies, the ultimate act of defiance against Caesar.[32]

Vengeance has already started for Servilia, who has used weaving and writing as her tools. Brutus is informed by Cicero that there is wide circulation of a manifesto against Caesar's tyranny, "a call to virtue," forged in his own name: "Sons of the Republic, the blood of our forefathers calls you to honor the memory and emulate the death of Porcius Cato, the last true Roman."[33] The pamphlet was composed by Servilia with the help of Quintus Pompey and Cassius (Episode 10). In her own defense, Servilia reminds an anxious Brutus that he has failed the Republic and his ancestors: "Rome has fallen into the hands of a corrupt monster. You are a direct descendant of the father of the Republic. Would your forefathers bend their knees to a tyrant? They would chase him out of the city like any mad dog."

With this weight on his shoulders, uncertain of his ability to become the liberator of the Republic, Brutus is slowly persuaded to participate in the conspiracy by breaking his ties with Caesar. This is the last time we see Servilia weaving, with one of her shoulders bare (Episode 11). By exposing part of her body, Servilia, who heretofore has always dressed very appropriately for a Roman woman of her age and status, indicates her full recovery from the shameful incident of her humiliation. She emerges as a seductress, who has ultimately succeeded in drawing her son into the murder plan. Then Servilia initiates Brutus, in a scene that evokes but also reverses the earlier episode of the composition of the lead tablets cursing the Julii (Episode 12). Now she invokes the ancestors of the Junii, in front of their wax images, and asks for their blessing: "Let his arm be strong, let his aim be true, let his heart be filled with sacred rage."

The plot of the series comes full circle with a reverse invitation (Episode 12). Servilia now invites Atia and her family for a visit, under the pretense of ending their feud: "the two families entwined must not be strangers." She signs her letter "with great affection." By now we are privy to the semantic (ab)uses of this word in the series: Servilia herself has learned how to abuse the word, just as Caesar had previously done without hesitation. Unsuspecting Atia accepts the invitation. As the camera cuts back and forth from the bleak events of the Forum to the seemingly peaceful private house of Servilia and to the tragic events at Vorenus' house, we can see how civil strife has permeated deep into Roman society. As Caesar falls dead, chaos erupts, while Servilia declares her victory to a stunned Atia and Octavian.[34] "So you see, the tyrant is dead. . . . The Republic is restored. And you are alone," Servilia says calmly and proceeds to confess and confirm her sworn eternal hatred against Atia and her family. She intends to make her suffer "slowly and deeply, as you made me suffer. . . . First I want to see you run, run for your life, to some rat hole in Greece or Illyria. I shall come and find you." The camera focuses intently on Servilia's face, as the audience sees her wearing pearls, a clear visual allusion to Caesar's gift. Servilia has completed her mission of revenge.

In my examination of the feud between Atia and Servilia, I have traced the emergence of these two women from the safely private boundaries of their households into the dangerous arena of the *res publica*, where public affairs are conducted. As both Atia and Servilia strive to promote the success of their sons in politics, these two prominent Roman *matronae* are seen to transgress the traditional gender roles ascribed to women of the period. Thus, these women do not hesitate to use and abuse their "traditional duties": while Atia exploits her charm and sexuality to seduce Antony in her desire to promote her family, Servilia manipulates her weaving by turning it into a trap to engulf Octavia, a ploy that eventually brings disorder to the house of the Julii. In the narrative trajectory of the series, however, there are no real winners or losers among the women characters: rather, it is the *res publica* itself that swiftly crumbles to pieces.

NOTES

1   In the television movie *Imperium: Augustus* (2003), Valeria d'Obici embodies Atia as an ideal model of the compliant mother and wife, in contrast to Atia in *Rome*, the scheming "harpy," as Antony calls her in Episode 06.

2   In the audio commentary of Episode 09, director Jeremy Podeswa praises Duncan as a fantastic actress and comments on the dynamic political and personal relationship between mother (Servilia) and son (Brutus).

3   See also Wyke (1997), 34–72, on the use of the body in the Spartacus films.

4   Cicero's characterization of Atia in *Philippics* 3.16.

5   See the entry in the *Real Enzyclopädie* under Attius 34; see also Becher (1996).

6   Note the poet Domitius Marsus' epigram of Atia: "Nevertheless, I am called fortunate before all other women because of him (my son), whether I, a mortal woman, bore a human being or a god" (fragment 8 in Courtney, 1993).

7   All translations of Suetonius are taken from Edwards (2000).

8   By contrast in *Rome* Episode 06, Atia asks Antony to marry her because of her money and status: "Allied with my house you'll have both coin and nobility to make yourself king if you wished so." On Atia's origins from Aricia, see Green (2006), 34–41.

9   It is agreed that Nicolaus based his biography on Augustus' thirteen-volume autobiography, *De Vita Sua*, "On His Life"; see also Toher (2006) on Julius Caesar's representation in Nicolaus of Damascus and its influence on the later tradition. Milnor (2005), 89, observes that Atia is represented by Nicolaus as taking "a singularly active role" in directing Octavian's activities. As Milnor notes, Atia is "not simply an over-protective mother, but a lively and intelligent ally to her son" (90).

10   See Appian, *The Civil Wars* 3.14: "She advised him to proceed craftily and patiently and for the moment avoid open or over-bold action." Translation by Carter (1996).

11   Translation by Hall (1923).

12   In Suetonius, *Life of Augustus* 8, and Velleius Paterculus, *Roman History* 2.60.1, Atia and Philippus opposed Octavian's decision to accept his uncle's inheritance and adopt the inauspicious name.

13   See the entry in the *Real Enzyclopädie* under Servilius 104; see also Hillard (1992), 53–54, who aptly remarks that Servilia's connections "ensured that she was center stage during much of her widowhood."

14   In fact, the historical tradition portrays Servilia having "maternal authority" (*materna auctoritas*) over her half-brother Cato (Asconius Pedianus, *Commentary on Cicero's Defense of Scaurus* 23), though we never see the two interact in *Rome*.

15   Note how the camera in *Rome* often centers on the wax images on Servilia's walls, as a reminder of the glorious past of the Junii. Servilia is more steadfast in her allegiances than Atia, who is depicted as more fickle. In Episode 03, for instance, Atia and her family take cover in their villa with Brutus and Servilia, as an angry Pompeian mob throws rocks and torches at their door. A frantic Atia curses her cousin: "If Caesar were here, I would stab him in the neck. He has ruined us . . . Our closest friends have abandoned us." Servilia and Brutus, on the other hand, declare their allegiance to Caesar, since they are not "slaves to fashion," as Brutus asserts. In Episode 06, after her split with Antony, Atia does not hesitate to switch sides and try to befriend Servilia: "The old crow stands well with Cato and the rest. When Caesar and his dog Antony are defeated, we'll need her good will!"

16   Servilia then married Decimus Junius Silanus (consul of 62 BC), who died in 60 BC. With Silanus, Servilia had three daughters, one of whom, Junia Tertia, married the conspirator Gaius Cassius Longinus. Servilia arranged Brutus' marriage to Claudia (daughter of Appius Claudius Pulcher), but his subsequent marriage to Porcia, Cato's daughter and his own first cousin, did not seem to have met the authoritative mother's approval. The series forges a powerful relationship between mother and son, while eliding the wives from Brutus' life.

17   Jonathan Stamp alludes to the legend in the audio commentary of the first episode.

18   Cicero calls it "nocturnal intervention" (*Letters to Atticus* 2.24.3). The rumor of Servilia's prostitution of her own daughter may also be reflected in Atia's offering Octavia to Pompey in *Rome*, while she is still married to Glabius (Episode 01).

19   As Vorenus comes to realize how much he loves his wife, deeply, so does Brutus come to the realization that the Republic is above friendship and family.

20   At Atia's party for Caesar's homecoming, the dancers perform the "Return of Ulysses," an appropriate theme anticipating Servilia's reunion with Caesar later that night.

21   Also compare another older couple, Pompey and Cornelia: Cornelia is portrayed as an older lady, fitting Pompey's age.

22   Actor Ray Stevenson (Pullo) says in the audio commentary: "It's quite breathtaking to realize they basically had four scenes to set up a relationship that

has been going for eight years." Note that Caesar plays *latrunculi*, a board game of strategy, with Brutus in Episode 11, just before Brutus finally decides to participate in his mother's plot.

23 In Episode 09, Servilia fights with Brutus over their respective political allegiances. Servilia insists her objections to Caesar are strictly political, denying she has any lingering sorrow or rage over "his lost affections."

24 Consider how Vorenus pities Pompey in the same episode.

25 At her party for Caesar's return from Alexandria, Atia pretends to welcome Servilia and hastens to comment on her shawl: "Is this a mourning shawl? It's very pretty. Has someone died?" Servilia immediately exploits the question and turns it into a biting comment of Caesar's recent victory: "A great many have died." Throughout the night, Servilia steals glances at the man who spurned her, but he avoids meeting her eyes.

26 Also in Episode 06, Atia chooses jewelry for Octavia and herself.

27 In the same episode, Calpurnia seeks Caesar's approval for her dress, which he finds "regal, but not excessively so."

28 See Vergil, *Aeneid* 4.698–706: by cutting Dido's hair, Iris facilitates the queen's death.

29 On *pudor* and *pudicitia*, see Langlands (2006); on Caesar's effort to protect his own *pudor*, see Augoustakis (2006).

30 The connection has been well explored in Livy's representation of Lucretia (*History of Rome* 1.58–59): see Joshel (1992).

31 Consider Lucan's description of Pompey's spirit transplanted into the hearts of Brutus and Cato (*Civil War* 9.1–18).

32 Caesar's arrogance is evident in Episode 11, when Atia pulls him aside to warn him about the wall-graffiti that portrays Brutus with a knife at Caesar's back. She believes Servilia will not rest until Caesar is dead. But he imperiously scoffs at her warnings: "I well imagine poor Servilia is not very fond of me, but really, wants me dead? You are a dramatist, Atia."

33 According to Plutarch (*Life of Brutus* 6), Servilia sent a wanton letter to Caesar in the Senate, as the Catilinarian conspiracy was being discussed, an act that enraged Cato.

34 As Servilia rises up from her seat, she looks like a snake ready to attack its prey. She evokes Colleen McCullough's portrayal of Servilia in *Caesar's Women* (1996); see Malamud (2001), 215–216, for an analysis of McCullough's Servilia.

10

Atia and the Erotics of Authority

Monica S. Cyrino

The first season of HBO-BBC's *Rome* is remarkable for its presentation of strong, multi-faceted, and impressively drawn female characters. The official series website declares its intention to explore the interlocking lives of ancient Roman women: "In a culture in which women lack formal power, and men leave for months and years on military campaigns, the wives, daughters, and mothers have built powerful networks of alliances completely independent of the men's worlds" (www.hbo.com/rome). *Rome* introduces us to several captivating female characters as the series explores their personalities, motivations, and relationships, with exceptionally talented actresses playing the roles of historical figures, such as Servilia of the Junii, Atia of the Julii, her daughter Octavia, and Cleopatra VII, as well as the roles of fictional characters, including Niobe, wife of the protagonist Lucius Vorenus, her sister Lyde, and the servant women Merula, Eleni, and Eirene. Society, class, sexuality, politics, and religion are all examined and vividly exposed though the narratives of these virtuoso portrayals of ancient women.

The Role

Foremost among the female characters in the series is the vigorous and brilliant portrayal of Atia of the Julii, the historical niece of Julius Caesar and mother of young Octavian, played by the gifted British actress Polly Walker. You may recall Ms. Walker from her role as a terrorist alongside Harrison Ford in 1992's *Patriot Games*; in the same year, more memorably, she played one of four London women who take a villa in Italy in the gauzy film *Enchanted April*. In the last few years, Ms. Walker has undertaken several roles in mainly British film and television productions; for example, she recently appeared in an independent British film, *Scenes of a Sexual Nature* (2006).

But playing Atia in the series *Rome* was definitely a high point in an acting career notable for its ups and downs. The actress herself agreed that the role was irresistible, even with all the cable-level nudity and the graphic sex scenes, as she made clear in an interview with London's *Evening Standard Magazine*. "When I read the script, my eyes got wider and wider. Although I never considered not taking the part because I didn't find it all that offensive. The guys that I was doing the scenes with were so brave and such a laugh. At one point, I sat on top of the actor (Lee Boardman) who played Timon, going, 'Please, for God's sake, make sure you cover my tits!' He went, 'Don't worry about your tits, cover my tits!'"[1] It came as no surprise when Ms. Walker was nominated for a 2006 Golden Globe Award, the only actor so recognized for the first season of the series.[2]

With all due praise to Ms. Walker's tour-de-force performance, it appears the role of Atia was intended from the very start to be flamboyant, sizzling, and a little extreme. In the cast summary section of the official website, this is how her character is described: "Niece of Caesar. Atia of the Julii is snobbish, willful, and cunning. She is also sexually voracious and totally amoral . . . Atia is among the women who serve as the shadow rulers of Rome."[3] Indeed, the figure of the sexy power-broker Atia is clearly meant to be one of the principal stars of the series. In the audience's very first glimpse of Atia, she appears wearing a long, red curly-haired wig and pretty much nothing else, astride the afore-mentioned Timon (Boardman), enjoying animated sex with him in front of her patient body slave, Merula (Lydia Biondi). Then the audience sees her in voluptuous, creamy-skinned, full-frontal nudity, savoring her midday bath, all the while chatting non-chalantly with her obviously mortified teenaged son, Octavian, the future Emperor Augustus (Max Pirkis). Later she gets soaked head to toe in steaming bull's blood – what the actress calls "my *Carrie* moment"[4] – in the sacred ritual of the *taurobolium*, to ensure her son's safe trip to Gaul. After that, viewers see her enthusiastically flogging her manservant Castor (Manfredi Aliquo) to sharpen her "coping" skills in the midst of a tense political situation. And that's just in Episode 01.

In an echo of the website blurb, critics and journalists writing about the series convey a gleeful unanimity in describing the role of Atia in terms of sheer feminine evil made manifest through her dangerous sexuality. Their comments also reveal a rather prejudicial opinion about women's hair color. James Poniewozik of *Time* magazine notes: "There [is] . . . a show-stealing turn by Polly Walker as Atia, Caesar's scheming niece; with her flaming red hair and willingness to trade sex for power, she's like a Latin version of *The O.C.*'s villain Julie Cooper."[5] Lynette Rice of *Entertainment Weekly* also provides her readers with a pop-culture analogy for Atia: "Think Alexis Carrington with red hair and less clothing."[6] Critics were apparently bewildered by this character – what, have they never seen a scheming temptress in a Roman epic before? – so they were reduced to comparing her to television vixens from tawdry prime-time soap operas. Then there's the entirely unsubstantiated equation between red hair and certain questionable moral qualities.

This chapter considers the character and actions of Atia as she appears in the series, and in particular, how she expresses her personal authority and self-determination through the complexities of her most intimate relationships. Even if it is agreed that Atia should be redeemed from the one-dimensional "she-devil" characterizations of the journalists, at the same time we must acknowledge that such seductive publicity was very useful for attracting viewers to the series. Actress Walker noted of her juicy role as Atia: "I saw it as a huge challenge, and I have huge admiration for this character. A lot of people might consider her to be sort of evil or bad, but I think she's wonderful. She's just a survivor, doing what she's got to do."[7] While the other female characters are shown to be motivated in their actions by conventionally "womanly" emotions, such as the narcissistic rage of erotic rejection (Servilia) or the fear of being detected in adultery (Niobe), Atia conveys a strong and almost masculine *virtus* – the Roman word expresses "courage" or even "heroism" – in the way her character's motivation is depicted. Most importantly, Atia's motivation is quintessentially Julian in nature, in that every action she takes in the series, whether extortion, assault, murder, or guerilla graffiti, she does in order to secure the shifting political fortunes of her loved ones and, especially, to establish a position of power for her son, Octavian. Atia's purpose is more than merely maternal: it is dynastic. In effecting her goals, Atia is certainly ruthless and indeed even ferocious, but she also exhibits the highest degree of purpose and loyalty to her family.

Chez Atia

Atia's role is most prominent in the first six episodes, where her strategies and maneuverings parallel, and in a real way also influence, the growing supremacy in Rome of the Julian clan under its most famous member, Caesar (played by Ciarán Hinds). At first it may appear that her function in the series is basically to host a succession of posh parties and private dinners at her sumptuous, ruddy-toned villa. But Atia's villa represents much more than just the luxurious hub of smart society: it is where some of the most important political meetings and decisions take place, as Caesar's authority is shown to increase over the first few episodes.[8] By making her villa the nucleus of political activity, it is clear that Atia wants to set herself up as the First Lady in Rome, but she does this with the principal goal of enhancing the status of her family. In Episode 01, Atia reads a letter from Caesar in Gaul, asking her to find a new Julian wife for his partner, Pompey, and adding that his wife Calpurnia is "no good at such matters." Thus the series immediately establishes Caesar's close relationship with and trust in his niece, a blood relative over a mere spouse of convenience, and the audience watches Atia happily assume the role of reigning Julian matriarch. In Episode 02, when Mark Antony (James Purefoy) returns from Gaul to hold secret negotiations with Pompey, Cato, and Cicero, they all meet at Atia's villa, while she can barely hold her excitement: "What a congeries of heroes! Such vim! I feel like Helen of Troy!" There are other benefits incurred when Antony enjoys Atia's hospitality, but we will return to that later.

By the time Caesar returns to Rome from Gaul in Episode 04, there is no question that his homecoming party will be hosted at Atia's villa. Caesar's chief slave, Posca (Nicholas Woodeson), brings the guest roster – "a very fancy list of people" – to Atia's major domo, Castor, and informs him: "Your lady should be aware of the honor done to her." While Atia is a bit perturbed to find the name of her rival, Servilia, on the list – "I'll not let that woman get between me and Caesar!" she declares – the meteoric rise of her family's status suffuses her with victorious glee. *Rome* stages the party scene at her villa in an elaborate and lengthy sequence, highlighting the intensely political nature of the event as Atia launches the celebration of the Julian takeover of Rome.

The scene encapsulates several of the most important themes about Atia's character as she appears throughout the series. Notice how the return of Caesar initiates a new and more dangerous turn in the rivalry between Atia and Caesar's mistress, Servilia (Lindsay Duncan), which will not be resolved but only intensified in its degree of toxicity by the end of the twelve-episode arc. But for now Atia veils the tension with diplomacy, air kisses, and *sotto voce* remarks to her body slave, Merula. Notice how Antony prowls around the villa like the man of the house, ever watchful of the various intrigues at play. And notice how Atia presents herself and her two children with the greatest grace and deference to Caesar, who murmurs with feigned modesty: "It's only your Uncle Gaius." After Caesar is forced to renounce Servilia for political reasons, his relationship with his niece and her status as the principal Julian female remain firm throughout the rest of the series. Atia takes a most prominent position in the executive box directly next to Caesar during his triumphal procession in Episode 10. At the end, it is Atia who warns Caesar that Servilia's vengeful anger will compel her son Brutus to betray him, but Caesar scoffs at the idea and scolds her genially: "Really, Atia, you are a dramatist."

Family Matters

In her relationships with her children, Atia expresses her confident authority, her candor about sexual topics, and something that comes close to maternal warmth and affection. Atia sees her family as a tightly knit unit of solidarity and personal loyalty, as she tells her daughter in Episode 01: "You and I and your brother are alone in the world. We have to be strong." Thus, Atia's main goal throughout the series is to strengthen their unified position.

With Octavian, whom she often astutely calls her "strange boy," Atia has two clear objectives in the first six episodes: to make a man out of her son and to secure his political position. In her very first act on the show, she has sex with Timon so that he'll sell her a magnificent white stallion, intended for Pompey's stable, but which she wants Octavian to take as a gift to Caesar all the way in Gaul. Atia jockeys, as it were, for political position, so that her son's risk-taking gesture will impress the general and "honor your beloved great uncle." As Octavian rides off on the horse, Atia exclaims: "Is he not perfect? Proper little soldier!" But she sighs and looks anxious as he rounds the corner, so she threatens the slave in charge of his security detail: "Andros, see that no harm comes to him or I'll use the eyes of your children for beads." Atia also seeks physical protection for her son in turbulent times. When Octavian is saved from captivity in Gaul in Episode 02, he comes home with his rescuers, Vorenus (Kevin McKidd) and Pullo (Ray Stevenson), insisting the soldiers stay and dine with the family. After a moment's hesitation, Atia soon realizes the benefit of having such sturdy men in her son's circle of trust. She enjoys their lively political debate over a meal of dormouse and tench (a species of freshwater fish), and as the men depart, she commands: "Do come and visit us again. Octavian needs reliable friends – he may depend on you, I trust."

Atia also desires to advance the sexual maturity of her teenaged son, whose "distinctly feminine *anima*" is of great concern to her. Before the party in Episode 04, Atia urges him to eat a pair of raw goat testicles, because, she says, "it puts oak in your penis." When Octavian refuses, she reminds him of the illustrious sexual proclivity of their family: "The men of the Julii are masculine men! When my mother's father was your age, there was not a slave girl in the house that was safe!" She stands watching imperiously as he is "forced to join the goat-testes Clean Plate Club,"[9] and when he is finished, she gives a satisfied purr: "That's my brave boy." Later, in Episode 05, she is thrilled and only a little bothered to hear a false report that Octavian has become Caesar's lover: "I'm not clear it is decent, him being your great uncle, but who's to say what is decent nowadays? Let's see Servilia compete with a soft young boy like you! What power we shall wield!" But in vehemently denying the rumor, Octavian stands up to his mother for the first time. Taking shrewd note of his growing maturity, Atia hires Pullo to teach Octavian "the masculine arts," as she says, "how to fight and copulate and skin animals." Indeed, Pullo, whom Atia calls "the cheerful brutish one," will supervise Octavian through a number of initiations, including the violent (and secret) murder of Evander, the adulterous lover of Niobe. A more amusing pedagogical moment occurs in Episode 06, when Atia orders Pullo to take a reluctant Octavian to a brothel for his first sexual experience: "You *will* penetrate someone today, or I'll burn your wretched books in the courtyard!" By the midpoint of the series, Atia is pleased enough by Octavian's successful passage to adulthood to send him away from home to an academy in Mediolanum (Milan), telling him: "You're a man now. Rome's not safe for men of the Julii." While Atia cannily hedges her bets about Caesar's chances against Pompey, the most important thing to her is the protection of her family, especially her son.

The parental bond with her daughter is shown to be more difficult, in that Atia's strength of purpose contrasts sharply with the weakness and gullibility of young Octavia (Kerry Condon). The complications start early in Episode 01, when Atia responds to Caesar's request by offering Octavia as a bride to his political rival. In a scene where she again uses her bath time to devise important strategies, Atia makes it clear to her daughter that it is a family decision: "Uncle Julius intends to marry you to Pompey Magnus." Unfortunately for Octavia, this entails getting her divorced from her beloved first husband, Glabius (Roberto Purvis).[10] "You'll be the first woman in Rome," Atia tells her reluctant daughter by way of inducement to marry the old man. "I know he's a touch low in manner, but I'm told he's a perfectly adequate lover." Like a good Roman daughter, Octavia obeys, but tearfully parts from her husband, to the disgust of her mother waiting in the well-appointed litter. "The man has tears in his eyes – tears! A womanish husband is no use to anyone." Although Pompey (Kenneth Cranham) agrees to the marriage, and Atia offers him an advance on the bargain by allowing him to have betrothal sex with her daughter, the deal is broken between the men and Octavia is repudiated. An enraged Atia comforts her humiliated daughter and promises with sinister accuracy: "Pompey will eat sand for this."

But rather than allow Octavia to reunite with Glabius, Atia wants to find her someone more appropriate to her status as a daughter of the ascendant Julii. When Atia discovers Octavia's secret rendezvous with her ex-husband, she sends Timon to kill Glabius. The death of Glabius not surprisingly initiates an intense conflict, with Octavia accusing her mother of complicity, and Atia denying any role in the murder: "Daughter, I swear on the masks of all my ancestors I did not kill Glabius." While Atia's cool lie may shock some viewers, it fits with her character as a parent fiercely defending the interests of her family. Later, at a subdued dinner party, a drunken Octavia gloomily recites lines from Vergil's *Aeneid* some twenty-odd years before it was written.[11] Still, Atia can't wait for Octavia's sullen mood to subside: with Octavian away, she needs her daughter to help protect the family. She sends her to Servilia bearing gifts, including a well-endowed, naked male slave whose appearance shocks the prim Octavia, while Atia calmly assures her she knows what she's doing: "Large penis is always welcome!" But even Atia cannot foresee the intensity of Servilia's manipulative rage, so she is devastated to learn of Octavia's erotic affair with her hated rival and Servilia's attempt to use the naive Octavia against the Julian family. In Episode 09, when Atia discovers that Servilia coerced Octavia – still distraught about the loss of Glabius – into seducing her own brother for information about Caesar's mysterious "affliction," in a fury she strikes both her children, and compels Octavia to see how cruelly she was used: "You abase yourself for a stupid lie!" Even Octavian, taking the protective role of man-of-the-house, urges his elder sister to put the family first and forgive their mother: "Whatever you think she may have done, consider the possibility she did it out of love for you." Through the force of her determination to sustain her family, Atia draws both of her children securely back into the Julian fold by the end of the series' first season.

An Affair to Remember

Rome also gives narrative prominence and a great deal of screen time to Atia's passionate – though unhistorical as far as we can tell – erotic relationship with the physically coarse, but brutishly alluring Mark Antony. From the very beginning of the series, a number of scenes show Atia and Antony engaged in scorching dialogue and graphic sexual activity, often at the same time. When Antony returns to Rome in Episode 02 to assume the office of people's tribune, he tells Octavian with a wolfish grin: "Boy, tell your lovely mother I will see her *later*." Antony's first night back in the city finds him at Atia's villa for the secret meeting with Pompey, and as he bursts through the door, to her obvious delight he bellows: "Good gods, woman, your beauty is painful!" Their love-making that night is so noisy, at dinner the next evening a spiteful Octavia is inspired to mock her mother's moans of pleasure – *à la* Meg Ryan in the diner scene in *When Harry Met Sally* (1989) – to which a blithe Antony remarks: "She has you exact."

As the political situation in Rome heats up, so do relations between Atia and Antony, but not necessarily in the way they would like. Caesar has left Antony in Rome "to keep the peace," but the warrior in Antony grows restless, bored with bureaucratic niceties, and anxious about the outcome of Caesar's battles against the Pompeians in Greece. In Episode 06, when Pompey sends an envoy to Rome to sue for a separate deal, the cagey Antony doesn't dismiss him right away. That night, Antony shares a tense dinner with Atia, and after another bout of raucous sex (no doubt to relieve the tension), Atia also makes him an offer. "I've been thinking," she says, "we should get married." Antony pretends surprise, but he knows where this dangerous scene is going. Atia suggests they join forces – "in case Caesar is defeated" – and take the city for themselves: "Allied with my house you'll have coin and nobility enough to make yourself king!" Although Atia mainly seeks the security of her family, her bold proposition strikes a guilty nerve in Antony, who sees his own venality reflected in the offer, as he seethes at her: "I had not realized until now what a wicked old harpy you are!" Stung by his remark, Atia slaps him, and when he slaps her back, she throws him out. The next day, a resolute Antony beats up Pompey's envoy, and leaves directly for Greece to join Caesar. With such an outcome, it appears Atia did her best to ensure a Julian victory.

By the time Caesar holds his triumph in Episode 10, the ex-lovers are stealing furtive glances at each other as they sit in the executive box. At

Figure 5 Caesar's triumph: Atia (Polly Walker) sits next to Antony (James Purefoy), with Calpurnia (Haydn Gwynne) in the background. Photograph from *Rome*^SM courtesy of HBO®. *Rome*^SM and HBO® are service marks of Home Box Office, Inc.

Atia's symposium in Episode 11, an improbably lovelorn Antony corners Octavia and asks for her help: "Your mother is a vicious and heartless creature, but I find I am wretched without her." Atia is eavesdropping by a column, as he continues dejectedly. "She refuses even to speak with me . . . Will you speak to her for me? Let her know how pitiful I've become?" Octavia answers in a stage whisper: "Her disdain for you is an act: she is entirely infatuated with you." Atia emerges from her hiding place and declares: "That is a wicked foolish lie!" and she brushes past him, ignoring his pleas to speak with her. Later, after the party, Antony waylays Atia in her bedroom, and after the requisite slapping, they fall into an enthusiastic embrace. In the relationship between Atia and Antony, the series presents an apparent reversal of the gender and power hierarchies between lovers that explicitly evokes the generic conventions of "gender slippage" in Roman love elegy, where the male poet describes his domination by the woman he loves.[12] While Antony pines for his cruel mistress, alternately despising and desiring her, his *domina* Atia controls the affair through the force of her charm and her considerable pugilistic skills. In the final episode, when Atia wonders why "the mad old turtle" Servilia has invited her for a visit, noting "she hates me," Antony serenely observes: "So do I – that's no bar to friendship." With this remark, Antony confirms the double-edged stance of the lover in Roman poetry.

A final point arises from a consideration of the erotic bond between Atia and Antony depicted in the first season of the show. Historical consultant Jonathan Stamp states on the DVD commentary that since we know very little about the real Atia, her character was based on more well-known Roman women of the period, and he says, by way of example, "like Clodia." It is not surprising that his one citation of a historical Roman woman would be to mention the infamous Clodia Metelli, mistress of the poet Catullus, and it fits well with the elegiac theme mentioned above, as well as the evocation of the poet's own verses in Episode 09.[13] But it also suggests that another "more famous" woman – one not cited by the series creators – may have also fleshed out the television character of Atia: this would be the notorious Fulvia, who was one of the best known of the politically active elite women of the late Roman Republic.

Fulvia was the daughter of one of the most distinguished of the plebeian noble families. She was intimately involved in the tempestuous politics at the end of the Republic through her marriages to three of the most influential men of the period, including Antony (her third husband), whose position and policies she zealously promoted.[14] Fulvia's energetic participation in politics would provide an apt analogy for Atia's maneuvering as it is portrayed on the show, and her notoriety as "a pro-totype of empresses"[15] would also correspond to Atia's voracious quest for power and status. Historians note that Fulvia may have been erotically involved with Antony long before she actually married him,[16] so this would be consistent with Atia's suggestion in Episode 06 of a potential marriage to her long-time lover. If the historical Fulvia does supply a narrative model for Atia, this explains many of the motivations, actions, and relationships of her character throughout the first season of the series *Rome*. Although the historical Atia died in 43 BC during her son's first consulship, the character of Atia – using the analogy of Fulvia – can thus be allowed a few more years of survival as she escapes Servilia's threats and seeks protection from Antony and his army. Ultimately, the Atia of *Rome* would have to decide between familial devotion and erotic love, and she would be forced to choose a side, her lover's or her son's. Under such circumstances, the stakes would never be higher, but that's just the way Atia of the Julii likes them.

NOTES

1 Quoted by Macdonald (2006), 29.
2 The series itself received a 2006 Golden Globe nomination for Best Television Series – Drama. *Rome* was also nominated for eight Emmy Awards in 2006, winning four statuettes.
3 Noted under "Cast and Crew" at www.hbo.com/rome.
4 The reference is to the climactic scene of the 1976 film *Carrie* by Brian De Palma, based on the 1974 Stephen King novel of the same name, where the main character is drenched in pig's blood.
5 Poniewozik (2005), 65. A parallel allusion can be found in the reviews of *Rome* on the website televisionwithoutpity.com, where Atia is called "Julii Cooper."
6 Rice (2005), quoted in box "Toga Parts," 29.
7 Quoted by Jay Bobbin in "Et Tu, HBO?" on the website Zap2It.com, August 27, 2005.
8 Likewise, in the second half of the first season, the villa of Servilia will foster the conspiracy against Caesar.
9 Flynn (2005), 51.
10 The character of Glabius is fictional: the historical Octavia's first marriage was to Gaius Claudius Marcellus, by whom she had three children.
11 Octavia's quote is from *Aeneid* 6.126–129.
12 On "gender slippage" in Roman love elegy, see the summary most recently in Skinner (2005), 212–238.
13 In Episode 09, Octavian reads Catullus' "sparrow" poem (Poem 2) to Octavia.
14 On Fulvia's control of her husbands' political aspirations, see Babcock (1965).
15 *Oxford Classical Dictionary*, "Fulvia," 614.
16 See Babcock (1965), 6; an early affair between Antony and Fulvia may be suggested by Cicero in *Philippics* 2.48.

11

Her First Roman: A Cleopatra for *Rome*

Gregory N. Daugherty

Cleopatra appears in only half of one episode of *Rome* (Episode 08, "Caesarion"), but for many viewers the image came as quite a shock. They saw a chained, drug-addled, whining waif with cynical schemes of seduction and a supposititious child sired by a fortunate soldier of convenience. It seems as if an amoral Forrest Gump has met an anorexic Theda Bara. Novelist Steven Saylor, who published a novel featuring his own Cleopatra, railed that "travesty is too kind a word for this wretched misfire."[1] In spite of some unique additions to the Cleopatra legend, what we see in this episode is not a complete departure from earlier traditions or even from the historical figure.

She does not look right. She is small, thin, and has short, spiky hair. While the remarkably accomplished British stage actress Lyndsey Marshal is by no means unattractive, what appears on the screen is no beauty. Her drug use, her sexuality, and her calculated plans to seduce Caesar in order to save herself shock us as much as her petulance, self-absorption, and violence. On the surface, this is not a Cleopatra whom the audience has seen before, and certainly not the Elizabeth Taylor version (from the 1963 Joseph Mankiewicz film, *Cleopatra*).[2]

In the series *Rome*, we first encounter Cleopatra when assassins arrive from Alexandria. She is chained to a bed and in an opium stupor. After Charmian (played by Kathryn Hunter) slaps her back to consciousness, she receives the notice of her death sentence and is reciting an Egyptian prayer when Titus Pullo and Lucius Vorenus come to her rescue. In a high shrill voice, she alternately insults and clings to her loyal but caustic slave, a doublet for Caesar's chief slave, Posca. The next morning we see her in the same chamber, smoking her opium pipe and hissing like a snake. Charmian chides her for being too weak to give it up and Cleopatra orders it thrown out, allowing the viewers to see that she is being carried in a massive, slave-borne litter escorted by her rescuers. Next, as Charmian assists in her detoxification, Cleopatra declares her intent to survive by seducing Caesar and having his baby. Charmian devises a plan to get her mistress pregnant by one of the Romans, and so orders Vorenus into the chamber. In the comic scene that follows, Charmian appears to be translating. Vorenus is appalled by the blatant proposal but allured by her open sexuality. After a shrill protest, he retreats and orders Pullo into the chamber. Pullo, of course, obliges.

Subsequently they smuggle Cleopatra into Alexandria in a bag rather than the traditional carpet. In this scene, Marshal does a brilliant job of inserting a great deal of Cleopatra's character into just a few actions and gestures. When the bag is opened before Caesar, she gasps for air and immediately attends to the grit coating her sweat-soaked and only partially detoxed body. It is not attractive; even Vorenus rolls his eyes. But then she realizes who is there and instantly channels the seductress, as she strikes an alluring pose. And, as Plutarch says, Caesar is charmed by her audacity (*Life of Caesar* 49). In the very next scene, Cleopatra appears transformed into the royal Ptolemaic princess, dressed and wigged before the astonished eyes of the other minions of the court. She terrifies her brother and con-demns his advisors to death. It is worth noting that she speaks to everyone in the third person, except for her equals, her husband/brother, and Caesar. Next, she and Caesar engage in a bout of verbal fencing that climaxes in her proclamation that, unlike her brother, she realizes that she is Caesar's client and slave. Sex follows and the episode ends with Caesar's presenta-tion of Caesarion to his troops, including his presumed "real" father, Pullo.

When approaching this episode, it is necessary to bear in mind that several themes occur here that run throughout the entire series. Pullo is a Roman "Forrest Gump," and thus he will have a pivotal role in every crucial plotline. He single-handedly "brought down the Republic" (Episode 02), so it is no surprise that he is the real father of Caesarion. Producer Bruno Heller set out to infuse humor – or the British equivalent – into every episode, and Pullo and Vorenus provide it, both in the fight scene against the Egyptian assassins and in the "audition for coitus" scene. The theme of "Rich Man/Poor Man" is also carried through not only by the staunch legionaries defending the palace full of preening elites, but also by the brilliant visual contrast between the decadent Macedonian court and the Bedouin peasants outside. Finally, the producers have maintained the interlocking storylines not only by flashing back to Rome to check in with Servilia and Brutus and Mark Antony and Cicero, but also by using the sex scenes to underscore the complex relations – past, present, and future – between Servilia, Octavia, Caesar, Atia, Octavian, and Mark Antony and how those relationships are going to be disrupted when Cleopatra is added to this potent mix.

This is not on the surface the conventional image of Cleopatra, but none of her various portrayals has ever been a mirror of the real person. An analysis of her characterization in *Rome* yields these results: Marshal's powerful portrayal is not a radical departure from the ancient evidence for the events in this episode; almost every element of the depiction of Cleopatra can be found elsewhere in the reception of her story, especially on stage and in film; and the essentials of this characterization are necessary to the structure not only of this episode but also to other plotlines in the series, in both the current and perhaps in future season(s).

The Real Cleopatra

Cleopatra VII Thea Neotera Philopator, the last Ptolemaic monarch of the Macedonian kingdom of Egypt, lived for barely forty years (69–30 BC), and died a suicide as she faced the unpleasant prospect of marching in chains in a Roman triumph to a death by strangulation. In her brief but eventful life, she managed to succeed Ptolemy XII Auletes (in 51 BC), her flute-playing, drunken, and bankrupt father, over the bodies of two older sisters (Cleopatra VI and Berenike IV). After marrying each of her two younger brothers in succession (Ptolemy XIII and XIV), she would dispose of them along with her ambitious younger sister (Arsinoe IV), but only with the direct assistance and interference of Julius Caesar (48 BC) to whom she bore an illegitimate and unacknowledged son, Ptolemy XV Caesarion (in 47 BC). When the Roman world split into two civil camps (32 BC), she cast her lot with Mark Antony, bearing him three children, buying him a navy, and sharing in his defeat and death (at the Battle of Actium in 31 BC). According to Plutarch, she was intelligent, multi-lingual, and had a lovely voice, but was not remarkable for her beauty as much as for her charm and wit.[3] These are the basic and brutal facts of her political career and could well have served as a reasonably complete summary of her existence, but for the fact that Antony's enemies turned her life into a legend.[4]

There are a number of ways in which Episode 08 of *Rome* is consistent with the historical Cleopatra. Most of the events and characters depicted are to be found in the writings of either Caesar himself or the ancient biographer, Plutarch.[5] The compression of the storyline, however, required some omissions. In the episode, she does not appear in the city of Rome as we know she did,[6] and as everyone remembers from the 1963 film, but it has been proposed that Cleopatra's visits to Rome were quite brief, low key, and entirely political in nature.[7] The loyal, carpet-carrying slave Apollodorus is replaced by Vorenus, and the character of the maid, Charmian, is portrayed as perhaps too old to still be around in 30 BC when she and Eiras attend to the final moments of their mistress.[8] Screenwriters almost never read Plutarch: but in the audio commentary of the DVD, director Steven Shill refers to the ancient biographer in his comments on the "carpet scene," and actually follows him in having Cleopatra brought in a sack, rather than a carpet.[9] Shill also notes that Plutarch had written that Cleopatra was not particularly beautiful: what enchanted Caesar was not her beauty but her clever audacity.

There are several other areas where the episode is refreshingly authentic. The creators of the episode are very careful to characterize the vast gulf between the royal court and the Bedouin-like people of Alexandria. They also went to considerable efforts to create an aesthetic look to the court that is a fusion of Macedonian and Egyptian elements, resulting in a style so bizarre that it appears alien and grotesque even to the Romans, and certainly to the viewing audience. None of the cosmetic face-painting or costumes are authentic to the period, but the producers deliberately tried to depict the Ptolemaic court as neither Greek, Roman, nor classical Egyptian but something different, decadent, and dangerous.

Since we know she spoke many languages, Cleopatra is depicted in the episode as speaking Egyptian and later not fully understanding Latin – perhaps part of the humor in the "audition for coitus" scene with Vorenus. Charmian appears to be translating as she explains what is expected. Cleopatra is correctly depicted as very young, with no attempt to portray her as a great beauty. She did bear a child whom she named Caesarion, but there is little evidence that Caesar ever took public notice, although Augustan propaganda may have suggested otherwise. Cleopatra's vicious and ruthless assaults on her brother and his counselors as portrayed in the episode are well established by the historical record. She was in fact responsible for the death and/or banishment of all of her siblings and their supporters. It is not a very flattering portrait of the "Tragick Queene," but it does not stray as far from our sources as most cinematic Cleopatras, where a stunning, raven-haired beauty usually urges a libidinous Caesar to join her to rule as god and goddess over a multi-cultural, multi-lingual, and multi-racial Shangri-La of gold lamé halter tops and jewel-tipped corn rows. The portrayal of Cleopatra in this episode of *Rome* raises intriguing possibilities for the second season since, as Alison Futrell notes, it "lays the ground work for an exploration of the contemporary construction of the Cleopatra legend as propaganda."[10]

The Reception of Cleopatra on Stage and Screen

Screenwriters and producers may not always read the ancient sources, but they do watch old movies and draw upon popular culture in general. This has clearly happened here, in the production of Episode 08 of *Rome*. Although the script is attributed to the American co-producer William J. MacDonald, it is evident from the director's commentary on the DVD that the story and concept involved Heller as well. This helps to account for the heavy influence of British stage versions of Cleopatra, especially the plays of William Shakespeare and George Bernard Shaw. Actress Marshal was already a stage veteran and Hunter (Charmian) played Richard III in an all-female cast.[11] The writers of *Rome* clearly had Shakespeare's *Antony and Cleopatra* in mind. The figure of Antony frames Cleopatra's appearances in the episode, and her erotic liaison with Caesar is interwoven with that of Servilia, Caesar's former lover and future nemesis, and Octavia, Antony's future wife and Cleopatra's rival. The influence of Shakespeare can also be seen in the depiction of her drug use, as Cleopatra says in the play: "Give me to drink mandragora . . . That I might sleep out this great gap of time my Antony is away" (*Antony and Cleopatra*, 1.5.4–7). Cleopatra's drug use in *Rome* may have shocked many American viewers, but the representation of opium-smoking has long been associated with Oriental settings in art, literature, and film: for example, in the Eugene Delacroix painting *Algerian Women in Their Apartments* (1834).[12]

Other Shakespearean allusions may be clever, "inside" stage jokes. When Charmian is trying to detoxify Cleopatra, Marshal hisses like a snake and Hunter remarks that she will turn green if she does not cooperate. I take this to be a humorous allusion to the scene in *Antony and Cleopatra* when Cleopatra recalls her time with Caesar: "My salad days, when I was green in judgment: cold in blood, To say as I said then!" (1.5.73–74). The serpentine hissing itself could be an allusion to the moment when Cleopatra wonders if Antony is looking for her: "*Where's my serpent of old Nile?* For so he calls me" (1.5.25). This last Shakespearean example may account for the high-pitched voice used by the diminutive and androgynous actress in the opening scenes of the episode in *Rome*. In *Antony and Cleopatra*, a horrified queen imagines her story portrayed on the Roman comic stage (5.2.214–221):

> . . . Saucy lectors
> Will catch at us like strumpets, and scald rhymers
> Ballad us out o' tune. The quick comedians
> Extemporally will stage us, and present
> Our Alexandrian revels. Antony
> Shall be brought drunken forth, and I shall see
> Some squeaking Cleopatra boy my greatness
> I' the posture of a whore.

Episode 08 of *Rome* is full of such esoteric allusions, which were perhaps intended for the mostly British, and thus most likely theater-trained, cast and crew.

In the same way we can detect the influence of Shaw's *Caesar and Cleopatra* (1901).[13] The character of Charmian was never part of the Caesar narrative, but in the *Rome* episode she seems to be playing a role similar to the fiercely protective and sarcastically manipulative nurse known as Ftatateeta in Shaw's play. Charmian also performs the function of Shaw's Caesar when early in Episode 08 she forces her charge to give up the opium pipe and cease to be "weak." Cleopatra hisses her response to the challenge: "Weak, am I?" After this, the thin and squeaky voice deepens, and a woman of steely determination replaces the frightened drug addict. The title of this chapter refers to a play based on Shaw: *Her First Roman* was a 1968 Broadway musical version of Shaw's *Caesar and Cleopatra*, which closed after only seventeen performances. Both versions, as well as Gabriel Pascal's 1945 film adaptation, emphasize Cleopatra's transition from girl to queen. The elaborate wig and heavy make-up worn by Flora Robson as Ftatateeta in Pascal's film appear to have influenced the imaginative head-dresses and face-paintings worn by the women in the Alexandrian court shown in *Rome*.

Another potent influence on the episode is more European than American. The depiction of Cleopatra as an Oriental vamp is evident in several sources, including the Victorian novel by British writer H. Rider Haggard,[14] the Victorien Sardou play *Cléopâtre* (1890) starring Sarah Bernhardt, and the silent film by Italian director Enrico Guazzoni, *Marc Antonio e Cleopatra* (1913). Since this phenomenon has been thoroughly discussed by Maria

Wyke,[15] I would only remark that in all of these works the aggressive eroti-
cism of these Eastern vampires entraps Western males and uses them
mercilessly. This concern for the dangers of Oriental females was repressed
in much of the reception of Cleopatra during the twentieth century, beginning shortly after the production of the quintessential vamp film, the now
lost *Cleopatra* (1917), starring Theda Bara. But the vamp image never
completely disappeared. The writers of *Rome* did not have to resort to
much research to encounter it, especially if they had visited the British
Museum exhibition *Cleopatra of Egypt: From History to Myth* (2001).
Wherever they encountered the idea, it clearly became central to their
portrait of Cleopatra and the establishment of her character. This image is
evoked most vividly and precisely in the carpet/bag scene when Marshal
transforms herself from a petulant teenager into the seductive vamp.

Big (and Small) Screen Cleopatra

The post-Theda Bara films were also very influential on the creators of
Rome. On first glance the Claudette Colbert *Cleopatra* (1934) might not
seem to be a candidate, since there is no child in the film and she was more
of a flapper with a big inheritance than a true vamp.[16] But here, too,
Cleopatra sets out to seduce Caesar and when her charms cannot distract
him from playing with his miniature war machines, she catches him with
the "gold of India." Sex follows, but off camera. Likewise, Marshal's Cleopatra bluntly addresses Caesar's financial needs before they become lovers.
In the film *Serpent of the Nile* (1953), we see a reptilian Rhonda Fleming
portray Cleopatra as a murderous manipulator of a loutish Antony
(Raymond Burr). The snake imagery used for *Rome*'s Cleopatra may have
been influenced by this very negative look at the queen. The Oriental vamp
reappeared soon after in an Alberto Sordi comedy where Sophia Loren
plays a double role as the deadly Cleopatra and her innocent body double
in *Two Nights with Cleopatra* (*Due Notti con Cleopatra*, 1953). This film
follows the Orientalist tradition as represented in the lurid novel by French
author Théophile Gautier, *One of Cleopatra's Nights* (1838),[17] which repeats
the slander of Augustan propaganda that Cleopatra would sleep with slaves
only to kill them in the morning. Since the Loren film merged the melodramatic and the comic, I see it as a forerunner of the amusing "audition
for coitus" scene in Episode 08 of *Rome*. Although Pullo, who previously
got the impression and informed a skeptical Vorenus that "She wants me,"
survives his night with Cleopatra, the scene presupposes her willingness to

have sex with inferiors; it also adds yet another "Forrest Gump" moment to the storyline, as Pullo appears to the audience to be the father of Caesarion. While comic at this point in the story, it raises the potential of a tragic arc in a plot yet to come: that the simple soldier Pullo, who has already formed a relationship with Octavian, might be commanded by his superior to be involved in getting rid of the child.

The most recent films and television miniseries have all returned to the depiction of a hypersexual Cleopatra played by stunningly beautiful starlets, such as Leonor Varela in *Cleopatra* (ABC miniseries, 1999), Monica Belluci in *Astérix et Obélix: Mission Cléopâtre* (2002), Samuela Sardo in *Julius Caesar* (TNT miniseries, 2002), and Anna Valle in *Imperium: Augustus* (2003). In all of these versions, the attraction is Cleopatra's beauty and the seductions are frankly rather abrupt. The Varela portrayal is based on the epic novel by Margaret George, *Memoirs of Cleopatra* (1997), where Cleopatra actually takes lessons from a prostitute on how best to seduce Caesar. The writers of *Rome* deliberately set out to portray a sexually experienced seductress in this same mode, but they also aimed to challenge our traditional expectations with a younger and somewhat androgynous character with bad hair in a perversely Shavian storyline.

It is quite clear from the DVD audio commentary by director Shill that they wanted their Cleopatra to be visually different. That seems to mean visually different from the cinematic version most familiar to the majority of viewers, the 1963 *Cleopatra*, starring real-life lovers Taylor and Richard Burton as Cleopatra and Antony, and Rex Harrison as Caesar.[18] But there are still several deliberate allusions to this famous film. After her rescue from Ptolemy's assassins in Episode 08, Cleopatra is carried in an elaborate, luxurious, and ostentatious conveyance which recalls the opulent barges in the 1963 film. When they first meet in the film, Cleopatra rummages among maps on a table and criticizes Caesar's strategy; Marshal does almost the same thing as she establishes her usefulness to Caesar, but her aim is more seductive. Although she does not appear as often in full regalia, Marshal wears outrageous wigs and elaborate make-up, as does Taylor in her film. Finally, as Rex Harrison does in the 1963 film, Ciarán Hinds as Caesar in *Rome* acknowledges the child to his men, including an enthusiastic Pullo, the boy's putative father. There are other allusions to "*Lizpatra*," such as the characters of the eunuch, Pothinus, and the teenage king, Ptolemy, as well as the insertion of a *testudo* or "turtle formation" at the defense of the gate, and there will doubtless be others in the second season when Cleopatra deals with Antony. I believe these flirtations with the familiar were intentional efforts to force the viewers of *Rome* to note how different is this Cleopatra. We should not be surprised if the character takes some other unexpected turns in the second season of *Rome*.

The character of Charmian is also a product of this performance tradition, as I have noted above, since she has taken on some of the characteristics – in particular, her wig style – from the Shavian character of Ftatateeta in the 1945 film version of *Caesar and Cleopatra*. British Shakespearean actress Hunter has turned this historical but minor figure into a crucial foil for the spoiled princess. Eiras is an uncredited extra in the *Rome* series, but she also follows the cinematic convention that, of the two handmaidens of Cleopatra, one must be white and one black. This convention seems to have originated – as far as I have been able to determine – with the 1963 *Cleopatra* where Eiras (Francesca Annis) is white and Charmian (Isabel Cooley) is black. This was continued in the television miniseries *Cleopatra*, although with a white Charmian and a black Eiras. In *Mission Cléopâtre*, neither character appears but the cadre of handmaidens is multi-racial, while in *Imperium: Augustus*, Cleopatra makes her entrance with two unnamed attendants, one black and one white. In earlier versions, such as the 1934 *Cleopatra* and *Serpent of the Nile*, the named handmaidens are all white. In spite of their efforts to counter iconic images from *Lizpatra*, the writers of *Rome* were still compelled by the visual tradition to follow this one.

Other Popular Culture Receptions of Cleopatra

Although the emphasis on the predatory sexuality of Cleopatra is not new to the big or the small screen, it has become the clearly dominant motif in other popular culture receptions, such as comic books, graphic novels, cartoons (especially Japanese), and pornography. As I have demonstrated elsewhere, the sanitized and deorientalized reception of Cleopatra prevalent in America from the 1920s and into the late 1960s was facilitated by the romantic vision projected in advertising, especially the Palmolive Soap ads masterminded by Albert Lasker.[19] Yet the backlash against the expensive failure of *Lizpatra* launched a darker, more sexual, and deadlier Cleopatra into the popular consciousness in the 1970s and beyond.

In comics and graphic novels in particular, the association with Egypt linked Cleopatra to mummies and vampires, as I have demonstrated elsewhere.[20] Anne Rice resurrects her to complicate the life of *The Mummy or Ramses the Damned* (1989); Vampirella, the heroine of the horror comics by Forrest J. Ackerman, discovers that she is the reincarnation of the queen;

and in *Bettie Page: Queen of the Nile* (2000), graphic artist Jim Silke styles her as a dominatrix as well as a double for his comic-book action heroine version of the famous model. The great Japanese animator Osamu Tezuka may have set this off in a bizarre mixture of humor, drama, and graphic sex in his film *Kureopatora* (1970). This masterpiece was unfairly labeled as pornography, but Cleopatra has been prominently featured in all kinds of sexually explicit material from the last forty years in almost every medium. For example, in print there is the pulp paperback by Walt Vickery, *Cleopatra's Blonde Sex Rival* (1962); among many erotic "films" we find *The Erotic Dreams of Cleopatra* (1983); and there is all manner of bad art ranging from calendar cuties to lurid paintings. I believe that we cannot ignore the impact of these various popular culture approaches to Cleopatra that are not far from what we see in the *Rome* series. Screenwriters don't all grow up reading Plutarch when their parents aren't looking. There are many trends in popular culture and media that help to account for the return to the representation of Cleopatra as the sexy, Oriental vampire in Episode 08 of *Rome*. This will perhaps come as a shock only to those whose principal contacts with the Cleopatra tradition are Shakespeare, Claudette Colbert, *Lizpatra*, the British Museum, and Steven Saylor. For those expecting to see the Cleopatra from Plutarch, or even less likely the real woman herself, Marshal's portrayal was quite a surprise indeed.

Cleopatra's Role in the *Rome* Series

Of course, every author and artist has the right to shape their worlds however they wish, and Cleopatra has fared no better or worse than other characters from the ancient world, real or imagined. Nevertheless, it is fair for us to evaluate how well this Cleopatra works as a character in the context of this episode and in the *Rome* series as a whole. Thanks to an intelligent and inspired actress and some clever writing, I think it works very well. Only part of the story of Caesar in Egypt involves her, and she does not even appear until halfway through the episode. Yet Marshal is a brilliant and nuanced actress, perfectly cast in the role. She can pull off the comedic scenes with Pullo and Vorenus. She is viciously arrogant in her treatment of her inferiors, addressing everyone but Caesar and her brother in the third person – and presumably in Greek. But she is also immature, as she clings to her nurse, then slaps her, and then succumbs to the most obvious of reverse psychologies. But when she and Charmian decide to guarantee her pregnancy, she can act with determination worthy of Servilia and ruthlessness worthy of Atia. She literally rises to the challenge. She does not appear standing until Caesar takes her by the hand and raises her from the sack. Within seconds she is in full regal panoply, confronting her child-ish brother/husband and his shifty minions. Her proposition to Caesar is as cold blooded as their sex scene is impassioned.

In the context of the episode, her role is to provide another "Forrest Gump" event for Pullo, which offers some of the most humorous moments of the series. Yet her role is also to disrupt the current triangle of Caesar, his lover, Servilia, and his wife, Calpurnia, and to lay the seeds for the coming conflict in the triangle of Octavian, his sister, Octavia, and his rival, Antony. This intersection of storylines is illustrated effectively in the montage of scenes at the start of the Alexandrian War that interweaves the sexual interlude of Caesar and Cleopatra in Egypt with the lovemaking of Servilia and Octavia back in Rome. Brief appearances by two key figures help to put this Egyptian interlude into its Roman context. Episode 08 begins with the return of Brutus to Rome and his strained reception by his mother, Servilia, and in the next to last scene he has an uncomfortable confrontation with a menacing Antony: this is the first time we have seen Antony since Caesar sent him from Alexandria just before Cleopatra makes her first appearance. Since the inner ring of the Cleopatra storyline is encircled by Antony, and the entire episode is bracketed by Brutus, the viewer is encouraged think ahead to the famous romance and tragedy that is to come.

NOTES

1 See www.stevensaylor.com/HBORome.html.
2 For other versions of Cleopatra – the history, the legend, and the image – see Hughes-Hallett (1990); Hamer (1993); Walker and Higgs (2001); Chauveau (2002); Royster (2003); Kleiner (2005), 157–282; and Jones (2006b), 205–306.
3 Plutarch, *Life of Antony* 27.2–4.
4 Some recent and reliable treatments of the historical Cleopatra can be found in Burstein (2004); Kleiner (2005), 1–156; Walker and Ashton (2006); and Jones (2006a).
5 Caesar, *The Civil War* 3.103, 107; Caesar, *The Alexandrian War* 33; Plutarch, *Life of Julius Caesar* 48–49; *Life of Antony* 25–36. The most convenient collec-tions of the ancient sources are found in Burstein (2004), 93–154; and Jones (2006b), 31–204.
6 For the evidence, see Jones (2006b), 78–87, especially the testimonies of Cassius Dio, Appian, and Cicero.

7   Gruen (2003); this was brought to my attention by Robert Gurval in "(Cast)igating Cleopatra: HBO's *Rome* and an Egyptian Queen for the 21st Century," paper presented at the APA meeting in San Diego, California (January 5, 2007).

8   Plutarch, *Life of Julius Caesar* 49; *Life of Antony* 60, 85.

9   Plutarch, *Life of Julius Caesar* 49.

10 Futrell (2006), 5.

11 At the Globe Theatre in London, summer 2003.

12 I owe this reference to Gurval (see note 7).

13 Note the film version of the play was directed by Gabriel Pascal, *Caesar and Cleopatra* (1945).

14 H. Rider Haggard, *Cleopatra: Being an Account of the Fall and Vengeance of Harmachis, the Royal Egyptian, as set forth by his own hand; Maiwa's revenge: a novel* (1889).

15 Wyke (2002), 244–278; an expanded version of Wyke (1997), 73–109.

16 Wyke (2002), 281–302.

17 Théophile Gautier, *Une Nuit de Cléopâtre* (1838).

18 Cyrino (2005), 121–157.

19 Gregory N. Daugherty, "Cleopatra Had Nothing On Me! 1920s Palmolive Soap Ads Define the Pop Cleo," paper presented at the CAMWS meeting in St. Louis, Missouri (April 16, 2004).

20 Gregory N. Daugherty, "The Greatest Story Ever Drawn! Cleopatra in American Comics," paper presented at the CAMWS-Southern Section meeting in Winston-Salem, North Carolina (November 4, 2004).

12

Gowns and Gossip: Gender and Class Struggle in *Rome*

Margaret M. Toscano

Power is the central theme of HBO-BBC's television series about ancient Rome: the struggle to get, keep, distribute, and even equalize power.[1] The initial words, spoken in the opening of the first episode of Season One, come from a male voiceover who asserts that "four hundred years after the last king was driven from the city, the Republic of Rome rules many nations, but it cannot rule itself. The city is constantly roiled by conflict between the common people and the nobility." Two visual images accompany these words: a map locating the ancient city and an unidentified male hand, undoubtedly of a plebeian – given the rough fabric of his clothing – who is making a crude drawing on stone of two men fighting with swords. Then the focus quickly moves from general class struggle to the conflict between the two men who dominate the city's turmoil: Caesar and Pompey. The "balance of power is always shifting," the narrator tells us.

In spite of the centrality of major historical figures to the plot, the genius of the series *Rome* lies in its depiction of power as intricately complex, many-layered, always shifting, unstable, and never focused on just the privileged few. Power is decentered throughout by both the narrative and visual movement away from the middle of major events to peripheral, private comments about them. For example, the Battle of Thapsus itself is never shown, only Cato's and Scipio's lament over its outcome. First the camera frames the two of them, standing near the body of a dying elephant; then it pans out to the common soldiers waiting and looking on (Episode 09). It is not only big personalities, like Caesar and Pompey, Antony and Cleopatra, who determine important events, as traditional history insists. Rather, cause and effect is a multi-dimensional interlinking of the wills and wants of many different characters of every size, shape, color, age, talent, ethnicity, and rank, who themselves are usually unaware of the part they play in larger events.[2] No one completely understands what forces are at work. The camera's lens captures so many different perspectives of Rome, high and low, interior and exterior, that we spectators begin to accept a world where the personal and political are not separable at all.

In this chapter, I focus on gowns and gossip as two central metaphors that demonstrate the complexity of power, the interplay of desire and action, in the episodes comprising the first season of *Rome*. Gowns and gossip, which are often seen as the trivial and stereotypical concerns of women – something hardly worth paying attention to – are depicted as central to the major historical event that ends the first season of the *Rome* series: the assassination of Gaius Julius Caesar. Who would think that the adultery of a plebeian wife, or the extreme love of a husband for this beautiful woman, or the gossip of slave women could influence such a monumental moment in time?

This series makes us believe such things are possible because it weaves a world of many colors and textures where events and objects small and great are all intertwined. There is no thread so slight that it does not matter to the larger tapestry. Whether it is a little bug in Titus Pullo's prison cell used to beseech divine favor, or a nameless boy with whom we watch Caesar's army crossing the Rubicon, or the younger daughter of Lucius Vorenus dodging soldiers as she runs through the streets of Rome with a ritual offering, all these small moments relate on some level to the big picture. Dwarves, prostitutes, children, Jews, barbarians, animals, and especially slaves play pivotal roles in the general movement of history as seen in this series' narrative and visual structure.

Gowns and Gossip

If we viewers miss the importance of seemingly insignificant people, or even everyday objects like dresses, wigs, and make-up, we are told directly why they matter by no less a male character than Lucius Vorenus, the last person one would imagine to be concerned with fashion. At an intimate evening supper with their elder daughter, Vorenus and Niobe tease her that since her father is now a Senator, they are finally going to find her a rich old husband (Episode 12). She can wrap him around her little finger so that he will buy her lots of dresses and jewels and slaves, Niobe says. When the girl answers that she wants no such things because they are trivial, her father contradicts her. "Trivial? Why, when I was your age, I had to eat bones out of the gutter. Dresses and jewels are not trivial. They show others that you are loved and protected and valued."

The series depicts dresses as one of the central concerns of women, something they use not simply to attract men but even more to compete with one another.[3] Servilia takes special care to dress attractively when she sees Caesar for the first time after his eight-year absence (Episode 04). Atia has her slaves fix Octavia up like a painted doll to win Pompey as a husband (Episode 01). But each woman is especially keen to maintain her beauty in front of her female rival. Atia grudgingly acknowledges Servilia's appeal while claiming its power is wasted. After she welcomes Servilia to her symposium, Atia exclaims aside to her body slave (Episode 04): "She has a good cosmetic slave, I grant you, but as a lover for Caesar – absurd!"

Still, the series breaks out of stereotypes about gender and fashion at several points, as with Vorenus' statement about the importance of apparel to his daughter. He knows that clothes make the man. They mark position and wealth in a society where certain colors and types of cloth were not only prohibited by lack of money but also legislated according to class and office. Vorenus' own dress changes along with his rise in status. He graduates from a simple, coarsely woven tunic to a white toga and finally to Senatorial purple stripes.[4] With this change comes a changing self-awareness too, as the series makes clear when Niobe holds a mirror up to let him take a look at himself in his new attire (Episode 12). The tension between Vorenus' pleasure at his class mobility and his shame about selling out on his Republican principles to achieve this status is already emerging in this scene.[5] Moreover, since mirrors are often symbols of female vanity and inferior identity in the Roman world, Vorenus in front of a mirror is thus another way the series creators challenge gender roles.[6]

Niobe's clothing also changes with the family's upward climb. But she finds that there is more to social acceptance than having money for nicer clothes and jewels. This is evident in a crucial scene where Vorenus and Niobe attend a symposium at Atia's house, invited at Caesar's request since Vorenus is his new magistrate (Episode 11). Because Niobe takes special care with making a dress fit to wear at an upper-class party, she is hurt when Atia and the other women gossip behind her back. "I don't see what's wrong with it," she mopes later, holding her dress as the camera moves up from the skirt, to the bodice, and finally to Niobe's forlorn but still striking face. Her natural beauty, noticed and commented upon by Caesar and even Atia, is not enough to give her access to the patrician world, even if it plays a role in her brother-in-law's preference for her over her sister Lyde.

Ironically, Niobe does seem to look better in her plain peasant smocks that fall fetchingly off her shoulder than in her stiff party costume, which may be a visual way the series offers a subtle questioning of class values.

Make-up is another metaphor for the interplay between status and identity in *Rome*. Cosmetic art is not simply about a beautiful appearance but about the kinds of social masks that are necessary for subtle negotiations of power. Once again, the series creators deconstruct gender stereotypes by playing against the notion that women alone manipulate image for certain effects. In Caesar's triumph episode, three scenes are closely juxtaposed (Episode 10). First Atia plays the role of slave to make amends to her daughter Octavia by offering to rouge her cheeks. Then Caesar's cheeks are reddened with ritual blood by the young pontiff, Octavian. And finally the half-dead Vercingetorix is dragged out with rosy circles painted neatly on each cheek, as Caesar had commanded the guards to liven him up a bit for public display. Men are as concerned with their dress in this sequence as are women. Caesar asks his chief slave, Posca, if he is wearing too much purple before his procession. Pullo, who earlier had scoffed at Vorenus' toga as making him look "like laundry," suddenly wants to dress up in his army red to show his soldier's identity in the parade, but is denied since he is now a civilian – a transition that also marks his emotional decline. And even Antony's vibrant royal blue competes with the bright colors of the women sitting next to him on the platform, though he earlier mocked Caesar for playing at being a god with his desire for ostentation.

Gossip, like clothing, deals with image and power. The Latin word *fama* is illustrative because it connects rumor with reputation and fame. I have chosen the term "gossip" to play on the way women's speech is often marginalized or downgraded.[7] The *Rome* series, by contrast, clearly connects women's gossip with important news and the official reporting of events, letter-sending, and all types of spoken, written, and visual communication. These communications are dominant visual and plot motifs from the opening credits to the closing credits: the moving, colorful graffiti and mosaics of the beginning titles sequence, the recurring public announcements given by the newsreader, the changing visual calendar, the letters Posca writes and reads for Caesar, the puppet shows and popular dramas, the private letters of the women, the public notices, the political handbills, and even Servilia's spoken and written curse deposited in a city wall. The abundance of such words and images in the series highlights the importance of perception for how power is maintained and transferred.

What is an official report? What is the truth? What is a lie or propaganda? And how does knowledge relate to power? These questions are the ongoing investigation of the series, which does not propose simple answers. The official news proclaimed by the corpulent town crier ironically contrasts with what is actually occurring in the city; and what is deemed legitimate shifts as power changes hands. The puppet shows and plays are reinterpretations of what has happened in previous scenes. Thus Cato and Scipio, depicted as the "last two Republicans" in one scene, become the enemies of Rome in the next when they are ridiculed by the actors in the mime after Caesar's power has become supreme (Episode 09).[8] In contrast, the fame of Pullo and Vorenus, portrayed in dramas and street drawings, reflects and sways public opinion to protect them from Caesar's punishment (Episode 12). The graffiti showing Caesar sexing Servilia and Brutus murdering Caesar are true on some level. It is the public reporting of private matters that makes these drawings disturbing to those who want neither their actions nor their motives exposed to public censure. Gossip's power relies on the threat of exposed secrets, as with the incest between Octavian and his sister and the adultery of Niobe and her brother-in-law. "What I tell you is the truth," the slave woman Eleni proclaims before whispering in Vorenus' ear (Episode 12).

Secrets are often the domain of slaves because their invisibility allows them to see and overhear things that would not be done or spoken in public, things the powerful patricians would not do in front of those of their own class. One of the most fascinating aspects of the series *Rome* is the way the creators lace slaves into almost every scene. They are everywhere, even in places the viewer does not notice at first. Of course most viewers were shocked by the watchful presence of slaves in the sex scenes, which shatters our modern notion of privacy and intimacy. But elsewhere, noticing the slaves is like looking for Waldo in the famous children's books. On close inspection, we suddenly realize slaves are all around, as silent backdrops, like scenery. It is only with repeated viewings that their names and their mumbled commentary are comprehensible. In the scene where the cook (Demeter) hears Caesar having an epileptic fit in the storage room with Octavian present, she assumes they are lovers from the groans and observes to herself, almost silently: "Mmh–" (Episode 04). Atia's body slave, Merula, though mostly taciturn, mutters just perceptibly that Servilia must still have "some juice in her yet" after Atia expresses her surprise that Caesar includes Servilia, "that rattled old sandal," on his guest-list for her party in the fourth episode.

The slave women, Merula and Eleni, may exert the most profound influence in the story as the instruments of revenge in the battle between Atia and Servilia, a contest for power that impacts all the major historical events

Figure 6 Atia (Polly Walker) and Antony (James Purefoy) enjoy dinner at her villa, while a servant attends them. Photograph from *Rome*^{SM} courtesy of HBO®. *Rome*^{SM} and HBO® are service marks of Home Box Office, Inc.

of the series.[9] These women are easy to overlook, not just because they are female slaves, but because they are older, dressed in muted colors, and usually hiding in the shadows. Merula, Atia's main body slave, is old and small and dark. She seems to fit the Greco-Roman literary role of the ancestral nursemaid who has been with Atia from birth, but we do not know this for certain.[10] She says little, but is ferocious. She draws a knife on Antony when he slaps Atia (Episode 06). And surely she is the veiled figure who cuts off Servilia's hair in the street attack (Episode 09).[11] Merula's face, when seen, is stern, hard to read, immobile, and mask-like.

Eleni, on the other hand, is more verbal and open; she smiles frequently. Closer in age to her mistress Servilia, they have several intimate conversations of the sort that could take place between close friends. In fact, the first picture we have of Servilia and her body slave is when Eleni reads Caesar's letter to her mistress, giving her own reassurances to quell Servilia's doubts about Caesar's intentions (Episode 01). "Do you think he says this to his wife?" Eleni asks encouragingly. But at other times, even after an intimate exchange, Servilia shows Eleni her place by suddenly giving orders in the mistress mode; this is something Caesar never does with Posca – but then Caesar has a natural reserve and unquestioned power.

Both slave women do the dirty work for their mistresses, seemingly without scruples. In fact, they both serve as psychological doubles for their owners.[12] They instinctively seem to know what to do in any given instance to play out the hidden desires of their mistresses, implied by the fact that they often seem to act without orders. Merula's and Eleni's actions reveal hidden motives and tactics and provide another level on which we may read and interpret the characters of Atia and Servilia. This is evident in the crucial scene where Atia comes to visit Servilia after she has been publicly attacked and humiliated.

The scene begins with Eleni waking Servilia to tell her Atia has come to visit (Episode 10). "Atia in my house!" the mistress says defiantly. Then the camera cuts to the faded image of an unknown slave, then to a close-up of Atia's face, then to her back, so we are looking from Atia's point of view when Servilia is brought in on a chair carried by two male slaves, with Eleni right behind her. "My dear Atia," Servilia exudes sweetly, as Atia crosses the frame. Servilia continues, "How lovely to see you," while a black-cloaked head follows Atia, barely visible at the bottom of the screen, evoking the dark veiled figure that cut Servilia's hair. The camera then cuts to Atia alone again. "*Bona Dea!*" she says, acting surprised. The camera moves to Atia in front of Servilia's chair, as the male slaves depart. Atia kneels, saying, "My poor friend." Then the camera provides a clear shot of the grim Merula; then across to Eleni, who crosses her arms defensively. The two slave women stand rigidly behind their mistresses, as though they are facing off for a duel. As the noble women keep up the polite talk of affected friendship and mutual concern, the hostile body language of the two slaves tells the real story of what is going on underneath the surface: both Servilia and Atia know the treacherous actions of the other and are on their guard. The fact that Merula's presence is not seen at first, and that she is clearly juxtaposed with Eleni, whose face is uncharacteristically stern, underscores the tension and the nature of the conflict. The careful movement and placement of the camera subtly evokes such an interpretation.

It is personal combat that connects the four women, as foreshadowed in the series' initial drawing on stone of men with drawn swords. Though the focus at first is on men's power in this series, the power of women quickly surfaces as equally important in the escalating conflict in *Rome*.[13] Their weapons may be different, but the women's aim is equally sharp.[14] Atia attacks Servilia with traditional women's arts, using both gowns and gossip. First, she authorizes the obscene graffiti about Caesar and Servilia (Episode 05). Later she has Servilia stripped and her hair cut off in a public attack as Servilia is carried on a litter through a district occupied by statue-makers (note the statuary lots in the background). Here the removal of

Servilia's clothing and the cutting of her hair do the opposite of what is done to Vorenus when he acquires a more elaborate and layered costume. Servilia's stripping denigrates her status and her ability to function in public. The fact that she is attacked on a street where sculpted images are created underscores her loss of face.

Servilia's revenge upon her rival is also double: she tries to take away Atia's children and plays a central part in plotting Caesar's murder. While not obvious in each instance, both gowns and gossip play a role here as well. It is while Servilia and Octavia are weaving, an intimate atmosphere conducive to gossip, that Servilia persuades Octavia to seduce her brother and that Octavia reveals the apparently insignificant story of Niobe's adultery (Episode 09). But it is this story that Eleni later whispers into the ear of Vorenus, taking him away from Caesar's side on that fatal and fateful day in March. Unknowingly and uncaringly, Servilia causes Niobe's destruction and hurts Vorenus more than she does her enemy Atia. Thus, Merula and Eleni, two seemingly powerless slave women, are instrumental in toppling the dictatorship of Caesar.

In many ways these two slave women parallel the figures of Vorenus and Pullo as fictional, lower-class characters played against the famous and historical aristocrats, though the slave women are more in the shadows than their male counterparts. Like Pullo and Vorenus, their small lives impact the larger events of history. The series creators establish multiple pairs of rivals like these who vie for power: the aristocrats and plebs, Romans and barbarians, Atia and Servilia, Antony and Cicero, Niobe and Lyde, Brutus and Caesar, Caesar and Cleopatra. Even those pairs that seem friendly, such as Octavian and his sister, or Caesar and Servilia, can quickly become at odds with each other. This tendency for partnerships to deteriorate into oppositions is a major concern of this series.

Gender and Class Struggle

In his commentary on the first episode, Bruno Heller, the executive producer, writer, and director of the series, says that he transformed the two centurions Pullo and Vorenus in Caesar's historical record into a centurion and legionnaire to show the tension of rank. The preponderance of such dualities in *Rome* also underscores the importance of gender. As feminist theory has demonstrated, gender as a social category is never simply about male and female roles but about any polarized division that can be used to create hierarchy.[15] Dichotomies, such as active and passive, hard and soft, reinforce traditional gender roles. Any kind of stratification fortifies gender divisions and inequity because all power structures give legitimacy to the idea of dominance and subordination.

For this very reason, it is no surprise that in the series *Rome* gender and class are intricately connected, though not identical. In general, all the slaves play womanly roles to their masters, male and female alike. It is telling, and believable in an ancient context, that the relationship between Caesar and Posca is depicted in many ways as that of an old married couple. Caesar calls his slave an "old woman" on more than one occasion and teases him about underestimating him after all their years together. In their study of women and slaves in ancient culture, Sheila Murnaghan and Sandra R. Joshel argue that the classical world "always combined slaveholding and patriarchy" in a way that "promoted a constant process of comparison and differentiation" where the categories male/female and free/slave "achieved their signifying power, not in tandem, but in combination with each other."[16] It is no surprise, then, that the creators of *Rome*, with their careful historical research, connect gender and slavery closely, both in the series itself and in their DVD commentaries and "Bonus Features" under the headings "Women in Rome" and "Slave Society." Both topics, of course, also demonstrate their interest in deconstructing categories of social power.

From the first episode of the series, the audience is given hints that slavery will be important to the plot: slaves are being sold in Caesar's camp in Gaul, Julia tells Pompey to be good to her slaves and to her father in her same dying breath, and the camera focuses on the brand on the bald head of Pompey's slave more than once.[17] Equally prominent in the first episode is the world of women: Servilia and Eleni discuss Caesar's return; Octavia is used as a sexual pawn to try to keep Pompey's political alliance with the Julii; later his elaborate marriage ceremony to Cornelia is shown; and Atia attends a symposium at Servilia's. "Lovely party," Atia tells her. "Not as lovely as you look in that dress," Servilia coos. The war of the women begins right alongside the rivalry between the men, and slaves are inextricably woven into this hostile network.

Power is complex because it is never simply a matter of strong versus weak, as one would expect of the categories master/slave and male/female. Sexuality, age, ethnicity, money, class, beauty, talents, intelligence, industry, facility in language are all factors that come into play to complicate the picture. Ironically, the more factors involved in creating power structures, the more unstable strict dualities and hierarchies become. Any difference can be used as a marker either to generate or subvert power. This is one reason gender relationships are never strictly linear.[18] As a Roman *paterfa-milias*, Vorenus always has the power to control and take Niobe's life. But because he wants her love, he also feels that he is at her mercy. On the one hand, he tells her when he returns home from Gaul: "Do as I say, wom-an . . . Do not question me in that tone" (Episode 02). On the other hand, he is desperate for her affection. So he tells Pullo: "I require my wife to love me; otherwise I'm her slave" (Episode 03).

Although a woman, Atia has more power than the horse trader Timon since she is part of an influential and rich Roman clan and he is a Jewish foreigner. Still, their sexual relationship in some ways breaks down hierar-chy because it breeds familiarity between them such that Atia must remind Timon more than once that he forgets his place. But her need for his talents, nerve, and connections to carry out her plans makes her dependent on him – a dependency that once again disturbs the balance of power. As a subtle contrast to and comparison with both the Vorenus/Niobe and Atia/Timon relationships, Pullo's attempt to win Eirene's affection as a marriage partner is undercut by the fact that he has already claimed her sexually as her master, though this was an accepted norm for slave owners in Roman society.[19] Pullo, the anti-authoritarian, never wants to treat Eirene as his slave; and, in fact, he seems attracted to her because she reminds him of his mother. Freeing Eirene is claiming his family's right to freedom, past and future.

The greater chasm between royalty and peasants in Egypt ironically makes the Romans look less autocratic in the series' Cleopatra episode (Episode 08). Her body slave, Charmian, is both bolder and more servile than the Roman slaves; she is both more intimate and more fawning. She uses Cleopatra's dependence on her, as well as her mistress' pride, to get Cleopatra to act in what she sees as her darling's self-interest: "Weak, I call it," Charmian wheedles. "She knows how to beat her slaves well enough but can't throw away the pipe." Then she smiles just slightly when Cleopa-tra responds in character: "Weak, am I? Insolent dwarf! Throw it out." Charmian manipulates her own servility to increase Cleopatra's mastery, and thus her own since their welfare is completely co-dependent.

The complex character and actions of Caesar himself illustrate the fact that power rarely flows from top to bottom only, nor is it concentrated in just one place. Though a patrician, Caesar sides with the plebs; and though a supporter of all classes according to the show's interpretation, still he opposes inequity through strong-armed threats that could be called tyran-nical. As he accepts the title "Imperator" in Episode 10, Caesar tells the Senators to join him in building a Rome "that offers justice, peace, and land to all its citizens, not just the privileged few. Support me in this task, and old divisions will be forgotten. Oppose me, and Rome will not forgive you a second time." The audience cannot fail to see the irony of Caesar's attempt to incorporate democratic policies through intimidation and imperial decrees.

Irony, a dominant trope in the *Rome* series, is used to show the tension between what we might expect if power always ran along strict hierarchical lines and what actually happens, given the complexity of human motives and the interdependence of all classes and people. As the actress Lindsay Duncan (Servilia) observes in the "Bonus Features" of the DVD: "Without the underclass there is no upper class. They couldn't live in their houses; they couldn't eat; they couldn't dress; they couldn't do anything." Lydia Biondi, the Italian actress who plays Merula, asserts that: "the slaves, they were perhaps the most important aspect of the city; without them the city couldn't exist." Still, the underclasses are at the mercy of the rich, demonstrating "the throw-away quality of human life" that Ray Stevenson (Pullo) refers to in his commentary on Episode 05. At the same time, the slaves are indispensable and enormously influential, as a character like Posca demonstrates not only by micromanaging Caesar's affairs but also by literally holding Caesar's life in his hands from day to day, as do any of the slaves who closely serve their masters. Yet the patricians rarely see their own vulnerability in this regard, just as they fail to see the suffering or lives of those beneath them. When Pompey is backed against the sea and receives Caesar's letter offering truce, he remarks about the carefree life of the messenger, a slave who faces no such dilemma as his (Episode 05): "How happy to be a slave and have no will, to make no decision, to be like driftwood, how restful!" How little Pompey seems to know or see of the slaves' real lives.

Pompey, though, has neither the hindsight of history nor the near omniscience of the camera's eye, which moves the audience around the set to see from every possible shot and angle. The camera brings the audience into the middle of things. Steven Shill, the director of the Egyptian episode (Episode 08), says in his commentary that he purposely placed the camera inside the scene, not outside, because he wanted no "fourth wall" between the action and the audience. He uses the camera to show the point of view of the actors so that we viewers almost become part of their world as we move with them. Ray Stevenson remarks that director Allen Coulter in Episode 05 does much the same thing, with the result that "the camera itself becomes a character," a shifting character whose role and point of view change as the camera moves position.

Such attention to artistic details creates subliminal subtexts that are transmitted through visual images and art direction. What is happening on a thematic and narrative level is iconically represented in the background. For example, Atia buying jewelry or choosing a wig may seem an insignificant detail, but it highlights the importance of women's wiles for the plot. This technique reinforces the intent and desire of the writers and directors to show the effects of small events and people on history, which Heller and others announce in their commentaries. That the series creators state explicitly that they wanted to show a different Rome, one that is colorful, cosmopolitan, multi-lingual, highly ethnic, and a contrast to the staid "classicism" of most Roman films, bears witness to their intentional dismantling of typical hierarchies.

In his commentary to Episode 09, director Jeremy Podeswa emphasizes the importance of the assistant directors who create the rich backgrounds where the texture of the many different worlds and classes of Rome is revealed. Podeswa explains that there are always unspoken elements shown visually in the background that tell a contrasting story to the main events. He illustrates his point with the scene in this episode where a slave steals bread while Cato commits suicide offstage in another room. "This is a lovely little moment that I always really liked in the script," he says, "where we have all these things of great import happening for the patricians, and yet for the people who are at the lower end of the economic scale, their daily issues are really about, 'Am I going to have enough bread to eat?'" Podeswa comments that the series overall is very successful in moving "between upstairs, downstairs, between the common man and patricians, the working class, the soldiers, the slaves, and counter-balancing that with the concerns of the wealthy and the important."

The upstairs/downstairs tension is shown visually in Episode 04 when the camera cuts back and forth between the dinner party at Atia's villa and the dinner party in the courtyard of the Voreni. Yet on the two occasions when the two worlds of patricians and plebs meet over food, they cannot meld. Though Atia agrees to dine with Pullo and Vorenus at Octavian's urging for saving his life in Episode 02, her statement that "we shall all dine together as equals" is clearly impossible as the scene progresses. The class divisions are too strong. Likewise, though Caesar wants his promotion of Vorenus to be accepted by the patricians, the way the women snub Niobe at Atia's party (Episode 11) shows the power of the resistance of those not directly in command.

The dichotomy of upstairs/downstairs is further reflected in the tension between private and political. On the surface, even the patrician women rule only on a domestic level, but the power of the women of all classes extends beyond this private realm in *Rome.* "Politics is for the men," Atia tells Servilia in surprise when she learns of her connection to Caesar's murder in the last episode (Episode 12). Her statement recalls Servilia's earlier comment to Atia that her objection to Caesar "is not personal but purely political" (Episode 09). In both cases the denial of interest, whether personal or political, is a ruse. However, Atia's assertion (when she visits Servilia after her public attack) that "men are so silly about their honor" may reflect a real difference between the two women. Atia sacrifices her dignity for her family's welfare on more than one occasion; Servilia sacrifices her son's honor to promote her own. Though Servilia plays more of the traditional "womanly" role on the surface, Atia's maternal instinct is a primary motivating force for her actions.

All categories in the end are unstable, as the final scenes of the last episode reveal. Caesar's bloody body is captured by a camera high above the Senate floor. Niobe topples from a height to her death below, once again wearing the simple homespun shift in her final scene. Together with her and Caesar, Vorenus topples too, though both his rise to and fall from power are illusory on some level. And as Vorenus' fortune crumbles, Pullo's begins to rise, not to the same heights, but just as he has lived, commonly, which is much safer. It is no accident, then, that Pullo is the one character whose costume – a simple, drab, soldierly tunic – barely changes throughout the first season.

On the official website for *Rome,* costume designer April Ferry states that she used costume to reveal class, family, and personality. She sought to recreate historical authenticity by using only the dyes and fabrics the Romans would have had at the time: cotton, linen, wool, and some silk for the very wealthy, like Caesar.[20] Costumes are clearly central in this series. They are part of the visual backdrop, like the graffiti, that sends both obvious and subliminal messages to the audience. While on one level truth always lies under the façade of visible power, on another level the façade of make-up and clothing tells the real story. Just as the real news is found in the interplay between the propaganda of the official newsreader and the exaggerations and simplifications of the graffiti and gossip, so also the real characters are more than their clothing but never apart from the social constructs that their clothes represent. Such material objects not only bring the ancient world alive, they also connect and intertwine all the elements in the story.

The weaving of cloth is an ongoing, subtle metaphor in this series that connects all classes and people and their assumptions, aspirations, and expectations in a complex tapestry of power. From the scenes where patrician women weave and gossip, to the scene where the plebeian dyers express their need for urine to wash their wool, to the scene where an old woman witnesses Pullo commit murder for hire as she sits at her loom, the fabric of human interconnectedness is depicted. The dominant picture on the tapestry only stands out against the negative space of its background. Likewise, the important historical events at the end of the Roman Republic cannot be separated from what is going on in the lives of all the people in Rome of every class, gender, ethnicity, age, and status. Power is dispersed throughout the complex social system of the ancient city, neither equally nor predictably. HBO-BBC's *Rome* is an effective critique on power because it realistically depicts its many facets, its subtleties, and its constant ironic elusiveness.

NOTES

1   I would like to thank my graduate student Cynthia Hornbeck for her help in compiling a bibliography on Roman slave and class issues. Special thanks to my husband Paul Toscano for being a springboard for my ideas and an astute reader of my manuscript.

2   Cyrino (2005), 115–116, emphasizes the importance of *Spartacus* (1960) as the first Roman film to deal with class struggle and to portray the plight of the common people.

3   See Sebesta and Bonfante (1994), 46–100, for a discussion of the way Roman dress marks gender, age, marriage, class, and social status. Bartman (2001) argues that hairstyles of Roman women "were highly individualized" as well as "gendered cultural markers" (1).

4   On the DVD commentary for Episode 12, historical consultant Jonathan Stamp explains that they made Vorenus' purple stripes broader than would actually have been allowed by law for the purpose of visual impact.

5   Stamp explains the importance of social mobility during this period of Roman history in his commentary on Episode 12.

6   Wyke (1994) explores Roman visual and literary texts that depict mirrors as objects representing female identity: "Placed before her mirror, woman is defined and recognized as less than a male citizen and disruptive of his pursuits, irresponsibly frivolous and dangerously seductive" (136).

7   There is a growing critical literature from a linguistic, literary, and sociological perspective that examines the importance of gossip as a primary form of social discourse. While women in the past have been blamed as its main perpetrators, Vermeule (2006) notes that "Everyone gossips" and that "Gossip is always concerned with power" (105). See also Spacks (1985) and Dunbar (1996).

8   On the DVD commentary for Episode 09, director Jeremy Podeswa uses this example to describe the importance of the "plays" for giving different points of view of the same action.

9   Actress Suzanne Bertish (Eleni) says in her commentary on the DVD "Bonus Features" that her character is "instrumental in leading up to Caesar's death."

10 In her "Bonus Features" commentary, actress Polly Walker (Atia) says that Merula "is like my mother; she has probably known me since I was a baby."

11 While the summary of Episode 09 on *Rome*'s website identifies the figure as Merula, the fact that the drama itself leaves the identity vague is an example of the shadowy presence of the slave women.

12 Fitzgerald (2000) explains how slaves in the classical world functioned as "the other self," as "part of the master's *mind* as well as his body, both an unruly part of the master's knowledge of himself and . . . knowledge of the world" (13).

13 In a general survey of women's influence in the classical world, Lefkowitz (1993), 59, examines the historical role of Servilia in mediating the relationship between Caesar and Brutus.

14 PBS's dramatization of Robert Graves' *I, Claudius* (1976) previously explored women's roles in shaping Roman politics. See Joshel (2001) for a discussion of the "villainesses" in this series who transgress against traditional femininity in their attempt to "wield financial or political power" (139).

15 Simone de Beauvoir's classic *The Second Sex* (1952) is foundational for defining the importance of dualities for feminine identity. Bergren (1983) shows how such categories function in the classical world. Hare-Mustin and Marecek (2001) discuss the complexities and paradoxes of difference and duality in postmodern feminism.

16 Murnaghan and Joshel (1998), 3.

17 Heller and Stamp begin their commentary on this episode by talking about the one million Gauls Caesar sold into slavery after he defeated them in war.

18 As Kampen (1996) explains: "Gender, thus, speaks constantly in the languages of age, status, ethnicity, and they in the language of gender; it exists only and always in relation to other social categories" (14).

19 This relationship is an ironic twist on the fact that historically slaves could win their freedom by being sexual pets for their masters, as Petronius' "Trimalchio's Dinner" indicates (*Satyricon* 76). Saller (1987), 72, uses the Trimalchio story to illustrate the "slave's vulnerability and resignation" in a system that accepted such exploitation without question.

20 On the "Wardrobe" commentary, one of the "Bonus Features," Heller says that they chose Ferry to do the costumes because "she came in not with the clichés but a fresh, imaginative take" that would reinforce the colorful, cosmopolitan, multi-dimensional Roman world they wanted to depict.

13

The Gender Gap: Religious Spaces in *Rome*

J. Mira Seo

The creators of *Rome* have discovered that historical authenticity is sometimes more exotic and titillating than fabrication. The series depicts many different types of religious activity to reveal the complex implication of religion in every facet of ancient Roman life, both domestic and public.[1] Not surprisingly, the rituals depicted largely feature blood, bloodshed, or at least murderous intentions; they seem to be chosen more for visual and emotional effect than to provide a careful survey of Roman religious experience. This seems fair enough: the show's creators generate thrills with effective reproductions of certain Roman religious rituals, and if they emphasize the differences between ancient religious practices and contemporary concepts of religion, this is clearly more desirable than offering a false picture of similarity.

Religion, "Belief," and Civic Cult

There is, however, one area in the representation of Roman religious practice that might give the scholarly viewer some pause: the prominence of personal devotionals in religious practice portrayed in the series *Rome*. Among scholars of ancient religion, one widely held view states that the notion of personal "faith" or "belief" is essentially a notion inappropriately applied to Greek and Roman religion from Christian ideology.[2] Given the show's general willingness to let "Romans be Romans," then, why is there such a strong emphasis on personal devotionals in the narrative of the series? When this fanatically well-researched series seems obviously to flaunt scholarly convention, rather than castigating *Rome* for its failures, we need to look deeper: who performs personal devotionals and in what contexts?

This chapter analyzes the religious rituals performed by men and women in the series, such as the presentation of Jupiter Optimus Maximus in Caesar's triumph, or Octavia's worship of Cybele, and how their depiction establishes polarities of gendered behavior. Though the male and female characters often interact socially and within the family group in environments relatively unmarked by gender – Atia's grand parties, Pullo's frequent presence in Vorenus' home – this impression of open male–female relations is counterbalanced by the strongly segregated religious behaviors that men and women exhibit. Space, therefore, is defined by religious activity perhaps more than by physical separation of the sexes.

In *Rome*, men dominate public ritual associated with political events. They conduct rituals in all-male environments at the heart of the city, like Caesar's ritual face-painting at the temple of Jupiter Optimus Maximus before his triumphal procession (Episode 10).[3] The proximity of this ceremony to the public spectacle of the military triumph effectively links Caesar's religious practice to his political victory and dominance. Caesar's own imminent deification is anticipated in his exchange with Antony before the procession. When Antony mocks the pomposity of "playing at being a god," Caesar indignantly retorts: "Playing? I'm not playing. This is not a game." For Caesar, the religious aspect of the triumph is an important symbolic affirmation of his political victory. Similarly, the induction of Lucius Vorenus into the prestigious ranks of the *Evocati* is accomplished through a solemn ritual in the temple of Mars (Episode 05), just as Antony's election to tribune of the plebs is marked by a religious induction into the sacred office by the priest of Jupiter Fulgor (Episode 02).

The two men's attitudes toward these events, however, could not be more different: while Vorenus kneels reverently before the priest of Mars, Antony seems less than impressed by his consecration, impatiently slouching in his seat during the ritual, and then declaring his urgent need for a drink upon its completion. Antony's disrespectful attitude toward the ceremony contrasts strongly with the portrayal of Vorenus as a devout, old-fashioned Roman. Vorenus' traditional Republican values are depicted through his reverence for Roman religious ritual, in direct contrast to the seemingly irreverent attitudes of both Antony and Caesar. Once in control of the city, Caesar demonstrates the political importance of religion when he administers a subtle bribe to the Chief Augur, offering a "birthday present" to his wife in exchange for favorable auguries (Episode 04).

Surprisingly for the former Chief Priest of Rome (Caesar had been elected *Pontifex Maximus* for 63 BC), Caesar protests a little too much when making his request, disingenuously asserting that "religion and politics should be kept separate." The very falseness of this claim, both historically and in the context of his portrayal throughout the first season of the series, underscores the mercenary nature of their exchange. This becomes clear in the staging of the auguries. As demonstrated by the elaborate choreography of the bird signs, the auguries are explicitly manipulated to provide good omens for Caesar's occupation of the city (Episode 04). Caesar's self-satisfied smile in the final frame of the episode reveals that the bribe has obviously succeeded. Earlier, Caesar had explained to the Chief Augur: "The gods know my intentions for the city are peaceful; the people must know it also."

Octavian, too, despite his adlection into the College of Pontiffs in Episode 09, exhibits a rather cynical attitude toward religion. When he confronts his sister, Octavia, in her refuge at the temple of Cybele, she refuses to return home with him for Caesar's triumph, protesting that the "priests will protect her." Octavian smoothly replies: "No they won't. I've bought them – quite cheaply" (Episode 10). This exchange encapsulates a strong polarity between male and female religious attitudes in the series: while his sister naively relies on sacral reverence and authority to protect her, Octavian, concerned only with the political performance of their family's ascendancy, cavalierly subverts the priests' religious duties through bribery. The series' depiction of male religious activity is rigorously true to scholarly consensus, if only a partial picture: men – especially aristocratic ones – in their religious practice are segregated from women, associated with prominent temples and public spectacle, and they accurately treat religion as an integral part of Roman political life. Priesthoods and the administration of public rituals were performed as political offices and constituted part of civic life quite apart from spiritual belief.[4] Given this historical condition, *Rome* goes further in characterizing their attitudes toward religious practice as cynical, at times even irreverent, with a few notable exceptions to be discussed below.

Women and the Subjective Style

As portrayed in the series, women's religious practice, however, seems to deviate more from scholarly convention. Although there were conspicuous roles for women in Roman religion, most particularly as Vestal Virgins and other priestesses of female-oriented cults, the series avoids depicting any of these more familiar institutions.[5] Instead, the first and perhaps programmatic portrayal of female religious practice is the unforgettable scene of Atia at the *taurobolium* of Cybele, the goddess known in Rome as the Magna Mater, or "Great Mother" (Episode 01).[6] Certainly, as far as television goes, the image is admittedly stunning: a gorgeous, aristocratic mother of two showered with the blood of a dying bull as body-painted, head-dressed priests in loincloths chant and gambol around the sacrifice. Quick cross-cutting between the images of the sacrifice and Octavian's misery on the road indicates the significance of this ritual: Atia is making the sacrifice for the safety of her son, Octavian, who is off on a dangerous trip to Gaul. Throughout the exotic ritual, Atia chants, *"meum filium, Magna Mater,"* "[save] my son, Great Mother," emphasizing Atia's maternal concern to the Latinate audience; to the Latin-less majority of viewers, this striking use of Latin only enhances the outlandish effect.[7] Immediately after the bloody shower, Atia soaks in a cleansing bath as though at the spa, casually discussing a new marriage with her daughter, Octavia. These contextual cues associate Atia's religious practice with her personal, family concerns, and the intimate space defined by the ritual becomes an ideal location for some serious mother–daughter bonding time.

Cybele, the Magna Mater, features prominently throughout the series as a goddess of personal appeal for the female characters, quite in contrast to the historical record of her cult at Rome. Many ancient sources testify to the popular legend that developed around the official importation of her cult from Asia Minor in 204 BC.[8] From the earliest period of her introduction to Rome, the Magna Mater was placed at the center of public worship; her first temple, built on the Palatine Hill in 191 BC (and rebuilt three times, including once by Augustus after AD 3), incorporated a piazza surmounted by steps leading to the temple building used for theatrical performances during the goddess' festival, the *Ludi Megalenses* (celebrated April 4–10).[9] In the first century BC, chariot racing in the Circus Maximus also featured as part of the festival activities.[10] As Lynn E. Roller concludes:

> The Magna Mater was a deity of patriotism. She was the Mother of the state, and literally the mother of the state's most important deity, Jupiter. The theatrical works produced at her Palatine temple reinforced the public perception of her importance to the state and the intertwining of her legend with Roman history. The political careers of virtually every politically important family, from the Scipiones through Augustus, touched on the cult of the Magna Mater.[11]

This institutional side of the cult, however, is distinctly neglected by the series. *Rome* systematically misrepresents the nature of the Magna Mater's cult, by anachronistically emphasizing certain television-friendly spectacles, as in the case of the *taurobolium*, and even presenting the goddess as a divinity of personal devotion for women. As a Near Eastern goddess of fertility, her cult was certainly important to women, but in the Roman context the cult became a central part of state worship and civic identity.[12] Octavia in particular turns to the Magna Mater in her many well-justified moments of emotional crisis in the series. At the height of her feud with her mother and her budding erotic liaison with Servilia, Octavia is shown briefly calling upon the Magna Mater at a small shrine in her bedroom (Episode 07). Although the source of Octavia's emotional conflict seems difficult to read – is it an expression of homophobic horror at her own same-sex attraction or guilt at potentially betraying her family through her connection to Servilia? – the message conveyed by her urgent chanting seems clear: Octavia needs help.[13]

Octavia's association with Cybele reaches its height after a highly overdue and well-deserved mental breakdown, when she leaves home and takes refuge at the temple of the Magna Mater (Episode 10); if being told that her mother had arranged the murder of her beloved – albeit fictional – first husband, Glabius, was not enough to send her over the edge, apparently the incest she committed with her brother as a result of this information was. The temple, however, is hardly loud with the urban clamor of the historical temple's central location on the Palatine; rather, as portrayed in the series, New Age-style wind chimes and gently flowing water suggest an idyllic, spa-like isolation.[14] Before her brother's intervention, Octavia is seen alone in a gauzy enclosure, hissing with pain as she slices into her forearms with a knife. Perhaps this self-mutilation implicitly recalls the notorious self-castration ritual undertaken by the *Galli*, foreign priests of Cybele, who, while flamboyantly attired, are not explicitly denoted as eunuchs in the *taurobolium* scene earlier (Episode 01).[15] Although this particular type of self-injury is unattested in the worship of Cybele, the behavior resonates with our contemporary awareness of self-cutting as an activity associated with adolescents, especially troubled young females.[16] The creators of *Rome*, therefore, have taken liberties with the historical information known about the cult of Cybele by representing the goddess as the object of personal, domestic worship and the practice of self-mutilation as a part of her rites.

These historical discrepancies reflect the writers' willingness to subordinate accuracy to character development in the narrative of the series.

While some types of female "religious" practice, like Servilia's *defixiones* (curse tablets) against Caesar, or Niobe's home extispicy (reading of animal entrails) about her illegitimate child, accord well with the immediate narrative aims without adaptation, the writers have clearly transformed Cybele's cult into one of personal, rather than communal or civic, worship, for the purposes of furthering Octavia's characterization as a disturbed and tormented young woman.[17] Atia, Octavia, Servilia, and Niobe all exhibit religious behavior in response to personal, emotional crises, and these ritual activities occur mainly in the home or in distinctly female-segregated spaces. Even Atia's *taurobolium*, which presumably took place in the temple to the Magna Mater on the Palatine, features the mystery-initiation aspect of the cult, not the more public face of the *Ludi Megalenses* celebrated by the entire city of Rome. Female religious practice in *Rome*, therefore, is strongly skewed toward the personal and minimizes the civic aspects of cult, focusing rather on individual devotions and more magical or mystical rites. These polarities may be illustrated in a proposed spectrum of gendered religious behavior:

MALE	FEMALE
Civic	Marginal/Domestic
Political	Personal
Cynical	Emotional
Institutional	Magic/Mystery Cult

This schematic representation illustrates the overarching principles underlying the gendered representation of religious practice in the series. Such stark dichotomies seem to invite narrative violation, however, an expectation the series fulfills at a number of significant moments. One anomalous instance is the propitiation of Janus, god of new ventures, which takes place before the party to celebrate the grand opening of Vorenus' business (Episode 04). His younger daughter retrieves an offering from the neighborhood shrine of Janus, and brings it back to the courtyard of their family's *insula* (apartment building), where a terracotta bust of the god has been arranged into a small shrine. Public and domestic space mingle as the camera follows the little girl through the city streets and back to the safety of her home. Niobe and the younger Vorena pray with Vorenus as he asks the god for a favorable beginning to his business venture. In this family ritual, men and women worship together. It seems, however, that the family-unit and its ties to the community legitimize this seeming violation, thus placing it precisely in the middle of the spectrum.

This example introduces another important aspect to religious practice as represented in the series: the function of class in religious ritual. Because Vorenus and his family are themselves solidly middle class according to the social stratification of the show, they are thereby perfectly placed to mediate between the male–female divide because of their explicitly middling, in-between status. The family worships together as a mixed-gender group again in the fertility ritual of Vorenus and Niobe at their farm outside the city, witnessed by the children and the attending priests (Episode 12). In this case, their programmatic middle-class status is further affirmed by their return to an idealized rural environment and the performance of an archaic Roman fertility rite, a lustration of the fields as recommended by no less an old-fashioned Roman as the Elder Cato (*On Agriculture* 141). So these mixed-gender rites, rather than violating the polarity of gendered religious practice, perhaps serve to affirm the poles by providing a secure and rational middle point.[18]

Gender Violation and Dramatic Characterization

More explicit violations of the gender schema in religious practice depicted by the series involve only the non-aristocratic protagonists, Vorenus and Pullo. Most memorably, Vorenus pauses in the street at a local shrine of Venus to offer his blood in exchange for Niobe's love (Episode 06). As he enters the house, Vorenus interrupts a guilt-stricken Niobe kneeling at her prayers at a shrine in the kitchen, and they tearfully reconcile. The parallel prayers of Vorenus and Niobe indicate the reciprocity of their desires for a harmonious marriage, but the juxtaposition of their similar devotional actions underscores Vorenus' gender transgression. Like the women of the series, Vorenus makes a personal prayer to Venus for a domestic crisis of his own; his strained relations with Niobe produce this somewhat surprising moment of vulnerability for the tough centurion. Nonetheless, Vorenus appeals at a handy roadside shrine, so although he makes a personal prayer in a feminine mode, he still remains in a public, albeit non-institutional, setting.

Titus Pullo also offers up personal prayers, which take the traditional ancient form of bargaining with divinities, the familiar *do ut des* ("I give so that you may give") formulation of Greco-Roman religion. On several different occasions, he promises modest offerings to the gods in exchange for a personal boon. In the first episode, the incarcerated Pullo's prayer for freedom is humorously and instantaneously answered when Vorenus arrives moments later to release him from the brig. Later, in a more desperate circumstance, Pullo calls on Janus, Gaia, and Dis to accept his offering of a large insect before his scheduled execution in the arena (Episode 11). Pullo's emotional appeals in this prayer for the loved ones he has wronged mitigate his recent portrayal as a violent, irrational murderer and cold-blooded assassin. Our affection for him is renewed, and this sentimental moment only increases our elation when Vorenus eventually leaps heroically into the arena to save his beleaguered comrade. In the final episode of the season (Episode 12), Pullo visits the country shrine of Rusina, an obscure rural goddess,[19] to make offerings in atonement for his crimes against his beloved, Eirene. This personal devotional moment affords an opportunity for Pullo's reconciliation with Eirene, who has come along with him for the fresh air and ultimately receives a proposal of marriage: here, narrative demands trump any necessity for overt religious accuracy.

These examples of Pullo's rituals further illustrate the boundaries of religious expression in the series. As a very low-ranking soldier, Pullo has little capacity to exercise the political aspect of male religious practice as seen in aristocratic figures like Caesar or Antony. As a result, his religious expression tends toward the more personal, and thereby female end of the spectrum, thus enabling dramatically conveyed emotional states that might otherwise seem incongruent with his gruff, soldierly persona. Similarly Vorenus, though he does participate in some state religious rituals due to his relatively respectable status and the fact that he enjoys Caesar's political favor, reveals his potential for greater emotional depth through his early breakdown at the street shrine of Venus. This moment forms part of a highly developed tragic arc: Vorenus wins his wife's love over the course of the series' first season, only to lose her forever in the final episode when he confronts her with the truth about her illegitimate child.

These gender transgressions of religious behavior can hardly be cited as evidence of effeminacy on Vorenus' or Pullo's part, and so other explanations are required. The depiction of religion in the series affords various opportunities for the creators: they can express the alienness of ancient Rome through the mingling of the political and the religious, or they can titillate, as in the case of the vivid and gory *taurobolium* scene.[20] By creating gender polarities for religious practice, they can underscore the female characters' emotional crises, or achieve powerful moments of characterization that might not otherwise be plausible for male figures such as Vorenus and Pullo. The audience is clearly meant to identify most closely with these two men, and it is to the series' advantage to afford them opportunities for emotional expression that make them seem more fully rounded as characters and thereby appealing to modern viewers. Although these emotional moments involve gods and rituals that we do not share, their religious expressions are portrayed as being similar in tone to our contemporary conceptions of personal faith.[21] This conveniently renders Vorenus and Pullo, in particular, more sympathetic to us in the viewing audience.

One further motive might be proposed for this gendered representation of religious practice in the series *Rome*. As many scholarly reviewers have observed, when this fine series takes liberties with the historical record, we should look for other reasons, especially dramatic ones, for these departures. In order to maximize the potential of female characters to participate in the events of the narrative, the show's creators have minimized the historically accurate separation of men and women physically and socially – it would seem alienating and create significant narrative problems for the contemporary Western audience if Roman daily life appeared as patriarchal and segregated as it historically really was. In other words, the degree of unmarked interaction between men and women in this show was not normal for a strongly patriarchal and gender-segregated society like ancient Rome. On the model of recent serial television dramas, such as *Dynasty* (ABC, 1981–1989) or *The O.C.* (Fox, 2003–2007), the women of *Rome* are powerfully and deeply involved in the narrative to an extent that a Roman like the historian Tacitus would shudder to contemplate. His depictions of women of the early imperial period (just a few years after the time setting of *Rome*), particularly Agrippina the Elder and her daughter Agrippina, the mother of Nero, express a typically Senatorial and essentially male horror of female interference in political activity.[22] For the series to present forceful aristocratic female protagonists mingling and conspiring actively in political events with little social restriction, I suggest that the creators perhaps have displaced and to a certain extent marginalized historical features of patriarchal gender segregation. We may interpret this spectrum of gendered religious behavior and its concomitant spatial segregation of the genders as a way to compensate for the surprisingly "free" nature of Roman male–female interaction portrayed in the series.

NOTES

1   On Roman religion as a system for generating social meaning, see fundamentally Beard (1987) on the festival of the *Parilia* and Wallace-Hadrill (1987) on the Roman calendar. More generally, see the introduction to Feeney (1998).

2   This position is strongly influenced by anthropological models, and is adopted as a principle in the reference text by Beard, North, and Price (1998). See the

debate and reassessment in King (2003), who suggests that while the concept of "belief" was not organized in Roman religion as centrally as in Christianity, it did form part of the Romans' experience of religion: "The Roman Pagans did not merely lack the Christian focus on orthodox sets of beliefs, but possessed specific alternative mechanisms for the organization of beliefs that allowed clusters of variant beliefs to exist within Roman society without conflict" (277).

3   Painting the face red in imitation of the cult statue of Jupiter is attested in many sources, although showing Octavian as one of the College of Pontiffs performing the rite in the temple is probably not accurate. The triumph began outside of the *pomerium*, or sacred enclosure of Rome, and the route ended at the temple of Jupiter Optimus Maximus, where the *triumphator* would lay his laurel wreaths on the cult statue's lap. Here, too, the show's creators have taken some liberties with the elements of the ritual in order to maximize the associations between male religious ritual and politics, as well as foreshadowing Octavian's succession to power. For a brief summary of the triumphal ritual, see Beard, North, and Price (1998); the most thorough account and analysis of the origins of the Roman triumph remains Versnel (1970).

4   One might compare here the Queen of England's position as "Defender of the Faith." Regardless of her personal belief, the monarch serves also, *ex officio*, as head of the Anglican Church.

5   Epigraphic sources for women's priesthoods in Republican Rome are collected in Schultz (2006), chapter 2; see also the broader range of sources compiled in Kraemer (2004).

6   Rutter (1968) hypothesizes that the *taurobolium* sacrificial ritual was only incorporated explicitly into worship of Cybele by Antoninus Pius in AD 159. Furthermore, evidence indicates that this ritual served an initiatory purpose and was not a vehicle for personal appeal to the goddess.

7   See Ward Briggs, chapter 15 in this volume, for the use of Latin in mystical and religious scenes throughout the series.

8   Roller (1999), 264–271.

9   For archaeological analysis, see Pensabene (1988); an overview in Roller (1999), 271–274.

10   According to Cassius Dio (*Roman History* 37.8), Julius Caesar presented magnificent games for the *Ludi Megalenses* as curule aedile to much public acclaim in 65 BC.

11   Roller (1999), 316.

12   Roller (1999): "the Mother's Roman cult offers no private inspiration by individual devotees; in fact, there is no indication that the Magna Mater was one of the deities to whom ordinary people turned for private consolation" (317).

13   The ambiguity of the purpose for her prayer provides a double possibility for the audience: Octavia's distress and turn to spirituality may disarm some

potential homophobic audience response, or rather enhance the transgressive thrill engendered by the explicit lesbian sex scenes that follow.

14   To the creators of *Rome*, the spa setting seems to be a highly marked indicator of female space.

15   Most famously, Catullus Poem 63 recounts the self-castration of Attis, the mythical consort and eunuch priest of Cybele; Roller (1999), 319, explains the Roman sources' contempt for the *Galli* as a response to the power inversion represented by foreign eunuchs (usually encountered as slaves) who held prestigious and influential positions as priests in a central Roman cult.

16   An Internet search for "adolescent self-harm" in the primary medical journal database PubMed (www.pubmed.gov) returned 183 results; a Google search returned a frighteningly large number of hits. In popular culture, the film *Secretary* (2002) featured an endearingly vulnerable self-cutter (Maggie Gyllenhall) as a protagonist.

17   LiDonnici (1999) examines women's public and private religious activities for the Greco-Roman world as a whole; on the aims and interpretation of magical rites such as curse tablets, see Graf (1997).

18   Servilia and Brutus also worship together when they propitiate their famous ancestors to affirm their conspiracy against Caesar (Episode 12); as Roman elites, their ritual serves an explicitly political purpose and engages motivations of personal and gentilic honor and tradition. The elite family, as much as the middle-class family, seems to justify religious gender violation in its own terms.

19   She is mentioned only once in the ancient sources: Varro, *Religious Antiquities*, fragment 164, as cited by St. Augustine, *The City of God* 4.8.

20   The phenomenon of state religion may well seem less unusual to the British creators and audience of the series (see note 4 above).

21   Note a similar stirring of audience empathy in the depiction of Maximus as a man of modern spiritual values in the film *Gladiator* (2000); see Cyrino (2005), 251–254.

22   For example, Tacitus describes how Agrippina the Elder, the wife of Germanicus, caused scandal by presiding over her husband's troops while accompanying him on campaign in Germany (*Annals* 1.69.4). Agrippina the Younger was infamous for her attempts to exercise power in the early days of Nero's reign; Tacitus describes her as imposing a *quasi virile servitium*, a "nearly masculine dominance," over the state (*Annals* 12.7.3) and mentions a potentially embarrassing incident when the young emperor was forced to remove his mother as she prepared to receive foreign emissaries (*Annals* 13.5.2). Kaplan (1979) analyzes the adjective *atrox*, "fierce," as an epithet applied to both women, almost as a family trait.

14

Staging Interiors in *Rome*'s Villas

Alena Allen

The artistic director and set designers for HBO-BBC's *Rome* have created lush interior spaces that support and develop the identities of the main characters of the series. Each character's home provides a rich stage upon which that character expresses his unique identity as well as his place in Roman society. Even today, an advertisement in the *New York Times* for a luxury condo states: "Where you live should be a perfect reflection of who you are." This was perhaps even more accurate in late Republican Rome because the home of a wealthy Roman was a very public place in which he carried on his business activities in addition to living his private life.

The *Domus* or City Villa

Wealthy Romans typically owned several houses, including at least one in the city of Rome and several country villas. By the late Republican period the prime location for this city villa or town house, the *domus*, was on the Palatine hill. The basic architectural plan for the town house had been developed over the centuries to meet the public and private needs of the wealthy citizen or aristocrat of Rome. The great Roman architect Vitruvius, writing in the first century BC, outlines the plan for an ideal *domus* in his work *On Architecture* (6.3). He emphasizes that only people who do business or who receive clients in their homes need worry about the plan and decoration of their *domus*. Vitruvius states that poorer people and people who are clients themselves have no need for such spaces since they leave their houses for work (6.5).

The single most important feature of the wealthy person's city villa was the view from the front entrance through the house to the main reception room where the master or mistress of the house sat or stood to receive visitors and clients.[1] Typically this reception of clients, the *salutatio*, took place every morning. The architectural plan of the ideal town house creates a long visual axis from the entryway, called the *fauces* or "jaws," through the central hall, the *atrium*, and into the main reception room, the *tablinum* (Figure 7). The viewer of the series *Rome* can appreciate the impact of this long visual axis in Episode 03, when Atia receives clients in her house after the Pompeians have fled the city, and again in Episode 06, when Antony receives clients in Pompey's former house. The client enters through the *fauces* into the *atrium* where, as he walks around the central pool or *impluvium*, he takes in the busts of the homeowner's family ancestors, the family shrine, and all the artwork. Also, expensive furnishings would be displayed here for public view. By the time the visitor reaches the head of the household, he has a good idea of the wealth and position of the family based upon the quality of their art and the identity of their ancestors.[2] The architecture of the house and its interior design set the stage upon which the head of the family greets the public.

The long visual axis from the front entrance often stretches beyond the head of the household seated or standing in the *tablinum* to a garden that provides a framed backdrop for the master or mistress. This garden is typically located in the center of a peristyle courtyard (Figure 7), where more private entertainment and dinner parties took place. The series viewer sees this part of Atia's house in Episode 02 when she invites Vorenus and Pullo to join the family for a symbolic meal after they return Octavian safely home. This long central axis – from the entryway through the *atrium* to the *tablinum* with a view of the peristyle courtyard and garden beyond – defines the core function of the affluent person's *domus*.[3] Thus, this staged public interior space establishes the fundamental identity of the family.

The more private rooms of the house open up off this central axis. A typical house would contain several small rooms, or *cubicula* – often identified as bedrooms, but in fact they were multi-functional rooms – as well as a bath, a kitchen, and dining areas.[4] Sometimes in large houses, separate slave quarters and another outdoor courtyard for animals, storage, and work areas were built. Interestingly, the *Rome* series presents some of the most private areas of Atia's house before the public ones. In Episode 01, for example, the audience first sees her astride Timon in a *cubiculum* and then later taking a bath. Atia's personal power is displayed before her public position is revealed.

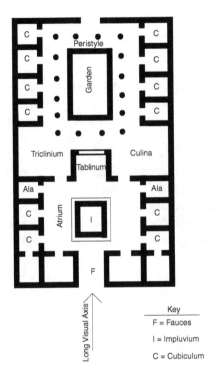

Figure 7   Plan of a typical Roman *domus*. Drawn by author.

Atia's Villa

It is not until Episode 02 that the public entryway and *atrium* of Atia's house are first presented. When Pullo and Vorenus bring young Octavian safely home from Gaul, the audience is shown the dark, heavy entry doors and the intense red walls of the *atrium*. There are black columns with red capitals around the central pool, the *impluvium*, as well as a black frieze accenting the ecru-colored beams of the coffered ceiling. Frescoes of large standing figures framed by bold yellow-gold bands decorate the intense red stucco walls. Figures of female goddesses or other mythological figures appear on one side of the entryway, while male gods, heroes, and actors stand on the other side. These frescoed figures create the image of opposed masculine and feminine power on the walls of this room, foreshadowing the ongoing amorous power struggle between Atia and her lover, Mark Antony. Set into niches on other *atrium* walls are black busts of the family's ancestors. The room is further decorated with expensive statuary, richly inlaid wooden benches and tables, and alabaster vases on pedestals. Atia's bold color scheme in red, black, and yellow-gold presents a powerful impression and a background setting worthy of so dominant a character in this series.

When Atia, at Octavian's insistence, invites Pullo and Vorenus to dine with the family, they all adjourn to the dining room, the *triclinium*, off the peristyle courtyard and garden. Here, strong light streams in from the open garden revealing the black walls of the dining room and the fluted red and dark-brown columns of the peristyle. In this brightly lit area of Atia's house, the black walls are defined by frescoed yellow-gold tracery and green garlands, similar to those that have been found in the excavations of a *triclinium* in an ancient Roman villa under the Villa Farnesina in Rome. Many slaves are present in the dining room tending to her guests, and their presence adds to the impression of the great wealth possessed by Atia's household.[5]

Both the color scheme and the frescoes in Atia's house are principally reminiscent of those that are found in many rooms of the houses excavated around Pompeii and in Rome.[6] The actor Ray Stevenson, who plays the soldier Pullo, confirms this impression in his audio commentary for Episode 05, when he describes how the cast and crew went down to Pompeii to get a feel for the streets and the textures and colors of the ancient city. The artistic care taken in reproducing frescoes, furnishings, and art objects adds a powerful sense of authenticity to the interior rooms of all the houses in *Rome*. Indeed, the historical consultant Jonathan Stamp, in the documentary entitled "When In Rome" that accompanies the series' first season released on DVD, states: "We wanted the show to be as historically authentic as we could possibly make it, and the distinction there for me is that while the characters there are dramatized characters, the world in which they are moving, the context in which they exist, was something that we could flesh out with historical detail, and that process was something that HBO backed to the hilt."

The Pompeian color scheme of Atia's red and black *atrium* and courtyard evokes the memory of the famous ruins themselves and the destructive eruption of Mt. Vesuvius that caused them. Not unlike the volcano itself, Atia smolders with both passion and rage that on occasion erupts with flaming outbursts. The audience witnesses such eruptions within the setting of her *domus* when in a fury she beats her slaves (e.g., in Episode 03) and her children (Episode 09), or threatens Octavia's beloved husband, Glabius, with attack dogs (Episode 02). Later Atia orders her hired hit man, Timon, to kill Glabius (Episode 03); she even orders Timon to have his men attack and humiliate her rival, Servilia, on a public street (Episode 09). Like the heroes on her frescoed red walls, Atia does not shrink from blood and destruction in order to accomplish her goals.

Servilia's Villa

The viewer of *Rome* first sees Servilia's city villa late in Episode 01 when her son, Brutus, who has just returned from Gaul, bursts through the entryway and into the *atrium* where his mother rushes to greet him. The *atrium* is bathed in soft, pale light which reflects off the creamy white marble and stucco columns, wide arches, and high vaulted ceiling. Delicate red lines frame the architectural elements of the arches, vaults, and walls. The diffused light streaming through the *compluvium*, the open space in the roof above the *atrium* pool, illuminates the sky-blue stucco of the walls decorated with frescoes of graceful standing or flying female figures. Similar figures can be found on the walls of surviving houses in Pompeii and the area around Campania, as well as in Rome, and they have been identified by art historians as figures of goddesses or other female divinities.[7] Servilia wears a gown of muted apricot-colored silk and she moves towards her son with an easy grace evocative of the female figures on her walls. More significant for her personal identity are the scores of ancestor masks that line other walls in her *atrium*.[8] On one wall, there is also an altar with everburning candles where Servilia and Brutus pray to their ancestors before Brutus goes off to the Senate to kill Caesar in Episode 12. The ancestor masks in the *atrium* appear translucent and are lit from behind by candles. The graceful goddesses on the walls of her *atrium* may well suggest Servilia's elevated status; but it is the presence of so many famous ancestors, descendants of the great and ancient family who deposed the Etruscan kings and first established the Republic, that truly defines her identity and that of her son, Brutus.

When Octavia, who has been sent by her mother Atia to ask a favor, sits with Servilia in her *atrium* (in Episode 07), the wall behind them across the room displays frescoes of two seated female figures facing each other on opposite sides of the family altar. These female figures in the background, which are replicas of those found in excavations at the Villa Farnesina in Rome, depict women at their dressing tables holding cosmetics or perfume vials in a very intimate moment. In Episode 01, Servilia was sitting at her own dressing table while she reads her letter from Caesar and talks about his love for her with her attendant slave, Eleni. Also, earlier in

Episode 07, Octavia is seen at her dressing table preparing to visit Servilia. Both suggest scenes of personal, private, and essentially feminine moments. By having such frescoed female figures visually presented behind the actual seated figures of Servilia and Octavia, the interior setting itself foreshadows the intimacy that will later develop between the two women.

Unlike Atia, Servilia does not have many servants standing around in her *domus*. They must be there when needed, however, since the job of keeping all the candles lit behind so many ancestor masks may well have occupied at least one slave. Yet Servilia's principal body slave, Eleni, always appears well dressed in a blue gown and, unlike the other slaves, even wears a blue beaded necklace. Eleni's speech indicates that she has been well educated and, given her name, she is perhaps of Greek origin. The furnishings in Servilia's house are made of expensive marble and there are vases of colored glass, as well as a large red-figured Greek vase, displayed on various pedestals. Perhaps most conspicuous of all is the prominent blue color of the stucco on her walls, both inside her *atrium* and even on the outside walls of her *domus*. In the ancient Greco-Roman world, pigments in blue, purple, and green were the most expensive and luxurious. Both Vitruvius and Pliny mention the expense and difficulties involved in creating such colors.[9] A few walls of blue fresco (from the period of the first century BC to the first century AD) have been excavated in Rome and around Pompeii.[10] Whereas the color scheme of Atia's house is bold, full of contrasts, and serves to arrest the viewer's attention, the color scheme of Servilia's house is subdued, but quietly asserts the wealth and elegance of its owner.

White marble with hints of blue-stuccoed walls have conveyed an image of aristocratic Rome from the time of Jacques-Louis David's neoclassical paintings in the 1780s through the time of Sir Lawrence Alma-Tadema's paintings in the late 1800s, and the image endures in the set designs of ancient-themed Hollywood epics and television series made throughout the last century. One of the most memorable cinematic epics set during the period of Republican Rome in the first century BC is Stanley Kubrick's film *Spartacus* (1960). In this film, the aristocratic general, Marcus Licinius Crassus, lives in a Roman villa characterized by white marble columns, pools, and statuary. His study is decorated with metallic-frescoed tracery and small, frescoed nude female figures on walls of blue stucco. Scenes for this film were shot at Hearst Castle in San Simeon, California, which was built by the publishing tycoon William Randolph Hearst in the 1920s to 1940s. These scenes in *Spartacus* depict the contemporary Anglo-American vision of classical aristocratic elegance and luxury. When the

BBC decided to produce *I, Claudius* (1976), it created an interior set of Augustus' Palatine villa characterized by white and bluish-gray marble columns and white-stuccoed walls with only a few small floating frescoed figures on them. The set reveals touches of red trim, some green garlands and draperies, but generally not much color. The study of his wife, Livia, has blue-gray frescoed walls, and so does one bedroom, while the peristyle garden is constructed of white and bluish-gray marble. The overall color scheme remains primarily shades of white and blue-gray, which is consistent with the popular artistic and cinematic image of the aristocratic classical world. The color scheme of Servilia's *domus* in *Rome* continues this convention of representing aristocratic elegance in a white and blue-gray setting.

In contrast to Servilia's house and its color associations with the villa of Crassus in the film *Spartacus*, the viewer may consider Atia's dramatic red and black interior color scheme. The walls of her *atrium* are highly reminiscent of the walls of the Villa of the Mysteries at Pompeii. One of the large female figures on Atia's wall resembles the figure of the goddess Aura and another resembles a winged divinity, both from Room 5 of the Villa of the Mysteries.[11] In *Spartacus*, the arch-enemy of Crassus is the populist Senator Gracchus, whom Crassus derisively describes as the "Master of the Mob." There are two scenes in *Spartacus* where the walls of Gracchus' *atrium* are visible, and they clearly present a replica of the entire famous fresco cycle from Room 5 at the Villa of the Mysteries. Thus, in the *Rome* series, Atia, the niece of Julius Caesar, the current populist leader in Rome, has an *atrium* that evokes the image of the one owned by this earlier populist film hero, Gracchus. Consciously or unconsciously, the artistic director and set designers of *Rome* have visually perpetuated the conflict between the wealthy, conservative aristocrats in their white and blue villas, Crassus in *Spartacus* and Servilia in *Rome*, with the populist villas displaying red and black frescoes from the House of the Mysteries, the villa of Senator Gracchus in *Spartacus* and Atia's villa in *Rome*.

After she has been rejected by Caesar, Servilia begins to plot her revenge in Episode 07. Having learned from Octavia that Caesar has "a terrible affliction," she attempts to gain more information from the girl. She engages Octavia in conversation while they are weaving together. Looms are set up in her *atrium* just as archaeologists have found evidence of them in the *atria* of houses in Pompeii.[12] For the ancient Greeks and Romans, weaving was considered the most traditional and honorable activity for women. It is an activity that Atia scorns, as she bluntly expresses when she tells Octavia in the same episode: "I know she's tedious, I mean, really, weaving!" The Homeric Penelope was famous for spending her time weaving as a device to stall her suitors as she loyally awaited her husband Odysseus' return. By Roman times, Penelope was deemed the model for a distinguished woman, and the activity of weaving became symbolic of female virtue. At the same time, however, Penelope's weaving was a trick to put off the suitors because at night she undid her day's work in order to buy time. Servilia's act of weaving embodies both aspects of Penelope's activity at the loom. She presents herself as a model of female Roman virtue while at the same time she weaves a web of intrigue involving Octavia. Servilia's weaving of intrigue will ultimately result in the plot to murder Caesar. This conspiracy will develop within her very own *atrium* surrounded by the masks of her ancestors and supported by the prayers that she and her son Brutus will make there at the family altar.

Caesar's Villa

The audience of *Rome* first sees Caesar's city villa from the outside in Episode 05 as he leaves the villa together with his wife, Calpurnia, and proceeds through the streets of the Subura district.[13] The foundation of the outside walls has a sky-blue base below walls of cream-colored stucco with intense red architectural accents. Once his wife sees the ubiquitous graffiti depicting the sexual affair between Servilia and Caesar, they return to the house where an ice-cold Calpurnia demands a divorce unless Caesar immediately ends his relationship with his mistress. This scene is set in an interior courtyard with a pool, a colonnade, and what appears to be the façade of a temple building complete with a sculptured pediment. This monumental white interior court resembles the one belonging to Crassus in *Spartacus*, and so this setting seems to support Caesar's increasingly regal aspirations, as he chooses political power over love and decides to forsake Servilia. Caesar further demonstrates his growing desire for power when he plays chess with Brutus on the pale-white colonnaded terrace of his villa, where he demands that Brutus leave Rome for Macedonia (in Episode 11). In the aftermath of this confrontation, Brutus finally joins his mother in plotting Caesar's death.

The setting where Caesar seems most at home, however, is in the tent at his military camp. The viewer sees him in his tent while in Gaul, when he is encamped with his army in Rome, and then later in Greece. In Episode 02, Brutus visits him in Gaul and comments that Caesar's tent appears "almost like a proper house." Indeed, Caesar's tent possesses most of the important elements of a permanent *domus*. The view from the entrance faces a massive, wooden table behind which there hangs a tapestry of a large golden eagle. Caesar sits behind this table and receives visitors in the manner of a *salutatio*. The desk is flanked by heavy, dark wooden columns with an altar off to one side, shelves for scrolls, pedestals with alabaster urns and portrait busts presumably of ancestors, a basin for washing, benches for sitting and talking, a couch for sleeping, and slaves standing ready to receive orders. Since the tent is made of leather, the interior glows with warm golden-brown colors accented by the intense red of military cloaks of the men and their martial standards. In this setting, surrounded by military symbols and the busts of his ancestors, Caesar early in the series demonstrates his powerful connection with his troops and thus with the common people of Rome. Later, however, by Episode 11, when not in the Senate, Caesar is more often seen in the regal setting of his villa, a setting that visually supports his imperial ambitions.

Pompey's Villa

The audience first sees the outdoor colonnaded courtyard of Pompey's villa, where Pompey is being shaved by his personal slave in Episode 01. The colonnade is made of gray-white marble and stucco, and the lower third of the columns are shaded a deep blue-gray with gold and red trim. Later, when Pompey is discussing the current military situation with Cato and other Senators in Episode 03, the viewer sees Pompey's peristyle courtyard composed of heavy black pillars and sienna-colored outer walls with inner walls of deep blue-gray. The garden displays life-sized sculptures of two martial figures bearing swords and shields, perhaps representing the Roman god of war, Mars, and his counterpart Minerva, goddess of military strategy. A low relief of shields and weapons decorates one deep blue-gray wall of his *atrium*, while a frescoed figure of a warrior adorns another wall. There are pedestals supporting large black vases as well as portrait busts around the *atrium* pool. One bust in particular is a Roman copy of a famous Greek bust of Pericles, the great general and statesman who defended Athenian democracy in the fifth century BC.[14] Pompey exhibits no ancestor masks or busts in his *domus* precisely because he is not a member of an aristocratic family. Instead, the artwork in his house evokes images of war gods and great martial figures of the past and thereby serves to support his position as a successful military general, which is his major claim to fame.

Once it becomes clear that Pompey will not return to Rome, Mark Antony takes over his villa, as the audience sees in Episode 06. Here Antony holds a *salutatio* assisted by the presence of Caesar's right-hand man, Posca, but Antony also has a dwarf and two scantily clad slave girls waiting on him as well. While he is attending to his clients and Senators, artisans are shown replastering and repainting the walls. Behind all the scaffolding, the visitors – and the viewers – see the bust of Pericles, the defender of democratic Athens, now reduced to an insignificant position. The walls are being repainted a bold green and bright golden-yellow covering their former dark blue-gray color. On one wall, an artist is painting the under-drawing for a fresco depicting an androgynous figure, perhaps an Amazon, down on one knee twisting back to look at her attacker. As Antony tells a Senator's wife: "I found Pompey's taste in decor rather dull. I like a little more color." Indeed, there is more than a change in color taking place in Pompey's former house. Pompey, who always seems dour and somber in mood like his black and dark blue-gray walls, earlier in the series told Cato: "You lack understanding of things military, else you would see that my actions have been perfectly correct at all times" (Episode 03). In contrast, Antony seems to delight in behaving in a shocking and incorrect manner. Instead of all the male warriors depicted on Pompey's walls, Antony chooses female warriors, and further he even has his slave girls don helmets and swords to stage a fight for him right there in Pompey's former villa. The redecoration of Pompey's house helps to define the characters of both men, and in particular emphasizes the irreverent, bold, and rather extreme nature of Antony.

Vorenus and Niobe's Apartment

The audience of *Rome* first views the block of apartment houses where Vorenus and Niobe live in Episode 02 when he returns home from eight years away in Gaul. Vorenus walks into the crowded central courtyard of the apartment block and greets his shocked wife, Niobe, who had been told by the Roman military over a year before that her husband was dead. Seeing the baby in her arms, Vorenus calls his wife a "whore" right there in front of all their neighbors. Niobe thinks fast and tells Vorenus that the baby is his grandchild, then rushes to hand the baby over to her elder daughter. The bustle and confusion of this crowded courtyard scene, where the viewer has a first glimpse of Vorenus' wife and family, helps to confirm the confused status of their marriage.

Most people in Roman cities lived in large apartment blocks called *insulae*, literally "islands," as they often took up an entire city block. Only the wealthy could afford even a modest *domus*. A typical apartment block was built mainly of brick and surrounded a large central courtyard.[15] It could be three or more stories high and had wooden stairs, some interior wooden walls, and often some wooden shacks on the rooftop accessible by ladders. Upper floors typically had only one outdoor stairway for access, with an outdoor balcony overlooking the central courtyard. In poor neighborhoods there was terrible overcrowding and there were frequent fires. What life must have been like in an *insula* apartment may best be appreciated today by a visit to the archaeological site of Ostia Antica, the ancient port of Rome. Here a tourist can still walk up stairs to upper-floor apartments and visit ground-floor shops.

Vorenus and Niobe clearly live in what an ancient Roman would recognize as a nicer apartment complex. They have a fountain in their central courtyard which provides fresh drinking water, life-sized stone statuary, and plants and vines for some shade. Since the family lives on the second floor, they have some respite from the commotion of the courtyard where ground-floor shops open onto the street. When Niobe introduces her stunned daughters to their father later in the episode, the audience first sees the interior of their apartment. It consists of one main room with a kitchen off to one side and sleeping quarters separated off by tan-colored hanging draperies. The walls are of brick partially covered by olive-green and dirty yellow stucco layered between dark wooden beams. Some walls are accented with red bands. The low ceiling is made of dark, roughly hewn wooden beams and the floor is made of broad wooden planks. Their sparse furniture consists of simple wooden tables, benches, beds, and the baby's crib. There is a small fresco above the family shrine depicting the household spirits, or *Lares*, and the ancestor of the family, or *Genius*. This particular painting is a copy of an actual fresco found in a kitchen in Pompeii.[16] The overall color scheme of Vorenus and Niobe's apartment is one of shades of brown, which is consistent with the colors available to poorer people since bright colors, dyes, and paints were so expensive. Indeed, Niobe and the girls wear plain, brown-toned clothing cut from simple material.

As the series shows Vorenus and Niobe reconnecting as a couple – albeit with some terrible secrets – the audience sees their fortunes improve. While Vorenus, now a prefect and an *Evocatus* in the army, spends two years off fighting with Caesar in Greece and Egypt, Niobe and her sister, Lyde, make money running a butcher shop. When Vorenus returns in Episode 09, this time to a loving wife and daughters, he walks into the apartment and exclaims, "*Bona Dea!*" or "Good Goddess!" Niobe responds with a smile: "It's nice, isn't it." In his two-year absence, she has repainted some of the walls, hung finer and more colorful draperies, and added houseplants. In addition, even the family's former dull brown clothing now is made of much richer color tones and finer fabrics. Finally, in what represents a significant step up in status, they own four slaves, who are shown busy about the much-upgraded interior space.

Once Vorenus is made a magistrate by Caesar, his status further improves. In Episode 11, he now receives clients during a morning *salutatio* in the courtyard of the apartment block. There he sits at the head of the courtyard surrounded by his very richly and colorfully dressed family. Niobe wears a sea-blue dress of fine fabric, Vorena the Elder a lavender dress, Vorena the Younger an orange dress, and all three are wearing jewelry. Vorenus himself is grandly dressed in a pristine white toga. No one in this family wears brown any longer. Later, when Vorenus returns home from a meeting with Caesar (in Episode 11), he discovers two exotic-looking slave women standing on either side of his door. He asks Niobe, "What are these?" and she responds, "Leased, at good rates too, and don't they look impressive." Clearly Niobe relishes her new-found wealth and status, and is busy redefining the family identity as indicated by the inside of their apartment. Now there are plaster ancestor masks on one wall, a partially completed fresco of a standing woman on another wall, and new rose-colored draperies. The entire apartment appears cleaner, brighter, and more colorful, more like an affluent person's *domus*. Yet by Episode 12, after an uncomfortable evening at Atia's party in the previous episode, even Niobe becomes somewhat destabilized by the rapid rate of the changes in their status and domestic environment. On a sleepless night, she expresses her fears to Vorenus, who tries to offer her comfort, not knowing that the next day will bring Caesar's death as well as the death of Niobe to end the first season of the series.

In *Rome*, the filming of a great number of scenes in the villas of either Atia or Servilia accentuates the intense rivalry between the two leading ladies of the series and indirectly helps to define the underlying power struggle going on at the end of the Roman Republican period. The color and decorative contrast between these two villas provides a visual dichotomy that highlights the conflict between old aristocratic wealth and new popular power. It is precisely this conflict, personified by Atia and Servilia and visually demarcated by their villas, that drives the major plotlines of *Rome*. In between these rival political positions, the audience watches as Antony renovates Pompey's villa; as Caesar becomes more identified with his imperial villa than his military camp; and as Vorenus and Niobe redecorate their apartment as their social status advances. Each interior set in *Rome*, like the ancient *domus* itself, visually defines the identity of its owner/s and reflects their personal status and political power. These staged interiors of the HBO-BBC production of *Rome* thereby function in the significant role of supporting actors for the main characters and their intersecting narratives in the series.

NOTES

1 Clarke (1991), 2–6, emphasizes the importance of the long visual axis through the ancient Roman house.

2 Hales (2003), 1–60, discusses how the arrangement and decoration of a house establishes the identity of a Roman family.

3 Hales (2003), 107–117, walks a visitor along this axis through a Pompeian house.

4 Allison (1997), 139–141, presents archaeological evidence that supports multiple uses of rooms in Pompeian houses.

5 Hales (2003) states: "Although elite families might have grown accustomed to looking straight through the slaves that surrounded them, it is also likely that slave presence was all part of family display" (125).

6 For examples of red and black rooms, see in particular the Villa of Agrippa Postumus in Boscotrecase, the Villa of Poppea in Oplontis, the Villa Farnesina in Rome, the Murecine complex in Pompeii, and the Villa of the Mysteries in Pompeii.

7 Clarke (1991), 402, identifies standing and flying female figures in his index of decorative motifs.

8 Hales (2003), 46, notes the importance of the presence of ancestor masks in the *atrium* to establish the family lineage visually.

9 Pliny, writing in the first century AD, offers many details about how blue pigment was made and gives its cost (*Natural History* 33.57). Pliny also lists bright colors including a rich blue that must be supplied by a patron at his own expense for wall frescoes (*Natural History* 35.12).

10 Rooms with predominantly blue walls can be seen in the Villa Arianna at Castellammare di Stabia, the House of the Orchard at Pompeii, and the Villa of Livia at Prima Porta in Rome.

11 See Mazzoleni and Pappalardo (2004), 102–124, for beautiful color photographs of Room 5 of the Villa of the Mysteries. This book also contains photographs of most of the other villas mentioned in the notes above.

12 Allison (1997), 135–137, describes how the main distribution patterns of artifacts in Pompeian houses indicate that domestic activities such as spinning

and weaving, in addition to public receptions, took place in the *atrium* areas.

13 Suetonius states: "Caesar's first home was a modest house in the Subura quarter, but later, as Chief Priest, he used the official residence on the Sacred Way" (*Life of Julius Caesar* 46); translation by Graves (1982).

14 The bust is a Roman copy of an original work of the mid-fifth century BC by the Greek sculptor Cresilas, now in the British Museum in London.

15 Wheeler (1964), 128–132, describes the architecture and construction of Roman apartment blocks.

16 Warrior (2006), 28–29, describes in detail this particular household shrine from the House of the Vettii in Pompeii. She identifies the *Lares*, holding their drinking horns, the *Genius* of the family, holding an incense box, and the serpent, a symbol of fertility, near the offerings on a small altar. She also explains the religious significance of such protective deities.

15

Latin in the Movies and *Rome*

Ward Briggs

While ancient Greece has seldom been portrayed on the screen,[1] Rome has always held a particular fascination for Hollywood, from the first filming of *Ben-Hur* in 1907. That fascination, however, extended only as far as the pagan Roman Empire provided an antagonist for the development of early Christianity. This view, largely present in the films made by Jewish producers and directors in Hollywood (such as Cecil B. DeMille, Sam Zimbalist, and Henry Koster), flourished from the original *Ben-Hur* through the great swords-and-sandals epics of the 1950s and 1960s, and was lately resurrected by Mel Gibson in *The Passion of the Christ* (2004). To reinforce the veracity of the portrayal of Romans as wicked, amoral, and/or anti-Christian, millions of dollars were spent on elaborate buildings, enormous arenas, historically accurate chariots, and Roman mansions faithful to history in design and detail. The more accurate the detail, the more truthful would seem the message. Despite these expenditures of time and money, identifying inevitable failures of historical accuracy, small or substantial, has been the sport of classicists, and sometimes the actors themselves.[2]

Most of these films are made not from works of ancient literature but from modern novels. Latin literature fights its way onto the screen, but is often wounded in the fray. In Joseph Mankiewicz's *Cleopatra* (1963), Rex Harrison as Caesar approaches Cleopatra (Elizabeth Taylor), who is lounging in her bathing room surrounded by her handmaids. A beautiful male rhapsode named Phoebus – whose blindness is hinted at by the actor's gestures – intones the following Catullan-Horatian rhubarb:

It is autumn again, my best loved Lesbia,
Look, the torrents of Roman leaves are falling, falling
And lovers revive in kisses the promise of spring
Which will end the winter world with new nightingales calling.
The seasons fall . . .
But love must bring despair one day as beauty, sorrow . . .

Evocative verses, but though it sounds like Lesbia on Mount Soracte, it's neither Catullus nor Horace.

Caesar decides to beard the queen in her bath and strides manfully into the room as Phoebus sings a version of Catullus Poem 5:

Ah then, let us live and love
Without one thought for the gossip of virgins
Now grown old and stale.
Suns go down and may return
But once we put out our own brief light
We sleep through one eternal night.

"A man!" the handmaids yelp as Caesar approaches; "Oh, it's *you!*" says a pouting Cleopatra as she recognizes the intruder. When Caesar speaks well of Catullus, Cleopatra remarks: "Catullus doesn't approve of you. Why haven't you had him killed?" "Because *I* approve of *him*," says Caesar, adding this version of Catullus Poem 93:

My desire to please you, Caesar, is very slight
Nor do I greatly care to know if you are black or white.

Caesar then asks Phoebus: "Young man, do you know this of Catullus?" and recites more:

Give me a thousand and a thousand kisses.
When we have many thousand more,
We will scramble them and forget the score
So evil envy will not know how high
The cost and cast its evil eye.

Of course Phoebus knows the passage, as it immediately follows the lines from Poem 5 that he was just reciting when Caesar interrupted him.

But this use of ancient literature is all too rare. If the literature is neglected (see the Cohn remark above in note 1), ancient authors on the screen are even rarer, the most notable example being the unforgettable Petronius of

Leo Genn in *Quo Vadis* (1951), with Nicholas Hannen as a conspiratorial Seneca and Alfredo Varelli as a sullen Lucan. In the BBC television mini-series *I, Claudius* (1976), Augustus (Brian Blessed) improbably goes to sleep at a banquet as Horace (Norman Shelley) recites. Upon awakening, Augustus opines, "Now that's what I call poetry" and disparages the future exile Ovid: "People say he has a lovely voice, but what does he do with that lovely voice? Writes a lot of smut!" (Episode 4). In the same episode, we find what surely must be the only cinematic appearance of Asinius Pollio (Donald Eccles), not to say of Livy (Denis Carey). Claudius (Derek Jacobi) judges a vanity contest between the two great figures in the Great Library. When the future emperor tells both men that they are the "two greatest historians," Pollio calls it "an abuse of the Roman tongue": there can only be one "greatest."

Latin in the Movies

The Roman tongue itself has fared no better in the great post-World War II movies than have the Roman writers. While no one can forget the "Latin lesson" in *Monty Python's Life of Brian* (1979) – the centurion is shown reading Brian's ungrammatical graffito: "People called 'Romanes' they go the house? What kind of Latin is that, boy?" – it is the exception. The only Latin in the film *Quo Vadis* is in the title, which comes from the Vulgate, not from classical literature. Likewise *Ben-Hur* (1959), *Spartacus* (1960), *A Funny Thing Happened on the Way to the Forum* (1966) – where the only Latin is in the names of its characters, like "Senex" and "Miles Gloriosus" – are all Latin-free, ancient-author-free, and with one exception (in *Cleopatra*, discussed above), free of quotation in English of a piece of Latin literature.

In the third episode of *I, Claudius*, after talking with the ingratiating young Herod Agrippa (Michael Clements), Antonia (Margaret Tyzack) tells Julia (Frances White): "What a polite boy and how well he speaks Latin." Of course we have only heard him speaking English. Historical fiction, whether books or films, performed in a language other than what the characters would normally speak involves the maximum suspension of disbelief. For example, in Charles Dickens' novel *A Tale of Two Cities* (1859) and its subsequent film versions, everyone in London and Paris, whether noble or low-born, speaks the same standard English; we only know we are in France by the costumes, scenery, and the occasional "Monsieur." We understand that when we hear or read d'Artagnan's or

Don Quixote's or Odysseus' English that the character would really be speaking French or Spanish or Greek. In that regard, to have the character Charles Darnay actually mouth some French when it is presumed that his English was being substituted for his French leaves the reader/viewer confused.

A prime example of this in Latin occurs in a non-classical-themed movie in which Latin is as omnipresent as in the original novel and presents the same problems. In *The Name of the Rose* (1986), based on the novel of the same name by Umberto Eco (1980), the murder mystery is close to a solution when Sean Connery as William of Baskerville reads the parchment that holds the secret to entering the final mirrored door where the answer to the mystery lies. " '*Manus super eidolum agit primum et septimus de quattuor*' is what?" he asks his assistant, Adso of Melk (Christian Slater). Adso ignores the wrong case of *septimus* and translates: "With the hand above the idol, press the first and the seventh of four." "Very good," replies William, though Adso mistranslates the Greek *eidolon* as "idol" instead of "image" or "reflection" (in the mirror). "The first and seventh of what?" Adso replies. As the race to solve the mystery heats up, William says: "Perhaps by pressing the first and the seventh letter of the word 'four.' " "But 'four' only has four letters," shoots back Adso. "In Latin, Adso, *quattuor*. Remember? The inscription above the mirror." Adso had forgotten that they were likely speaking Latin and certainly were reading it. "Pray God we are right," says William, as he presses the Q and, inexplicably, the R of the inscription above the door, and in they go.

Mel Gibson has no such problem of linguistic crossover in his film *The Man without a Face* (1993). Here Latin is clearly used as a separate language. Gibson plays Justin McLeod, a Latin teacher from a fine preparatory school who was disfigured in an automobile accident and ensuing fire that killed the student who was accompanying him. Convicted of manslaughter, he now lives in seclusion in a house full of spooky relics with his dog and his text of Vergil in translation, which he also presumably keeps in his head. Perhaps the spookiest of his relics appears in an early scene in which McLeod, sitting at his desk by a crackling fireplace listening to "Ch'ella mi creda" from Puccini's *La Fanciulla del West* (1910), stares at a clock given him in happier times by the students of his former school. He recites, in English, with the good side of his burned face to the camera: "Arms I sing and the man who first from the shores of Troy came fate-exiled to Italy and her Lavinian strand; much buffeted he on flood and field by constraint of heaven and Juno's unslumbering wrath." When he finishes, he holds a bi-fold mirror to the good half of his face and he seems for the moment unscathed; Vergil has lustrated his crime and made him whole again. But then he opens the mirror wider and sees that his scars remain and he curses.

But back to the clock for a moment: the prologue to the *Aeneid* is inscribed on a brass plate on the front of the clock, but this is how the Latin reads: *Cano, arma que virum qui profugus fato, / primus venit ab oris Troiae Italiam que Lavinia / litora multum iactatus et terris et alto / vi superum ob memorem iram saevae Iunonis.* What is behind this barbaric rearrangement of this famous prologue? Would one begin reading Dickens' novel with "Of times the best it was, of times it was the worst"? Closer examination shows that Vergil's prologue is rearranged into English word order and obviously was taken from the nineteenth-century Hamilton, Locke, and Clark series of interlinear ponies.[3] What school administration would create such an abomination as this inscription? What Latin teacher would be proud to have it?

Later, to his troubled tutee (played by Nick Stahl), McLeod cites the motto of Winchester College: "This is the way it works: *aut disce aut discede,* learn or leave." The kid resists and is dismissed. When the boy visits McLeod later and learns that his tutor's dog has been injured by a porcupine, he says "*Excrementum,*" to which the teacher rejoins: "*Stultus puer.*" Later, while hiking, McLeod keeps the lesson up on the trail, since the boy will have to translate Cicero's *De Amicitia* ("On Friendship") for entrance into military school. McLeod asks him to translate "*Quidem magistri discipulos tanta cum arte docebant ut ipsi discipuli quidem discere cuperent*" ("Certain teachers used to teach their students with such great skill that the students themselves indeed desired to learn"), a sentence directly out of the standard school textbook, *Wheelock's Latin* (Exercises, Chapter 29, #13).[4] In saying goodbye to the boy in profile against a shimmering sea, McLeod leaves him with the Senecan motto "*Sequere Deum.*"[5]

Gibson continued his obsession with the sound of the Latin language in some of his other films, for example in his Oscar-winning film *Braveheart* (1995). In this film, a priest speaks Latin at the funeral service for young William Wallace's father, and again later at the burial of Wallace's wife, Murron, though they'd likely have been speaking Gaelic. Early in the film, Uncle Argyle Wallace (Brian Cox) asks young William (James Robinson): "You don't speak Latin? Well, that's something we shall have to remedy, isn't it?" This narrative set-up anticipates the moment later in the film when the adult Wallace (Gibson) surprises and impresses Princess Isabelle (Sophie Marceau) by speaking to her in Latin: "*Ego sum homo indomitus.*" The Latin spoken by the English King Edward Longshanks and his crew needs its own remedy. Edward decides to solve "the Scotland problem" by invoking against the Scots people the right of a sovereign to spend the wedding night with the bride of any of his subjects. The Latin term is *ius primae noctis*, "right of the first night," which comes out of Edward (Patrick McGoohan) as simply "*prima nocte*" (subtitles: "*prima noctes*"). The English nobleman who crashes the country nuptial festival to announce Edward's decision and seize the Scottish bride calls it "*prima nocta.*" Was Gibson intentionally showing the ignorance and impiety of the English through their imperfect Latin?

Gibson dealt with the suspension-of-disbelief issue both summarily and radically by scripting *The Passion of the Christ* entirely in Latin, Aramaic, and Hebrew.[6] The success or failure of that unique venture deserves a separate treatment and another occasion. Suffice it to note here that the film's main character, like Wallace in the earlier film, uses Latin to surprise his interlocutor: when Pontius Pilate (Hristo Shopov) interviews his prisoner in the Fortress Antonia and addresses him in Aramaic, Jesus (James Caviezel) responds in perfect Latin.

One great success breeds a thousand successors, as Seneca might have said, and we can certainly look to Ridley Scott's *Gladiator* (2000) as the first English-language epic film set in the Roman world to employ Latin (and other languages), though in idiosyncratic ways. In many respects the film is an homage to a myriad of heroic cinematic predecessors. It is interesting to watch the overlay of allusions not only to John Wayne westerns – Maximus finding his family slaughtered recalls a similar scene in *The Searchers* (1956), while the general's faithful dog recalls Wayne's desert-crossing dog in *Hondo* (1953) – but of course also to its noble cinematic predecessors set in ancient Rome: *Ben-Hur* (chariots, male bonding) and *I, Claudius* (survival of the Republic), but mostly *Spartacus* (gladiator school, body daubing by tough trainer, black–white gladiatorial pair, throwing spear at noble's box).[7] There is, however, one way in which it is distinct from these predecessors: there is actual Latin in *Gladiator*, though usually only in writing either on walls or as signage or on "paper." We see signs like the battlefield standards of the Praetorian Guard behind Marcus Aurelius that read "PRAETORIA IV," or the "FELIX III" in camp, or the handbills handed out at the Colosseum that say "*Gladiatores – Violentia*," and above the citizens' entrance to the Colosseum, a pediment supporting a quadriga (four-horse chariot) reads: "*Vi Roma cadit ita orbis terrae.*"[8]

Over the gladiators' entrance, an ungrammatical inscription reads: "*Ludus magnus gladiatores.*" Inside the citizens' entrance the bettors and bookies are wildly yelling in English to bet on the reenactment of the Battle of Carthage (wouldn't this be like betting today on the outcome of the 1932 World Series?), and the chalk board reads "*Hodie – Speculatum* [*sic*] *Carthaginiense.*"[9]

Languages other than English pose something of a problem in this movie. All the characters speak English with the exception of Maximus' young son, who, like his father, is supposed to be Spanish (although Maximus has no accent). When the young Italian actor Giorgio Cantarini, who also played the protagonist's son in the film *La Vita è Bella* (1997), sees Commodus' soldiers coming to kill him and his family, he thinks it's his "Papà," and somehow reverts to Italian: "*I soldati! I soldati!*"

Before the battle in Germania that opens the film, the Romans are taunted by barbarians yelling a kind of proto-German, but Roman superiority is signaled at the end of the battle when Maximus (Russell Crowe) yells in triumphant Latin, "*Roma Victor!*" In Zucchabar, an exotic Roman province in northern Africa, the slave-dealer Proximo (Oliver Reed) interrupts his conversation to greet another friend with a mysteriously Teutonic "*Guten Tag.*" He later describes a Latin word to a fluent speaker of the language when he tells Maximus that Marcus Aurelius gave him a "*rudius,*" explaining, "it's just a wooden sword, a symbol of your freedom," as if the gladiator did not know the name of the item he had been using for months to train for the arena. The most obvious Latin tag line appears only in English translation: in addressing his gladiators, Proximo tells them they are about to die and says, "Gladiators, I salute you," reversing the direction of the well-known Latin phrase that the gladiators will later proclaim to the chief of the games (in English) before the Battle of Carthage sequence in the Colosseum: "We who are about to die salute you" (*Morituri te salutamus*).

Latin as simply Latin shows up nowadays quite commonly in the film world, from catch phrases like "*Carpe diem*" in *Dead Poets Society* (1989) and *Clueless* (1995),[10] to the names of the spells in the numerous Harry Potter movies (2001–2008), to the various mysteries of *The Da Vinci Code* (2006), and even to the tattoo visible on actress Angelina Jolie's abdomen (*Quod me nutrit, me destruit*: "What nourishes me, destroys me"). It should be no surprise that, with all the Latin in films set in post-classical times, Latin should reappear in the sudden burst of films and television programs set in antiquity that have been made in the last decade, climaxing with HBO-BBC's great series, *Rome.*[11]

Latin in *Rome*

The series *Rome* goes further than any of these earlier films and television shows. Again Latin appears written on walls, either as inscriptions, such as on the Mars Gate in Episode 03, or in the ubiquitous graffiti, for example, *Atia amat omnes* ("Atia loves everyone") and *Caesar tyrannus* ("Caesar is a tyrant") in several episodes, or on documents, such as Caesar's written announcement "*In Italiam regressus sum*" ("I have returned to Italy"), which Lucius Vorenus posts on the door of the Curia in the Forum in Episode 03.

The graffiti shown in many episodes deserve a separate study, but one inscription is of interest. In Episode 03, after Pompey has abandoned the city and taken his forces and supporters south of Rome, Titus Pullo (Ray Stevenson) and Lucius Vorenus (Kevin McKidd) enter the deserted Forum to post Caesar's announcement through a gate that did not exist in Rome but was copied by the set designers from the Porte de Mars located in Rheims, France.[12] They enter through an arch in the gate above the keystone of which is an inscription that reads:

MARTI INVICTO PATR
ET AETERNAE URBIS SUAE
CONDITORIBUS
DOMINUS NOSTER
INVICTUS CN. POMP. MAG.

("The unconquered Gnaeus Pompey Magnus, our leader, has given this to unconquered Mars the father and to the founders of his eternal city.")

This inscription is taken from a rectangular statue pedestal found in the Forum today, near the Curia Julia, except that there is a line between the fourth and fifth lines above that has been erased apart from an initial "I," and the last line reads "INVICTUS AUG."[13] Clearly the set designers of *Rome* saw the "AUG" and assumed it referred to the first Caesar Augustus. The name was then cleverly changed to "Pompey" to provide an ironic note to his disastrous withdrawal from the city and Caesar's entry through the gate dedicated by his arch enemy. Unfortunately, the back of the pedestal gives the date of its actual dedication, which works out to April 21,

AD 308.[14] Thus, the missing line should be restored to read "Imp[erator] Maxentius P[ius] F[elix]" ("Emperor Maxentius the Pious and the Happy"), for the statue set on this pedestal was dedicated by Marcus Aurelius Valerius Maxentius who was Emperor of Rome (AD 306–312) preceding Constantine. He proclaimed himself "Augustus," a cognomen which by this time merely meant he was emperor, not that he was related to the former Octavian. He won a string of victories (hence "*invictus*," "unconquered") and tried to reinstate the foundational cult of Romulus (hence the reference to "*conditoribus*," "founders"), but after his death and Constantine's accession, he was declared a public enemy and an enemy of the church (hence the erasure of his name). The blend of arch and inscription is a typical example of the anachronisms and anomalies of architecture, fact, and language that characterize the series *Rome* and, to be fair, many films set in an ancient Roman context.

A certain amount of the spoken Latin in the series is what linguists call "code switching," the tendency of a bilingual person to alternate in the course of a conversation or statement between two (or more) languages.[15] Sometimes this is done because the speaker feels the foreign word or phrase is more appropriate, or perhaps less (or more) vulgar, or because he simply wants to impress his audience. Code switching is nothing new to the dramatic stage. One of the most famous examples in literature is in William Shakespeare's play *Julius Caesar*, when Brutus and the other conspirators stab Caesar and he cries out: "*Et tu, Brute?* Then fall, Caesar!" (3.1). Clearly the Latin here is made to stand in for the historical Caesar's code switch to Greek, quoted by the biographer Suetonius: "*Kai su, teknon*" ("Even you, my son?").[16] In both cases, not only the words themselves but also the fact of the code switch (he did not change languages for anyone else in the play) indicate the special affection and intimacy Caesar had for Brutus. More modern, frequent, and colloquial code switching occurs in the musical theater world of Gilbert and Sullivan, where everyone from the writers and producers to the actors and maids pepper their conversation with French and Italian in Mike Leigh's *Topsy-Turvy* (1999).

The most common code switching in *Rome* seems to occur with expletives, exclamations, and greetings. The plebeian characters Pullo and Vorenus both frequently use the expletive "*kak*" ("shit"), perhaps from Latin "*caco*," a Greek derivative meaning "to shit." In the butcher shop where Vorenus and Pullo are learning to be butchers, a woman uses a vulgar, Greek-derived term for buttocks: "You'll never learn a trade sitting on your *pugas*" (Episode 09).[17] When the reprobate ex-soldier Mascius (Michael Nardone) asks, "Where's that old Titus Pullo?" Vorenus replies:

"I haven't seen him." Mascius smirks and replies with "*Gerrae*," a comic word of Greek origin used by Plautus to mean, well, "nonsense" (Episode 11).[18] Perhaps Mascius does not want to use his own language to accuse Vorenus of lying, or perhaps the word is intended to show Mascius' coarse nature or common origins.[19]

Masters in the series are referred to as "*dominus*" and addressed in the vocative case as "*domine*," as a slave addresses Caesar while he's having a seizure, and Atia and Servilia are regularly called "*domina*" by their servants. "*Salve*" is used a great deal as a greeting, though in one case it occurs in English, when the adulterous butcher, Evander Pulchio (Enzo Cilenti), says "Good health, soldier" to Pullo (Episode 05). In another instance, Vorenus not only switches language but makes a grammatical error in doing so when he greets Appius (Bruno Billotta) and the footmen stealing Rome's treasury for Pompey with the singular form "*Salve*, citizens" (Episode 03), where the correct form would be the plural, "*Salvete*."

In Episode 04, Atia (Polly Walker) blames her son Octavian's disinterest in sex on his "distinctly feminine *anima*" and obliges him to eat a plate of warm goat testicles to counteract it. Can Atia be referring to the anima–persona arguments of Carl Jung (1875–1961), implying that femininity is Octavian's "archetype"? She seems to be a couple of millennia ahead of her time, as this sense of *anima* seems more specific than the normal Latin meanings of "breath," "soul," or "spirit."

Code switching at its illogical extreme is found in Episode 02. Cato (Karl Johnson) upbraids Antony for wearing his military cloak within the city limits. Antony (James Purefoy) responds in boisterous Italian, "*Che brutta figura!*" Antony's next line is: "Oh, *bene*." Where did Antony learn a language that did not then exist? Assuming that the "*bene*" is also Italian, not Latin, are we to assume that this lapse into Italian is intended to result from his seven years in Gaul? If so, then why does he not use French? In another episode, two Greek house slaves greet each other, one saying, "How be, *paisan*?" (Episode 04). Immigrants in any society will unthinkingly revert from their new to their native language. Can butchered English grammar plus an Italian dialect form in this case stand for the slave's code switch from Latin to his native Greek?

Latin is used in several scenes of religious rituals in *Rome*. During the famous *taurobolium* sequence in Episode 01,[20] the priest, eunuchs, and celebrants of the Magna Mater cult depicted in the scene are derived from Phrygia (Turkey); but even with alien priests in the alien temple of the Magna Mater dancing to non-Roman music, Atia repeatedly chants in Latin, "*meum filium, Magna Mater*" ("[save] my son, Great Mother"), as she prays for her son Octavian who has been kidnapped by Gauls. Again comes the suspension-of-disbelief problem. Is Latin supposed to represent the alien language she chants in this alien ceremony or are we to assume that she is chanting in her own tongue? If the latter, why is she not chanting in English? If the former, are we to believe that Latin here in this scene represents non-Latin? Another religious example involves the great native goddess of Rome, the *Bona Dea*, or "Good Goddess," who is portrayed in a later episode as a fat, naked, Buddhaesque woman presiding over a street shrine visited by Vorenus' distraught wife, Niobe (Indira Varma). The patrician female characters in the series often invoke the goddess' Latin name in times of shock or stress. For example, Octavia (Kerry Condon) uses the exclamation "*Bona Dea!*" on numerous occasions. After Servilia (Lindsay Duncan) has been stripped and beaten in the streets in Episode 10, her rival Atia visits her and, observing the damage, sighs, "*Bona Dea!*" Most rituals, however, like Vorenus' blood-oath at the street shrine to the goddess Venus (Episode 03), are conducted in English.

Ritual and literature can overlap. In Episode 08, when Caesar (Ciarán Hinds) cremates Pompey's severed head, he recites in Latin not a religious chant, as the series would make you think by his somber tone, but listen closely and you will hear that it is Catullus' poem blessing and taking leave of his brother (Poem 101.9–10): *Accipe fraterno multum manantia fletu, / atque in perpetuum, frater, ave atque vale* ("Accept these tears with much brotherly weeping and forever, brother, hail and farewell"). So on this religious occasion, Caesar uses secular verse for his litany, while the fact of the code switch itself (compare the effect of Shakespeare's "*Et tu, Brute*") and the subject matter of the poem suggest the intimate and nearly fraternal relationship he shared with Pompey. On the other hand, at Atia's banquet to celebrate Caesar's return to Rome, she turns to her daughter Octavia and demands: "You there, some poetry, nay?"[21] She confides to Calpurnia (Haydn Gwynne): "She can rattle off pages of this stuff." Octavia suspects that Atia has just had her husband killed – indeed, Atia had given her henchman Timon the task – and is in no mood to join her insouciant celebration. She recites in English the Sybil's famous words to Aeneas before he enters the Underworld in Vergil's *Aeneid* (6.126–129): "Easy it is to go down into Hell, the gates of death are ever open; to climb back out again, that is the difficulty" (Episode 04). Atia ignores this "go to Hell" message and responds: "It's a touch dark, my love, but never mind." She then says softly to Calpurnia: "She lost her husband, you know." Octavia exits the party before we realize that she has lost not only her husband but also her place in time. The dramatic date of the episode must be 49 BC with

Pompey maneuvering outside the city and preparing to lead his army to Greece. Yet Book 6 of the *Aeneid* was only read to Augustus and his entourage sometime after the death of Marcellus in 23 BC.[22] In 49 BC, Vergil was only 21 years old and still ten years away from publishing his first work, the *Eclogues*.

Another literary plot point occurs in a later episode, when the poetry-loving Octavia is bored, lingering in the outdoor aviary of their home with her brother. To entertain her, Octavian reads to her in English Catullus Poem 2: "Little sparrow, my lover's love, with whom she plays, permits to lie in her lap . . ." (Episode 09). While the selection of the poem may be appropriate to the setting, and also recalls the "quotation" of Catullus in the film *Cleopatra*, the erotic/phallic qualities of the "sparrow" discomfit Octavia. This sibling sex talk is later taken a step beyond mere poetry when Servilia persuades the horrified girl to lure her brother into revealing his secrets by making sexual advances toward him.

Despite anachronisms and grammatical slips, classicists will agree that *Rome* is moving in the right direction by employing colorful vernacular, ritual prayers, and high literature in a series that sets a new standard for historical and cultural accuracy. Whether Latin is used in films for code switching, or to add solemnity to the context of ritual, or to indicate the reading pleasure and practices of the aristocracy, the occurrence of the genuine language is now, after *Gladiator* and *Rome*, firmly established as part of the milieu of movies and television series set in ancient Rome. The signs do not augur a diminishment in the future.

NOTES

1 The most notable example before Wolfgang Petersen's *Troy* (2004) was Kirk Douglas' *Ulysses* (1955). When Harry Cohn (1892–1958), the head of Columbia Studios, thought that the *Iliad* might have film possibilities, he told his writers: "Now, boys, I want a one-page treatment of this by tomorrow." The next day he was given the treatment, but tossed it, saying: "There are an awful lot of Greeks in it." See Boller and Davis (1987), 68–69.

2 "Sometime in 1949 [Peter] Ustinov had taken a screen test for the part of Nero in *Quo Vadis*. However, the film ran into administrative difficulties and it was a year before he heard from the film company saying that the test was very good, but he was perhaps a little young. Ustinov replied by cable: 'If you wait much longer I shall be too old. Nero died at thirty-one.' To this he received the answer: 'Historical research has proved you correct.' He got the part." See Willans (1957), 85–86.

3 *The Works of P. Virgilius Maro, with the original text reduced to the natural order of construction; and an interlinear translation, as nearly literal as the idiomatic difference of the Latin and English languages will allow* (Philadelphia, 1882). This series "improved" upon the educational theories of the English businessman James Hamilton (1769–1829), who came to America after being wiped out in the War of 1815. In the Hamiltonian method, developed out of John Locke, the teacher goes through a passage of Latin, first dictating a Latin word, then translating it while the student writes down the word and translation beneath it. The student then reviewed his transcriptions. See Latimer (1952–1953), 80–81.

4 The first edition was published in 1956 but the latest edition, the sixth, was published by HarperCollins, New York, in 2005.

5 This old Stoic maxim, "*deum sequere*" (Seneca, *Dialogues* 7.15.6.1), was the motto of both Giacomo Casanova and Francis Cardinal Spellman.

6 Latinists who can stomach the scourging of Jesus scene in this film will note that the Roman soldier counts the twenty-eighth lash with the more colloquial cardinal number "*viginti octo*" rather than the more elevated locution of "*duodetriginta.*" *Viginti* in compounds normally appears with an *et*, and frequently with the smaller number preceding, for example, *duas et viginti linguas* (Quintilian, *Oratorical Training* 11.2.50).

7 On *Gladiator*'s debt to *Spartacus*, see Cyrino (2005), 228–229, 242–243.

8 This is probably intended to mean "The whole world falls to Roman force," requiring "*Romanae*" or "*Romae*" rather than just "*Roma.*"

9 The word should be "*spectaculum,*" a performance devised for entertainment.

10 In *Dead Poets Society*, when teacher John Keating (Robin Williams) shows his class faded photographs of earlier generations of classes at the school, he tells them to make the most of their time, and adds the advice "*Carpe diem.*" In *Mrs. Doubtfire* (1993), Williams as Mrs. Euphegenia Doubtfire drops her false teeth and picking them up says, "*Carpe dentem.*" In *Clueless*, when Cher Horowitz (Alicia Silverstone) is asked by a friend if a jacket is "James Dean or Jason Priestley," she replies, "*Carpe diem*, okay? You look hot in it."

11 Perhaps the current popularity of films set in the ancient world will direct Hollywood to the large number of recent popular novels set in the ancient world by such talented writers as Colleen McCullough, Steven Saylor, and Lindsey Davis.

12 Though the Porte de Mars ("Mars Gate") in Rheims, which served as a model for the gate in *Rome*, was thought for a time to be Augustan, it probably dates from the third century AD. It has many exterior carvings, but no inscription over any of its three arches.

13 Platner (1929), 484.

14 Ashby (1900), 237. April 21 is the traditional birthday of Rome.

15 See Crystal (1987), *s.v.* "code switching."

16   Suetonius, *Life of Julius Caesar* 82.

17   See Horace, *Satires* 1.2.133.

18   The word *gerrae*, "nonsense," in its literal meaning refers to any lightweight wicker construction made out of twigs: compare the English expression "fiddlesticks." See Plautus, *Epidicus* 233; *Poenulus* 137; *Trinummus* 760 (*Oxford Latin Dictionary*, s.v. "*gerrae*").

19   The one use of Greek (not counting "*kak*") in the first season of *Rome* would fall into this category. In Episode 07, Lysandros, a vulgar-speaking (in English) Greek who leads Pompey and his family to the seashore, is ordered by Pompey to try to get the family to Amphipolis. He turns to his men and says, "*Provati, kaunoproktoi*," or "Move it, you wide-asses." Still, this is more Greek than is to be heard in Petersen's *Troy* or Oliver Stone's *Alexander* (2004).

20   The occurrence of the *taurobolium* at this period is problematic. It is a picturesque scene, but unfortunately, the practice is not known in Rome until AD 134 and the person drenched with the blood of the bull was the priest, not the suppliant. Of course, no Roman could be a priest of the Cybele cult, as it was an import from Phrygia (they worship a black stone). The chief description is from the late fourth century AD, in Prudentius, *Crowns of Martyrdom* 10.1006–1085. See Duthoy (1969); and Showerman (1901).

21   Several characters in the series punctuate the end of their questions with the word "nay," which sounds like an approximation of the Latin direct-question particle *-ne*.

22   See the biography of Vergil by Aelius Donatus, *Vita Donati* 32; also Servius' commentary on the *Aeneid* at 6.861.

16

Spectacle of Sex: Bodies on Display in *Rome*

Stacie Raucci

In the initial scenes of the series *Rome*, a virile voiceover introduces us to Julius Caesar and Pompey Magnus; a child's hand draws in the sand the image of two people fighting; Roman soldiers engage in fierce battle with the Gauls; their conquered leader, Vercingetorix, kneels stripped before the conqueror, Julius Caesar, who is surrounded by his throng of loyal soldiers chanting his name. These opening scenes probably strike a familiar chord for modern audiences. They are reminiscent, for instance, of the beginning of the most recent toga epic to arrive on the big screen, *Gladiator* (2000).[1] In both productions, the viewers are introduced to the Roman world with a bloody battle, where disciplined Romans fight against a crowd of rowdy barbarians, who are (literally) coming out of the woods, located up on a hill on the right side of the screen. Viewers of the initial scenes of *Rome* might therefore anticipate that the series will continue in line with the epic image of ancient Rome prevalent in the cinema for decades, where the crux of the movies lies in spectacular battles, where relationships between men are essentially of a political and military nature, and where the honor of men and the image of their manliness is fought for and won on the battle-field with their blood and guts. Yet in the next scenes of Episode 01, the action quickly turns to the personal world, showing the great soldier Pompey weeping over the body of his dying wife, Julia, daughter of Caesar. *Rome* moves now clearly along the path of the PBS televised series *I, Claudius* (1976), as it conflates the private world with the public into a familial soap opera.[2] Between *Gladiator* and *I, Claudius*, the series *Rome* lies at the nexus of television and cinema. But how can this series coherently articulate the distinct expectations created by these two media?

It is through the spectacle of sex, and especially of the male body, that *Rome* manages to find a solution to this question, a solution that sets the series apart from earlier screen representations of Rome. There is in *Rome* a rather conventional narrative and visual emphasis on the Romans' sex lives, and this is obviously most important for the success of the series with a modern audience accustomed to being entertained by the display of bodies. In *Rome*, moreover, the spectacles of battle are reduced to a few scenes with little bloodshed, while the spectacle of sex moves front and center, present in every episode. What is more original in these sex scenes is the presence and prominence of the male body, which up until now had been displayed either at war or crucified on a cross.[3] Beyond its entertainment value, sex in *Rome* appears to have another function: the virtue and strength of men are contingent upon sexual prowess, and their arena is the bedroom, not just the battlefield. This characteristic of sex is perhaps best encapsulated in the titles that begin each episode, where graffiti on the wall show a man with an exaggerated penis and proportionally large testicles, and where the word *arma*, Latin for "weapons," is written under the image. The power of a man is represented by his phallic prowess. *Rome*, like a big screen toga epic, insists on the male body showing off its power and virtue; but, like a televised series, it stages this body in the personal and sexual sphere.

Mark Antony

More often and in more explicit ways than traditional screen productions, *Rome* provides an erotic feast for the eyes of the viewers. It is through these corporeal displays that *Rome* establishes Mark Antony (James Purefoy) as the primary sex symbol of the series. Even when Antony is clothed, his body more than those of all the other elite male characters is clearly signaled as a spectacle. The camera focuses lovingly on his handsome face for many a close-up shot, as it does for few others in the series. He is set apart from the other Roman men by the essential force and intensity of his physical stance. In Episode 10, for example, when the Senate is gathered and the camera pans the crowd, all the Senators seem to sit properly, backs straight and many with hands folded neatly in their laps. By contrast, Antony sits slumped against a wall, with his feet up in a casual position. In another instance in the Senate (in Episode 02), Antony sits with his legs spread apart and his arms outstretched behind him, as if he were a spectator at an entertaining show. In the same episode, when he is inducted as a tribune of the people, a high political office, he merely looks bored as his body strains against the confines of his seat. When he receives visitors who need his official help in Episode 06, he fidgets and looks annoyed, holding his chin in his hands. He is more interested in the slave woman behind him, Cynthia, than in the official business at hand. In almost every scene in which he appears, Antony speaks primarily with his body.

Although Antony is supposed to be a fierce warrior and is an omnipresent figure on the screen, he is in fact rarely seen fighting. In Episode 02 there is a scene where he appears in full battle gear, helmet on, but instead of fighting, he is shown having sexual intercourse with a peasant woman as his whole army watches and waits for him. After a rather subdued orgasm, he rejoins the troops, throwing his arms in the air and roaring noisily as if he had won a battle. The armor he wears is an obvious symbol of his power, but it is displaced from the military to the sexual realm. In Episode 06, war again appears symbolically in a sex scene. Two of Antony's slave women play "sword fight" at his command, but with real swords. Sitting on his bed half-naked and eating, he watches nonchalantly and cheers the women as they slash at each other. He sets up a triangle in which he sits back, directing the viewer's attention at least momentarily to these powerless, whimpering young women. It is only when one slave, Cynthia, is struck and wounded that Antony enters this arena fully. More vampire-like than soldierly, he rises to lick the bloodied belly of Cynthia. Throughout the first season, *Rome* significantly plays down Antony's military prowess by alluding to it with hints and symbols, but never showing it in action.

It is by exhibiting his body, not by fighting, that Antony demonstrates his virility. Antony's body is carefully put on view in several erotic scenes with his patrician lover, Atia. In Episode 04 he is in bed with her, lying on his stomach, sleepy-eyed, hair mussed, and unshaven. In these sex scenes, the camera focuses more on the body of Antony than on that of Atia. In another sequence (in Episode 02), the camera even cuts off the view of both their faces and merely shows his unclad body. During these scenes, there is always at least one slave present, usually Atia's female body slave and guardian, Merula. The voyeuristic presence of this third-party viewer provides Antony with an internal audience for this display of his virility.

But the most striking spectacle of Antony's body is in Episode 04, when he addresses the centurion, Vorenus, while standing in a courtyard completely naked and being oiled by a slave. His nudity is made all the more obvious by the fact that every person around him is fully clothed. Antony's hair is wet and carefully mussed in the style of a male model and his recently oiled chest glistens in the sunlight. The camera faces Antony and for a few moments shows the entire front of his body, allowing the audience to view his full-frontal nudity.[4] He is positioned with his arms outstretched to the sides at shoulder level and his feet spread, as the slave rubs him down. One might imagine that a naked man would appear uncomfortable standing outdoors with his body on display for the gaze of three dressed people – all the more so since he stands in the symbolic position of a crucified victim. Yet Antony continues to bark orders with unfazed confidence: note the irony when he comments to Vorenus that he could have him "crucified." This scene brings to the fore Antony's role as a spectacle of powerful masculinity in the series. Just as Vorenus and the slave watch from within the scene, the spectators watch his body from their living rooms. Antony is the object of the viewers' gazes, yet he retains his absolute power in this exposed stance.

The camera even makes sure to show the most salient image of his masculinity, his penis. For an American audience, the penis remains "the last great taboo in our culture"[5] and is still almost never seen on television or in the cinema. On the major networks the penis has been discussed at length, for instance on shows like *Ally McBeal* (Fox, 1997–2002) and *Chicago Hope* (CBS, 1994–2000),[6] but the organ itself remains unseen. Thus, by actually showing the penis, this scene in *Rome* is going to jolt the sensibilities of its modern viewers. Precisely because the sight of the penis onscreen is taboo, its appearance has a powerful impact.[7] The magnitude of Antony's masculinity is proportional not to the size of his penis, but to the size of the taboo broken by the visibility of his penis.

There is an intriguing parallel with the full-frontal nudity of a slave in Episode 06. Atia, Caesar's niece, is sending the slave as a gift to make amends with Servilia, the former lover of Caesar. Like Antony in the scene described above, this slave is the only naked figure in this particular scene. But here the other characters comment on his naked body, while he stands with his head lowered, body oiled and decorated with various adornments, including ribbons on his penis. As Atia examines him, the camera mirrors the movement of her eyes, scanning the slave's body from his head downwards and stopping at the tip of his penis, emphasizing the unqualified power of this elite woman's gaze. When her children question the appropriateness of her gift, Atia states: "A large penis is always welcome." She orders that before being delivered, the slave be well oiled and his toenails groomed. The body of the slave is clearly meant to be the erotic object of the gaze of those present, including Atia, Octavia, and Octavian. During the inspection, the camera shows the front side of his body. As he exits the room, the camera follows him as he turns, showing his well-shaped but-tocks. After the slave is given as a gift to Servilia, the camera again shows his body as a montage of parts. Inside Servilia's villa, the camera provides a close-up of his body, starting at his toes (which are now well-groomed), moving past his large penis, and only then moving out away from his body to show more of the interior setting as it reaches his head. His body is presented as a product to be consumed, first by the women who purchase and give him as a gift, and then by the viewing audience. Much like the gladiators depicted in films like *Spartacus* (1960) and *Gladiator*, the slave is there as "nothing more than a spectacle for Romans' desiring gaze."[8]

While the state of being naked for this slave clearly shows his lack of power, for Antony, it is his very nakedness that represents his power. Antony's penis is a symbol of his authority, and for the slave, his gift-wrapped penis is a sign of his subservient state. Antony well handles his status as object of the gaze, what Monica Cyrino appropriately terms the "visual negotiation between strength and vulnerability."[9] He controls the eyes of the viewers and compels them to continue watching his masculinity. The slave, on the contrary, is not in control of anything, and the visibility of his body signifies only his lower social status. His penis has as much agency as an appetizing piece of meat dressed for sale in a butcher's window. It is not the mere state of being nude which makes one vulnerable, but rather the social status of each man that determines whether he will manip-ulate or be manipulated through the spectacle of his sexual organs.

Caesar

The narrative of the first season of *Rome* ends unsurprisingly with the iconic death of Caesar (Ciarán Hinds). Caesar is killed during a meeting of the Senate, at the hands of other Roman men – including his dear friend, Brutus – as his body is penetrated both by the knives of his murderers and the gaze of the viewer. Although this final scene is not directly of a sexual nature, it offers the conclusion to a constant and recurrent emphasis throughout the first season on the close relationship between Caesar's political power and his sexual life.

Unlike Antony, little of Caesar's body is shown early in the season, and his sex life appears to be driven more by emotion than by sexual instinct. In more than one instance, he is seen locked in a passionate embrace with his mistress, Servilia. Since Caesar already has more power than anyone else, the depiction of his character at first does not require the display of the body, and therefore of his virility, in the same way as the depiction of Antony. But once Caesar's emotional affair with Servilia becomes publicly known (in Episode 05), Antony remarks while in bed with Atia: "Every dog in camp knows that Servilia has unmanned him." Antony reinforces his own masculinity by telling Atia as he penetrates her: "As you can tell, I am not unmanned." As if to contrast Antony's vigorous masculinity with Caesar's progressing emasculation, the camera cuts from Antony in bed discussing his erection to Caesar quietly asleep in bed with Servilia. Obscene graffiti also appear in the streets depicting Caesar in an unflattering manner, as an older man with a large, paunchy stomach, just the opposite of the pin-up model image of Antony.

As a protection against this apparent emasculation, Caesar cruelly renounces Servilia later in the episode. In Episode 08, he regains his manhood not by going into battle, but by sexually conquering the Egyptian queen, Cleopatra. While his soldiers fight against Ptolemy's followers, he fights the battles of love with Cleopatra. These Alexandrian sex scenes are unlike the calm interludes he shared with Servilia back in Rome; rather, they show a passionate Caesar aggressively seizing and making love to the young queen. It is precisely this powerful image with which Cleopatra is concerned, as she must ally herself with a strong Caesar for the sake of her own rule. Before Cleopatra even meets him in this episode, the focus is on the image of Caesar and not the man himself. Cleopatra is shown staring at a Roman coin with his likeness and remarks that he is "not a bad-looking man." Cleopatra is not interested here with how handsome Caesar is, but with his larger public image. By referring to a widely distributed image on a coin, she refers to the extent of his public power. The more powerful Caesar appears politically and militarily, the greater Cleopatra's chances of gaining protection for her rule. The display of Caesar's sexual prowess simply solidifies for the audience what Cleopatra has already recognized.

The result of Caesar and Cleopatra's union is the ultimate display of virility, the exhibition of a healthy son. At the end of Episode 08, Caesar faces the Roman army with Cleopatra at his side and shows off their male child, Caesarion. In this scene, Caesar takes care to keep the blanket of the baby open, so that the whole army can see the baby's penis. The camera even moves in to emphasize it, as all the soldiers cheer loudly. The image of this particular penis represents the masculinity of two individuals at once. First, it demonstrates the undisputable male sex of the baby Caesarion. By publicly claiming the child as his own, Caesar shares by blood his own masculinity and the assumed position of legitimate heir.

At the same time, the penis also represents Caesar's own virility and his ability to produce offspring of the appropriate, that is, male, sex.

But this particular representation of masculinity is not so straightforward. *Rome* overturns other historical and cinematic versions of the Cleopatra/Caesar saga by casting doubt on Caesar's virility. In fact, the narrative of Episode 08 has somewhat comically suggested a different paternity for the son of the Egyptian queen. As Caesar holds up his supposed newborn child, it is implied – and the audience is to understand – that the baby is actually the offspring of the grunt soldier, Pullo. By casting such doubt, *Rome* anticipates Caesar's downfall and death in the final episode of the season with a foreshadowing of a sexual nature. Thus the series indicates that Caesar is, technically, still a man without children, and as Cleopatra had warned him earlier: "A man without sons is a man without a future."

Octavian

When the viewer first encounters Octavian (Max Pirkis) in Season One, he appears as a scrawny young man with a baby face, and his rather powerless body is hidden under the heavy folds of his boyhood toga. In the first episode, Octavian is captured on his way to visit Caesar in Gaul, and is predictably saved by the manly soldiers Vorenus and Pullo. One might imagine that the radical transformation of this boyish figure into the great Emperor Augustus of Roman history must have involved many political, social, and cultural factors. In *Rome*, however, it is essentially Octavian's access to a sexual life that catalyzes his gradual ascension to masculine authority and power.

In Episode 04, the camera opens the scene with a close-up of the hand of a servant cutting off the testicles of a dead and skinned goat. These testicles are then served to the young Octavian to inspire strength in his penis. His mother, Atia, makes clear that Octavian's masculinity is at stake: "You've been developing a distinctly feminine *anima*, and I do not like it. The men of the Julii are masculine men!" In Episode 06, Atia again states her concern regarding Octavian's virility and commands that he will "penetrate someone today." Pullo, following Atia's order, leads Octavian to an upscale brothel where he can display his masculinity to the television audience for the first time. While Octavian chooses a prostitute, all the choices are lined up and the camera scans them for Octavian's eyes as well as for the viewing audience. These figures are meant to be penetrated both figuratively and literally, first by the gaze and then by the male penis. Once Octavian enters the bedroom, his half-naked body is visible for the first time in the series.[10] He undresses as the camera focuses on him, rather than on the young female prostitute, and the audience clearly sees his bare chest. The naked body of the prostitute is only shown after sex, in order to confirm Octavian's virility. And in case there were any doubt, she emerges from the room to tell everyone that Octavian was "like bull." It is also at this point in the series that Octavian begins to wear the *toga virilis*, the toga worn by an adult male. The series has tied Octavian's transition into adulthood to the ritual of having sex for the first time, rather than to the familial and military rituals which are traditionally part of donning the *toga virilis*.[11] Yet Octavian's visit to the brothel is an age-appropriate rite of passage for an American audience familiar with movies dealing with teenagers and the loss of their virginity.

But this is not the end of sex for the young Octavian in the first season. Octavian's transformation into a virile figure is apparently not complete until he has incestuous sex with his sister Octavia in Episode 09. Octavia, manipulated by her mother's rival, Servilia, is desperately trying to coax Octavian into telling her a secret, so she lures him into bed with her. When Octavian seems confused by her enticements, she verbally completes his transformation into a man when she says: "You are a man now, you can take what you want." After the sex is over, the camera again favors the male body and follows the length of Octavian's body in bed, displaying him in his post-coital triumph. The audience sees his chest, but not Octavia's breasts. At this point, Octavian immediately becomes manlier, and more aggressive in his speech, telling his sister that she knows what they did was wrong. It is only after these sex scenes that Octavian takes on the male role in the household, a transformation that foreshadows his rise to power in the next season.

Vorenus and Pullo

The exhibition of the male body in *Rome* extends past the elite Roman men to the characters of the soldiers. As they are of a lower class than Caesar and his circle, Vorenus (Kevin McKidd) and Pullo (Ray Stevenson) start out as objects of the gaze. In Episode 02, after they have saved Octavian from captivity in Gaul and delivered the boy safely to Atia, she stares at them and refers to them as "good fearsome specimens," a phrase that dehumanizes them. She looks at them with only slightly more respect than she looks at the naked male slave in Episode 06. And while Pullo remains in the same rank and status throughout the first season, Vorenus' social and political status will climb and so does the presentation of his masculinity beyond this initial image.

As the series progresses, and as his status grows, more of Vorenus' body is indeed shown. In Episode 02, he is shown having sex with his wife, Niobe, with only his torso revealed on screen. The experience is clearly not a successful one, since Niobe, anxious over the strains on their marriage, appears disengaged at best. Later, in Episode 06, Vorenus is shown being bathed by Niobe in their bedroom. She appears in a subordinate position, lowered to the ground on her knees, lovingly washing his feet and lower legs. He stands straight, looking at her below him. The camera moves slowly from his feet up along his legs, showing a clear view of his buttocks and finally arriving at his torso and face, as Niobe rises to kiss him. Just as his wife now desires him, ideally so should the viewing audience. It is only when Vorenus has assumed this new, more sexually virile persona that he joins Caesar's political slate, runs for office, and is eventually named Senator. He has proven his sexual strength, and is only then worthy of political power.

Pullo, on the other hand, is often shown having sex in the early episodes, but he never advances above his status as a legionary soldier. Pullo's nude body is seen in Episode 02, when he visits a brothel upon his return from Gaul. He is depicted having vigorous intercourse with a prostitute, as the camera shows the whole of his body from the back. He is again shown having sex in Episode 08: this time he appears in an extremely energetic erotic sequence with Cleopatra in her tent (this is the scene where the series hints that the conception of the child, Caesarion, takes place). But before they begin having sex, Cleopatra lies on her back and imperiously examines Pullo as he stands naked before her. This highly sexualized shot of Pullo is the last one in the series where his nude body is completely exhibited. Later, as his status falls from soldier to criminal hit-man to gladiator, less of his body is displayed in a sexual way. By the time he is convicted of murder in Episode 11 and sentenced to die in the gladiatorial arena, he appears fully clothed. The decrease in the frequency of the displays of Pullo's body seems to correspond to his decline in social status. Even in the gladiatorial arena, Pullo appears fully clothed. He is only saved by Vorenus, who by this point in the series has proved himself sexually and politically. When Vorenus saves Pullo in the arena, he lifts him to his feet and places his arm around his shoulders, as the dead bodies of the slain gladiators are shown in the background. Pullo is only redeemed by the association of his degraded body with that of Vorenus' more powerful one.

One Last Look

In the end, what is the significance of displaying the male body as if a commodity to be purchased and enjoyed by cable television subscribers?[12] The omnipresence of the male body puts *Rome* in proper cinematic company. It becomes part of a distinguished reception of the ancient world on screen, including films such as *Ben-Hur* (1959), *Spartacus*, and *Gladiator*. Such films are part of the "body genre," in which "sweat, muscles, shows of strength, tunics, and loin cloths" are the norm.[13] In these films there was already a trend to focus the "erotic gaze on the male, rather than the female, figure."[14] Yet *Rome* surpasses the projection of these epic images by further sexualizing the display, showing even more skin, as expected by an audience in the early twenty-first century. Moreover, like the television series *I, Claudius*, the series *Rome* brings these soap opera images every week into the living rooms of British and American families. With each display of the male body it uses to drive the narrative, *Rome* compels the viewer to come back each week for more.

In their homes, modern viewers bridge the distance between their own lives and ancient Rome by performing an activity common both to the ancient Romans and to us: watching others closely and judging them. Celebrities and politicians in the present day are constantly under the eye of the paparazzi, who obtain images to sell and share with the larger public. These images often focus not on the achievements of the observed individuals but on their private, and sometimes even their sexual, lives. In the eye of the media, the sex lives of politicians can even determine political outcomes. President Bill Clinton is perhaps the prime example of the modern intermingling of sex and politics, as the US Congress and the American media in the late 1990s became obsessed with the smallest details of his affair with Monica Lewinsky.

In ancient Rome it was the norm for a person, male or female, to be constantly on display to another's gaze: "Being, for a Roman, was being seen."[15] David Fredrick aptly termed ancient Rome a "society of spectacle and surveillance."[16] People who had publicly proven themselves were referred to in a visual way: men were *spectati viri*, "observed men," and women were *spectatae feminae*, "observed women."[17] Such terms indicate that a person needed to be noticed and scrutinized in public to gain and retain power and status. Yet by being observed, one was left unprotected against the possible attack of other gazes. Scholars have accurately characterized the difficulties for a Roman in navigating the proper balance between being the observed and being an observer. Holt N. Parker writes about the "double bind" of the Romans,[18] and Carlin Barton refers to this paradox as the "risky oscillation of exhibition and inhibition."[19] Much like modern celebrities, ancient Romans were constantly in a precarious position, in between the need to be seen and the danger of being seen. In order to survive in society, a Roman must be the object of the gaze of others, while enduring the judgment of those penetrating gazes.

In *Rome*, the cable television audience acts in place of the approving and disapproving Roman eye in seeing and being-seen situations. In the occasional scenes, modern viewers see the male body on display in the traditional, public, and often risky ways that they were actually displayed in Roman society, and also in the ways most often portrayed on screen in toga epics: in triumphal processions, walking through the Forum, speaking in the Senate, and sometimes fighting battles. But perhaps because of the influence of contemporary paparazzi culture, with its craving for a glimpse into the private lives of the individuals it observes, *Rome* insists on relocating the Roman visual dynamics to the less grandiose, more intimate, and more modern context of the bedroom. Sexual display becomes the primary indicator of manliness.

NOTES

1   On the typical openings of toga movies, see Fitzgerald (2001), 23.
2   Joshel, Malamud, and Wyke (2001), 15. As Joshel (2001) notes, the medium of television changed "the cinematic spectacle of Roman imperial power and corruption. . . . In *I, Claudius*, the family becomes the spectacle. . . . The spectacle of *I, Claudius* consists primarily of sex and talk – with a dose of dastardly deaths" (120–121).
3   Fitzgerald (2001), 42.
4   Note there are two instances of female full-frontal nudity in Episode 01, when Atia rises out of the bath and when Octavia is disrobed in preparation for sex with Pompey.
5   Lehman (2001), 28.
6   Lehman (2001), 37.
7   Lehman (2001), 33.
8   Hark (1993), 154.
9   Cyrino (2005), 120, on the display of the nude body of Spartacus.
10 Note that while the bodies of the young prostitutes in this episode are shown in various states of undress and even nude, the body of Octavian is never seen fully naked. Perhaps more of his body is not shown here since showing the

body of such a young boy who is also a main character would not be accept-able to the audience. In addition, note that while Octavian may be of an age similar to that of the young prostitutes, their bodies seem more developed, further emphasizing that their bodies are for sale.

11 On the *toga virilis* during the Roman Republic, see McDonnell (2006), 177–178.
12 On Hollywood's consumerism, see Joshel, Malamud, and Wyke (2001), 21.
13 Hunt (1993), 66.
14 Cyrino (2005), 87.
15 Barton (2002), 220.
16 Fredrick (2002b), 13.
17 On being tested visually, see Barton (2002), 220–222.
18 Parker (1999), 167.
19 Barton (2002), 227.

17

Vice is Nice: *Rome* and Deviant Sexuality

Anise K. Strong

When I first began watching *Rome*, I expected to be entertained as an American television viewer and intrigued as a Roman historian. I had not anticipated, however, being disgusted or outraged, priding myself on my equanimity and open-mindedness about modern interpretations of the ancient world. Yet in the middle of Episode 09, "Utica," I found myself shocked by an intense scene in which the teenaged Octavia seduces her barely pubescent brother, Gaius Octavian.[1]

My discomfort was twofold. As an early twenty-first-century American, I was repulsed by a scene of consensual incest between two characters I had previously liked and admired. As a classicist, I was startled by the complete invention of a sexual relationship between two well-known historical figures where no evidence or even hint of such a liaison existed. I had been relatively pleased by the historical accuracy in *Rome* until that point and tolerated fictional intrigues and romances like the numerous affairs of the Octavii's mother, Atia. Little historical data survive about Atia, leaving a wide canvas for the artist's brush. While Augustan propaganda paints her as a virtuous Roman matron, there is little reason to take this version more seriously than that of the television series.[2] Yet while we know little about Atia, we know much about her son, the future Emperor Augustus, including his numerous romantic escapades with a variety of women. No ancient or modern author ever suggests that he had an inappropriate relationship with his beloved sister, the famously virtuous Octavia.[3]

I quickly moved on from my initial vague distaste to the larger question of why HBO-BBC had chosen to depict such a relationship. The Octavia–Octavian incest represents a nexus of two separate goals for the creators of

Rome, both of which concern issues of representation and identity. Both the HBO network and ancient Roman society are associated in modern culture with sexual decadence and deviance. Portrayals of ancient Rome in American mass media over the past century have repeatedly depicted Rome as a center of exotic fornication and immoral sexual practices, often involving sexually aggressive women. Over the last six decades, the means of depicting such decadence has shifted in tune with evolving American social and sexual mores. Representations of ancient Roman sexuality have been carefully tailored to shock contemporaneous social norms, ranging from the depictions of female voyeurism in the 1951 film *Quo Vadis* to the scenes of partial nudity and group sex in the 1970s miniseries *I, Claudius* (1976).

HBO has built its original programming reputation over the last decade not only on the artistic qualities of its shows but also on its willingness to depict material that the broadcast networks shunned, whether the female masturbation of *Sex and the City* (1998–2004), the ubiquitous obscenities of *Deadwood* (2004–2006), or the graphic violence of *The Sopranos* (1999–2007). Its slogan, "It's not TV, it's HBO," reflects the channel's emphasis on the importance of the divide between its shows and other television programs. However, the networks have begun imitating the cable channels, especially HBO, in the last few years, gradually introducing more sex, violence, and obscenities in order to attract and retain viewers wanting more sophisticated adult fare. In order to maintain its cutting-edge reputation with *Rome,* HBO needed to reposition itself as more daring than any other television channel. It did so by showing sexual relationships previously unseen on network television. As the third section of this chapter will establish, incestuous themes and a general increase in deviant sexuality on television have been a mainstay of the most popular and critically praised television shows of the past two years, whether network or cable. However, previous shows all hedged their incest plotlines, whereas *Rome* dealt with the issue unambiguously.

This simultaneous double escalation of representations of sexual deviance came to an intersection in this scene of sibling incest in *Rome.* Incest has become both the new topless dancing girl and the new lesbian kiss, at a time when both have become passé in their respective genres of togate epic and prime-time drama. The next logical question is whether incest is indeed merely another point on the scale of television depictions of sexual behavior, from the separate beds of married couples in 1950s television to the lesbian kisses and single mothers of the early 1990s. I seek to construct a schema whereby it is possible both to criticize the narrowness of those who condemn *Ellen* (1994–1998), the first television show to star an openly lesbian character, and yet to discourage representations of incest on television as just another exotic lifestyle choice, much less one evocative of the ancient world. If the bar of representations of sexual deviance is continually raised, we must ask what might be the next step, and whether any of us would be comfortable watching it.

Historical Incest in Ancient Rome

Ancient Roman attitudes toward incest were relatively similar to common modern mores. The surviving laws on marriage, although they date from the later Roman Empire, are explicit in their ban on close-kin unions. Marrying a close relative was both sacrilegious and illegal in Rome. The Roman jurist Paul considered parent–child unions and deliberate fraternal unions to be against the *ius gentium*, the common set of moral and legal doctrines that bound not only Roman citizens but all civilized people.[4] Several Roman prosecutions for cases of incest survive, including a case brought before the Roman Prefect in Egypt that involved two Roman citizens.[5]

Such accusations, whether true or false, also formed a frequent source of political invective in Roman speeches and writing. The most notorious example is Cicero's mockery in the *Pro Caelio* of young Publius Clodius' habit of sharing a bed with his older sisters.[6] It is possible that some incestuous relationships, like the alleged one between the siblings Clodius and Clodia, actually occurred. However, Cicero was extremely fond of salacious gossip, and we have little evidence for this incest except for Cicero's speeches and letters.

Incest was also used as a political excuse when Senators or emperors desired to charge their enemies with suitably horrific crimes. Tiberius, for instance, executed Roman citizens on the charge of incest. Tacitus and Cassius Dio describe Tiberius' execution of Sextus Marius and Marius' daughter for the crime of incest, an accusation apparently motivated by Marius' refusal to allow Tiberius to seduce the young woman himself.[7] Regardless of the factual circumstances, the case was publicly prosecuted and deemed worthy of a death sentence, showing the emphasis Romans purported to place on such crimes. While this was not a brother–sister liaison, we may infer that such relationships would also have been harshly prosecuted in Rome, unless, of course, they involved the emperor himself, as in the supposed case of Caligula and his sisters.[8]

The general Roman social attitude toward incest was one of condemnation and horror. While it may have been more common in the Eastern provinces, such as Roman Egypt, where as much as 20 percent of the Greek Egyptian population may have been involved in sibling marriages, or in Greece, where half-siblings were allowed to marry, in Rome itself incest was definitely not best.[9] Although in the series *Rome* Atia reacts with shock at the discovery of her children's affair and Octavia herself seems remorseful, even the existence of the relationship does not echo actual Roman society or sexual values. Since *Rome* tries elsewhere to be reasonably historically accurate, particularly in its representation of interpersonal relationships like the affair between Caesar and Servilia, the creation of the incest storyline implies a particular agenda on the part of the creators.

Sexual Deviance and Rome in Film and Television

Since the beginning of the twentieth century, modern media have portrayed Rome as a cesspool of extreme sexual behavior and exotic styles of intercourse. These representations of Roman orgies and other sexually exotic practices in film and television evolved along with American sexual mores. The early cinematic Cleopatras such as Theda Bara (1917) and Claudette Colbert (1934) wore outfits that left little to the imagination; Bara's costume involved small metallic breast cups designed to resemble snake coils. However, the actresses themselves did little more than kiss their Roman paramours on screen; their sexuality was more suggestive than explicit.[10] Colbert, in particular, may have been restrained by the recent adoption of the Hollywood Production Code (1930) from anything racier than sultry glances and suggestive dialogue.

The Code continued to moderate and censor films about the ancient world for several decades, despite a continued thematic emphasis on Roman debauchery and decadence.[11] In the film *Quo Vadis* (1951), the decadence and perversion of the Empress Poppaea were implied by the active role she takes in her adulterous liaison with the hero Marcus and her frequent voyeuristic appreciation of his body. However, the audience saw remarkably little of Poppaea's own body. In the film *Spartacus* (1960), Stanley Kubrick depicted the corruption of the Roman elite through the homoerotic "snails and oysters" bath scene between M. Licinius Crassus and his handsome young slave Antoninus. This scene, despite its lack of anything approaching actual homosexual intercourse, was deemed so scandalous that it was cut from the film until the video re-release in the early 1990s.[12]

Federico Fellini's *Satyricon* (1969) celebrated Roman decadence with vivid scenes of homosexuality, nudity, group sex, and anal intercourse, as well as allusions to pedophilia. For the late 1960s, these acts marked the height of sexually transgressive behavior, but many scenes in the film *Satyricon* are echoed or exceeded by Atia's frequent and exotic sexual encounters in the HBO-BBC series *Rome*. The first episode of *Rome* alone features Atia trading vigorous sex with a lower-class tradesman in return for a particularly nice horse. The sexual extravagances and grotesquerie of the *Satyricon* were echoed in 1970s and 1980s soft-core pornography films depicting the Roman era, such as Derek Jarman's *Sébastiane* (1976) and Bob Guccione's *Caligula* (1980). While *Caligula* does explicitly depict the emperor's incest with his sister, it never possessed the mainstream audience of HBO-BBC's *Rome*, giving it less influence over the general Anglo-American imagination and conceptualization of ancient Roman society and sexuality than this series may ultimately have.

Rome's direct predecessor and inspiration, the BBC miniseries *I, Claudius* (1976), closely associates ancient Rome with sexual debauchery, nudity, and deviance. The first shot of the Augustan court zooms in on the bare breasts of a group of African dancers, whom both the camera and the Roman elite characters casually objectify.[13] Other scenes in the series feature a variety of more and less risqué orgies, although they generally do not show any nudity by principal characters or any unorthodox sexual acts or partners.

The most provocative and disturbing sexual moment in the series *I, Claudius* is the lengthy kiss and breast-fondling of the elderly Livia by her teenaged great-grandson, Caligula, a sexualized act that thankfully for the viewer's eyes goes no farther.[14] This scene is one of the first introductions of Caligula to the viewing audience, and it successfully paints him as the most depraved and perverted of the Julio-Claudians. Claudius, the protagonist and narrator, reacts in horror to this kiss, and the audience is certainly intended to share his outrage and distaste. In any case, it set a high bar for any attempt by HBO-BBC in 2005 to depict an even more extreme representation of Roman sexual decadence than previously displayed on the small screen.

Incest and Modern Television

Since the beginning of the Nielsen ratings in the early 1960s, television shows have repeatedly attempted to lure in extra viewers during the crucial "sweeps seasons" of February, May, and November by running brand-new programming or injecting novel elements into existing shows like weddings, births, and tragic deaths. In addition to these rites of passage, television writers have used depictions of sexual deviance to stir up, titillate, and attract new viewers.

In February 1991, for instance, the television drama *L.A. Law* (NBC, 1986–1994) attempted to engineer a ratings boost during sweeps in a lackluster fifth season by featuring the first same-sex kiss on television.[15] The kiss was a brief exchange in a parking lot between one bisexual female attorney and a "bi-curious" fellow female attorney. Out of 14.6 million households who watched the show, 84 contacted the network with their comments, 51 negative and 33 positive.[16] Nonetheless, under pressure from the American Family Association, NBC hedged its support of the show and emphasized that the regular character was not lesbian but merely experimenting with her sexuality.[17]

However, the political backlash did not stop the rise of the so-called "lesbian sweeps kiss," in which network television shows featured women kissing each other as a means of generating buzz about their show and garnering a larger audience to boost their ratings at critical times. An early and prominent example was a kiss between Roseanne Barr and Mariel Hemingway in a 1993 episode of *Roseanne* (ABC, 1988–1997). More recently, in February 2005, television featured at least six lesbian-kiss storylines in shows as wide-ranging as the venerable daytime soap opera *All My Children* (ABC, 1970–current), and evening programs such as *The O.C.* (Fox, 2003–2006), *Jack and Bobby* (WB, 2004–2005), *The L Word* (Showtime, 2004–current), *The Simpsons* (Fox, 1989–current), and *One Tree Hill* (WB, 2003–current).[18] Few of these liaisons continued beyond the end of the sweeps month of February, suggesting that they existed more for erotic appeal than character development.

This plethora of recent same-sex kisses on television implies that they may have become passé in terms of their shock value. The continued popularity of the scenes suggests that these moments may still be sexually appealing to American audiences, whether gay or straight, but the same-sex kisses of 2005–2006 are now almost routine fare on television. In order to portray shocking sexual behavior on television, screen writers have moved onto a new type of unorthodox relationship: incest.

In 2005, a variety of both cable and network shows featured incest storylines, often without significant condemnation of the relationship or characters involved. In January of 2005, the hit ABC drama *Lost* (2005–current) depicted a sexual relationship between step-sibling characters Shannon and Boone.[19] Although the writers emphasized repeatedly in the episode that the pair shared "no blood relationship," they had been raised together and their dynamic on the show was very much one of confused siblings. At the end of the second season of the critically acclaimed comedy series *Arrested Development* (Fox, 2003–2006), the non-biological teenage cousins George Michael and Maeby kiss, and during the third season the pair was accidentally legally married.[20] Indeed, the plot twists and relationships in this show were almost as complicated as those of *Rome* itself.

Incest was even more popular among minor characters and shorter story arcs in recent television. The long-running British soap operas *Brookside* (1982–2003) and *EastEnders* (1985–current) both featured sibling-incest storylines for minor characters, *Brookside* in 1997 and *EastEnders* in 2003.[21] This may indicate that British television is more sexually adventurous than its American counterpart, given the earlier date of these shows. A five-episode arc in 2006 on the ABC show *Boston Legal* (2004–current) featured the firm representing a defendant who was secretly involved in an incestuous relationship with his mother. In the last scene of the arc finale, mother and son shared a passionate kiss to celebrate his acquittal on murder charges.[22] A one-episode incest plotline also appeared during February 2006 sweeps on the Fox medical drama *House* (2004–current).[23]

HBO itself has used incest plotlines in a variety of its original dramas. In one of the last episodes of HBO's *Six Feet Under* (2001–2005), the character Brenda had an incestuous and explicit erotic dream about her brother Billy, who had previously expressed sexual desire for her.[24] While the relationship was not consummated during the series, it formed a major part of the dynamic between the two characters. During the second season of the disturbing apocalyptic series *Carnivàle* (2003–2005), Brother Justin, the "Avatar of Darkness," and his sister Iris had an erotic aspect to their relationship, although any sex remained off screen. Unlike other television series, the writers here used incest as a sign of the characters' villainy, rather than merely to discomfort or titillate the audience. Meanwhile, HBO has also begun experimenting with depictions of polygamy in the series *Big Love* (2006–current), perhaps as yet another means of recapturing the title of the network with the most sexually deviant content.

Incest in *Rome*

Rome crossed new barriers in the fall sweeps season of 2005 by depicting an actual sexual liaison between two blood siblings, an act that earlier American television series had carefully sidestepped. While the shows *Lost* and *Arrested Development* emphasized the non-biological relationship between their couples and *Six Feet Under* portrayed the incest in a dream sequence, *Rome* made it very clear that consensual sex takes place between two blood siblings, Octavia and Octavian.

Within the context of the series, the incest was merely another sally in the war of intrigue between Atia, the Octavii's mother and Caesar's niece, and Servilia, Brutus' mother and Julius Caesar's former mistress. Servilia has earlier seduced Octavia herself, a relationship used both as a weapon against Atia and in the interest of possibly learning scandalous information about Caesar. When Servilia discovered that Octavian knew a secret about Caesar's health (his epilepsy), she persuaded her young lover, the pliable Octavia, to seduce her younger brother in order to find out the secret.

Initially, Octavia refuses; she is horrified by the idea of incest. She does, however, reluctantly acknowledge her brother's apparent sexual attraction to her, a desire already hinted to the audience in Episode 06, where Octavian chooses a prostitute who closely resembled Octavia for his first sexual experience. However, Servilia reveals to Octavia that Atia arranged the murder of Octavia's first husband, and in bizarre revenge Octavia decides to pursue the incest as a means of retaliation against her mother. The twists and convolutions of this elaborate plot suggest that the real goal of the scriptwriter, Alexandra Cunningham, was to create justification for such a shocking scene during November sweeps month, rather than as a necessary and logical outgrowth of character development.

The seduction scene itself takes place in two sections in Episode 09. In the first section, Octavian reads to Octavia Catullus' first "Sparrow Poem" (Poem 2) in the garden while the siblings flirt with each other in a silent dialogue of exchanged glances and alluring poses. The choice of this poem connects Octavian and Octavia with the presumed inspiration for Catullus' poetry, Clodia, who was herself famously accused of incest with her brother, Publius Clodius, in one of Cicero's speeches (*Pro Caelio* 36). While presumably a deliberate allusion, this is a reference that would go over the heads of most non-classicists unless they happened to be familiar with both Catullus and Cicero's speech. However, *Rome* has shown a tendency to insert subtle references to minor but telling historical details, such as the dark toga worn by the character of Cato.[25]

The garden scene is followed by a scene in Octavian's bedroom, where Octavia initially claims to be looking for reading material, specifically a comic play. After some light banter, Octavia propositions her brother (Episode 09):

OCTAVIA: Come lie down with me.
OCTAVIAN: Why?
OCTAVIA: Why not?
OCTAVIAN: I can think of several reasons.
OCTAVIA: When you were little you would come to my bed every night.
OCTAVIAN: Not every night. Only when I was scared.

In the *Pro Caelio*, Cicero claims that Publius Clodius, as a young boy, would sleep with (*cubitabat*) his elder sister Clodia every night out of childish fears and "night terrors" (*Pro Caelio* 36). Cicero then goes on to insinuate that this was not just a relationship of childish comfort but one that evolved into adult incest. The direct parallelism suggests that writer Cunningham may have lifted the entire brother–sister incest plot from the accusations in the *Pro Caelio*, despite the total lack of evidence for any such relationship between Octavian and Octavia. When Octavian initially hesitates and rebuffs Octavia's advances, she urges him to "pretend," although what he is supposed to pretend is unclear. Finally, she flatters his masculinity: "I thought you wanted me. You're a man now. You can take what you want." This blatant appeal is sufficient to produce first a kiss and then intercourse.

Immediately after sex, the siblings discuss the nature of incest itself. After first trying to rationalize their act, Octavia later becomes hysterical, while her brother remains icily calm and analytical:

OCTAVIAN: Now comes the price.
OCTAVIA: What do you mean?
OCTAVIAN: You're a virtuous woman, so you must know that seducing your brother is wrong.
OCTAVIA: You and I are above such petty social convention.
OCTAVIAN: But incest is not merely wrong in convention, it is wrong in essence. It must be, else why so many idiots and monsters among the children of incest?
OCTAVIA: [*stricken look*]
OCTAVIAN: Don't worry. It's unlikely I've seeded you. Not with the moon in transit. The point is: you're not the woman to do such wrong out of mere lust. Ergo, you must have another reason. I suspect you shall renew your strange interest in Caesar's health.
OCTAVIA: [*cries*] What have I done? Promise you won't tell Mother.

While Octavian apparently desired his sister, he regards the consequences of their intercourse in an entirely detached and dispassionate light. He notes that Octavia should have refrained from incest because of its immorality, but Octavian never himself claims to be moral. Indeed, *Rome* portrays Octavian as increasingly callous and selfish; earlier, in Episode 05, he participates in the torture and murder of the adulterer Evander largely as a means of gaining worldly experience.

In Episode 09, Octavian reacts similarly to the prospect of incest. The young atheist and natural philosopher explains that incest is wrong because of its dangerous reproductive results, rather than out of any respect for law or piety. While the "wrong in essence" claim might refer to the Roman belief that incest went against natural law, as mentioned earlier, Octavian bases his evidence not on universal social principles but on scientific evidence. This is somewhat anachronistic, as the correlation between incest and birth defects does not seem to have been known to ancient writers. For instance, the children of the famously incestuous Oedipus and Jocasta, while socially dysfunctional, are normal in appearance. The young scholar Octavian also apparently knows more about Octavia's menstrual cycle than she herself does, and he refers to the prospect of incestuous parenthood with bluntly clinical terminology.

Octavian's lecture on the nature of incest serves not to reassure the horrified audience but rather to suggest that we are ourselves irrational for being repulsed by non-procreative incestuous sex. It also further distances us from Octavian's character. Since he is one of the major protagonists of the series, this act must be interpreted as a significant clue to his character and suggestive of further deviant behavior.

Although Octavia is initially the one to claim exemption from "petty social convention," she is ultimately a reluctant pawn retroactively shamed by her deed. The siblings present a stereotypical representation of the difference between Roman men and women in the ancient imagination. Octavia fails miserably in her plan to be subtle and sophisticated and finishes the scene by weeping all over her little brother's shoulder, yielding to her weak feminine emotions. When Atia, their mother, finds out about the incest from a slave, she similarly reacts with extreme emotion and outrage, even threatening to whip Octavia and punching Octavian in the jaw amidst a storm of curses and tears. Although she is normally scheming and rational, the news of incest reduces Atia to hysterics and violent rage. Even under his mother's abuse, Octavian remains poised and rational; he is a proper Roman gentleman.

Although Atia describes the incest as "perverted," it is hard to sympathize with a woman who calmly encouraged her adolescent son to prostitute himself to his great-uncle in return for political favors (Episode 05). The audience is left to wonder what, precisely, the reaction of the

Roman community would be to such an act. While the Octavii have apparently performed the one deed repulsive to Atia, sex queen of Rome, by the very next episode she is frustrated by Octavia's repentance and religious retreat, calling her daughter a "poor little grump" (Episode 10). Atia takes revenge against Servilia, but she makes no attempt to separate her children or prevent further sexual incidents. The incest itself is never directly mentioned again, and it vanishes into the list of Octavian's bizarre educational experiences and Octavia's various psychological traumas.

The creators of *Rome* would like the audience both to be shocked by the incest of *Rome* and to discuss it gleefully the next morning over the proverbial office water cooler. Cunningham, the screenwriter, presupposes a twenty-first-century world in which the depiction of incest on television is merely one step farther along a spectrum that began with the bouncing breasts of *I, Claudius*. The incest plotline is not intended to tar Octavian or Octavia as depraved villains like Caligula, although Octavian's emotional detachment may presage further acts of cold calculation and manipulation. While incest is used as a device to depict the sexual decadence of ancient Rome, HBO-BBC does not seem to intend viewers to condemn the evils of ancient society. We lack the virtuous Christians or faithful philosophers of earlier cinematic versions of the ancient world who might offer a more chaste and moral alternative. All that is left is titillation and entertainment, and HBO-BBC expects us to be entertained by a plot involving consensual sex between siblings.

This leads to the obvious question: "Are you not entertained?"[26] HBO-BBC wants their audiences to find incest as exciting as attractive women kissing and as redolent of ancient Roman decadence as nude bath scenes. However, this attempt, even though it is similar to the devices used by many other current television shows, fails to understand the difference in societal perception between these types of sexual acts. Lesbian romantic interludes excite many viewers, especially voyeuristic heterosexual men seeking both unusual depictions of sexuality and a multiplicity of female sexual objects for the viewer's gaze.[27] Presumably, it also draws an audience of lesbian women, but they are a much smaller percentage of the viewing audience, and their identity as viewing subjects is more complex and questionable, particularly in the case of shows not primarily intended for a gay or lesbian audience.[28] Meanwhile, the nude bathing scenes and dancers in the earlier representations of ancient Rome provided more conventional erotic stimulation by exhibiting attractive bodies engaged in sexualized movements.

However, the only distinction between an incestuous sexual act on television and a conventional heterosexual liaison lies not in its visual representation but in the dialogue and the fictional relationship between the characters. Incest cannot be visually erotic; it can only provide shock value due to the audience's knowledge of the characters' consanguinity. If the incest plotline had been crucial to the overall story arc of the series, it might have been justifiable. But its absence from later episodes suggests that it was merely an aberrant incident marking the beginning of November sweeps and the fevered imagination of a scriptwriter fond of Cicero's more vituperative accusations. In her review of the upcoming second season, Alessandra Stanley in the *New York Times* dismisses *Rome* as "X-rated Masterpiece Theater," more notable for spectacle than for artistic quality.[29] In the end, the incest and other shocking sexual moments in *Rome* serve more to distinguish HBO-BBC from PBS than either to illuminate ancient society or address important issues about the nature of sexual relationships today.

If incest plotlines are accepted as the new "lesbian kiss" of 2000s television, we must ask what form of sexual deviance will eventually supersede them. The series *Rome*, and Episode 09 in particular, demonstrates the constant re-creation of ancient Roman society according to modern sexual and societal prejudices. When I asked students in an anonymous survey in the spring of 2007 to list three terms they associated with the Roman world, several surveys included "incest" as an answer, suggesting that *Rome* has succeeded in falsely associating this practice with Roman society. Meanwhile, the legality of incest has become a popular topic in mainstream news articles, suggesting that the portrayal of incestuous relationships may lead to greater toleration in American and European society.[30] The *Rome* or *I, Claudius* of the next generation may have to dig deep to find sexual practices so appalling to contemporary audiences that they can be used to represent the purported decadence of ancient Rome. Perhaps, in the end, they will have to scale back and realize that the Romans were not all that different in their perversions from their modern descendants.

NOTES

1   While the historical figure would have been known as Gaius Octavius during this period, the series simplifies matters by referring to him as Gaius Octavian, and so I have followed suit.

2   Tacitus, *Dialogue concerning the Orators* 28.

3 Suetonius, *Life of Augustus* 69.
4 Justinian, *Digest* 23.68; see also Strong (2005), 32.
5 *Berlin Griechische Urkunden* 4.1024.
6 Cicero, *Pro Caelio* 36.
7 Tacitus, *Annals* 6.19; Cassius Dio, *Roman History* 58.22.4.
8 Suetonius, *Life of Caligula* 24.
9 Hopkins (1980), 304.
10 Wyke (1997), 89–97.
11 Wyke (1997), 93.
12 Cyrino (2005), 109; Winkler (2001), 52.
13 Episode 1, "A Touch of Murder."
14 Episode 7, "Queen of Heaven."
15 Episode 5.12, "He's a Crowd." See Kennedy (1997), 319.
16 Mayne (2000), 100.
17 Lo (2005b).
18 Lo (2005a).
19 Episode 1.13, "Hearts and Minds."
20 Episode 2.18, "Righteous Brothers"; Episode 3.10, "Faking It."
21 *Brookside*, Episode 1761, "Misjudgement"; *EastEnders*, "September 29, 2003."
22 Episode 3.06, "The Verdict."
23 Episode 2.13, "Skin Deep."
24 Episode 5.11, "Static."
25 Plutarch, *Cato the Younger* 6.
26 The quote is from the film *Gladiator* (2000).
27 Mulvey (1975); de Lauretis (1984), 118–119.
28 de Lauretis (1990), 144–145.
29 Stanley (2007).
30 Lindenberger (2007).

Bibliography

Adams, J. N. (1982). *The Latin Sexual Vocabulary*. Baltimore: Johns Hopkins University Press.

Allison, Penelope M. (1997). "Roman Households: An Archaeological Perspective." In Helen M. Parkins (ed.), *Roman Urbanism: Beyond the Consumer City*. London and New York: Routledge, 112–146.

Anderegg, Michael (1999). *Orson Welles, Shakespeare, and Popular Culture*. New York: Columbia University Press.

Anderegg, Michael (2005). "Orson Welles and After." In Zander, 295–305.

Ashby, Thomas (1900). "Recent Excavations in Rome." *Classical Review* 14.4: 237.

Augoustakis, Antony (2006). "Cutting Down the Grove in Lucan, Valerius Maximus, and Dio Cassius." *Classical Quarterly* 56.2: 634–638.

Babcock, Charles L. (1965). "The Early Career of Fulvia." *American Journal of Philology* 86.1: 1–32.

Barnouw, Erik (1970). *The Image Empire: A History of Broadcasting in the United States*. Volume 3: *From 1953*. New York: Oxford University Press.

Barthes, Roland (1977). *Image, Music, Text*. Trans. Stephen Heath. Ann Arbor: University of Michigan Press.

Bartman, Elizabeth (2001). "Hair and the Artifice of Roman Female Adornment." *American Journal of Archaeology* 105: 1–25.

Barton, Carlin A. (2001). *Roman Honor: The Fire in the Bones*. Berkeley and London: University of California Press.

Barton, Carlin A. (2002). "Being in the Eyes: Shame and Sight in Ancient Rome." In Fredrick 2002a, 216–235.

Beard, Mary (1987). "A Complex of Times: No More Sheep on Romulus' Birthday." *Proceedings of the Cambridge Philological Society* 33: 1–15.

Beard, Mary, North, John, and Price, Simon (1998). *Religions of Rome*. Volume 1: *A History*. Cambridge: Cambridge University Press.

Beauvoir, Simone de (1952). *The Second Sex.* Trans. H. M. Parshley. New York: Bantam.

Becher, Ilse (1996). "Atia, Mutter des Augustus – Legende und Politik." In Ernst G. Schmidt (ed.), *Griechenland und Rom: Vergleichende Untersuchungen zu Entwicklungstendenzen und höhenpunkten der antiken Geschichte, Kunst und Literatur.* Tbilissi: Erlangen and Jena, 95–116.

Bergren, Ann L. T. (1983). "Language and the Female in Early Greek Thought." *Arethusa* 16: 69–98.

Boller, Jr., Paul F. and Davis, Ronald L. (1987). *Hollywood Anecdotes.* New York: William Morrow.

Borgeaud, Philippe (1996). *La Mère des dieux.* Paris: Seuil.

Bosworth, A. B. (2003). "Plus ça change . . . Ancient Historians and Their Sources." *Classical Antiquity* 22: 167–198.

Bourdieu, Pierre (1999). *On Television.* Trans. Priscilla Parkhurst Ferguson. New York: New Press.

Bowersock, G. W. (1984). "Augustus and the East: The Problem of the Succession." In Fergus Millar and Erich Segal (eds.), *Caesar Augustus: Seven Aspects.* Oxford: Oxford University Press, 169–188.

Brice, Lee L. (2003). "Holding a Wolf by the Ears: Mutiny and Unrest in the Roman Military, 44 BC–AD 68." PhD dissertation. University of North Carolina, Chapel Hill.

Brown, Les (1977). "TV's *I, Claudius* Will Test the Boundaries of Public Broadcasting." *New York Times* (November 6): D1.

Brunt, P. A. (1993). "Cicero and Historiography." In P. A. Brunt, *Studies in Greek History and Thought.* Oxford: Oxford University Press, 181–209.

Burns, Ken (1996). "Four O'Clock in the Morning Courage." In Robert Brent Toplin (ed.), *Ken Burns's The Civil War: Historians Respond.* New York: Oxford University Press, 153–183.

Burstein, Stanley M. (2004). *The Reign of Cleopatra.* Westport: Greenwood Press.

Caldwell, John Thornton (1995). *Televisuality: Style, Crisis, and Authority in American Television.* New Brunswick: Rutgers University Press.

Canfora, Luciano (2007). *Julius Caesar: The People's Dictator.* Edinburgh: Edinburgh University Press.

Carter, John (trans.) (1996). *Appian: The Civil Wars.* London and New York: Penguin.

Carter, John (trans.) (1998). *Caesar: The Civil War.* Oxford: Oxford University Press.

Chauveau, Michel (2002). *Cleopatra: Beyond the Myth.* Trans. David Lorton. Ithaca: Cornell University Press.

Chrissanthos, Stephan G. (1999). "*Seditio*: Mutiny in the Roman Army, 90–40 BC." PhD dissertation. University of Southern California.

Clarke, John R. (1991). *The Houses of Roman Italy, 100 BC–AD 250: Ritual, Space, and Decoration.* Berkeley: University of California Press.

Clarke, M. L. (1981). *The Noblest Roman: Marcus Brutus and His Reputation.* Ithaca: Cornell University Press.

Coleman, Kathleen M. (2004). "The Pedant Goes to Hollywood: The Role of the Academic Consultant." In Winkler, 45–52.

Cook, David A. (2000). *Lost Illusions: American Cinema in the Shadow of Watergate and Vietnam, 1970–1979.* Berkeley: University of California Press.

Courtney, Edward (ed.) (1993). *The Fragmentary Latin Poets.* Oxford: Oxford University Press.

Crystal, David (1987). *The Cambridge Encyclopedia of Language.* Cambridge: Cambridge University Press.

Cyrino, Monica Silveira (2005). *Big Screen Rome.* Oxford: Blackwell Publishing.

Daly, Gregory (2002). *Cannae: The Experience of Battle in the Second Punic War.* New York: Routledge.

Daniell, David (ed.) (1998). *Julius Caesar.* London: Arden Shakespeare.

Davies, R. W. (1989). *Service in the Roman Army.* Ed. D. J. Breeze and Valerie A. Maxfield. New York: Columbia University Press.

de Lauretis, Teresa (1984). *Alice Doesn't: Feminism, Semiotics, Cinema.* Bloomington: Indiana University Press.

de Lauretis, Teresa (1990). "Eccentric Subjects." *Feminist Studies* 16.1: 115–150.

Derrick, Thomas J. (1998). "Teaching Julius Caesar." In *Understanding Shakespeare's Julius Caesar.* Westport: Greenwood Press, 133–194.

Dobson, B. (1974). "The Significance of the Centurion and *Primipilaris* in the Roman Army and Administration." In H. Temporini and W. Haase (eds.), *Aufstieg und Niedergang der römischen Welt: Geschichte und Kultur Roms im Spiegel der neueren Forschung.* Berlin: Walter de Gruyter, II.1: 392–434. Reprinted in Michael P. Speidel (ed.), *Roman Officers and Frontiers. Mavors* 10 (1993): 143–185.

Dunbar, Robin (1996). *Grooming, Gossip, and the Evolution of Language.* Cambridge, MA: Harvard University Press.

Duthoy, Robert (1969). *The Taurobolium: Its Evolution and Terminology.* Leiden: E. J. Brill.

Edel, Peggy Goodman (1987). "Julio César *et al.*: The 1986 Florida Shakespeare Festival." *Shakespeare Quarterly* 38: 214–217.

Edwards, Catharine (trans.) (2000). *Suetonius: Lives of Caesar.* Oxford: Oxford University Press.

Feeney, Denis (1998). *Literature and Religion at Rome: Cultures, Contexts, and Beliefs.* Cambridge: Cambridge University Press.

Finley, M. I. (1983). *Politics in the Ancient World.* Cambridge: Cambridge University Press.

Fitzgerald, William (2000). *Slavery and the Roman Literary Imagination.* Cambridge: Cambridge University Press.

Fitzgerald, William (2001). "Oppositions, Anxieties, and Ambiguities in the Toga Movie." In Joshel, Malamud, and McGuire, 23–49.

Flynn, Gillian (2005). "Roman Scandals." *Entertainment Weekly* (August 26): 51.

Fornara, Charles W. (1983). *The Nature of History in Ancient Greece and Rome.* Berkeley: University of California Press.

Fredrick, David (ed.) (2002a). *The Roman Gaze: Vision, Power, and the Body.* Baltimore and London: Johns Hopkins University Press.

Fredrick, David (2002b). "Introduction: Invisible Rome." In Fredrick 2002a, 1–30.

Freedberg, David (1989). *The Power of Images: Studies in the History and Theory of Response.* Chicago: University of Chicago Press.

Fuller, J. F. C. (1965). *Julius Caesar: Man, Soldier, and Tyrant.* New Brunswick: Da Capo Press.

Futrell, Alison (2001). "Seeing Red: Spartacus as Domestic Economist." In Joshel, Malamud, and McGuire, 77–118.

Futrell, Alison (2003). "The Baby, the Mother and the Empire: Xena as Ancient Hero." In Frances Early and Kathleen Kennedy (eds.), *Athena's Daughters: New Women Warriors on Television.* Syracuse: Syracuse University Press, 13–26.

Futrell, Alison (2006). "Shadow Government: HBO's *Rome.*" *Amphora* 5.2: 1, 4–5.

Garrison, James D. (1992). *Pietas from Vergil to Dryden.* University Park: Pennsylvania State University Press.

Geiger, Joseph (1975). "Zum Bild Julius Caesars in der römischen Kaiserzeit." *Historia* 24: 444–453.

Gilbert, Matthew (2005). "Weak *Empire* is Ruled by Inadequacy." *Boston Globe* (June 28): E1.

Gilliver, C. M. (1999). *The Roman Art of War.* Charleston: Tempus.

Gilliver, Kate, Goldsworthy, Adrian, and Whitby, Michael (2005). *Rome At War: Caesar and His Legacy.* Oxford: Osprey Publishing.

Goldberg, Lee (1990). *Unsold Television Pilots: 1955 Through 1988.* Jefferson: McFarland.

Goldenson, Leonard H. (1991). *Beating the Odds: The Untold Story Behind the Rise of ABC.* New York: Charles Scribner's Sons.

Goldsworthy, Adrian (1996). *The Roman Army at War: 100 BC–AD 200.* Oxford: Oxford University Press.

Goldsworthy, Adrian (2006). *Caesar: Life of a Colossus.* New Haven: Yale University Press.

Graf, Fritz (1997). *Magic in the Ancient World.* Trans. Franklin Philip. Cambridge, MA: Harvard University Press.

Graves, Robert (trans.) (1982). *Suetonius: The Twelve Caesars.* New York: Penguin.

Green, C. M. C. (2006). *Roman Religion and the Cult of Diana at Aricia.* Cambridge: Cambridge University Press.

Greenwald, Michael L. (2005). "Multicultural and Regendered Romans." In Zander, 319–332.

Gruen, Erich (2003). "Cleopatra in Rome: Facts and Fantasies." In David Braund and Christopher Gill (eds.), *Myth, History and Culture in Republican Rome: Studies in Honour of T. P. Wiseman*. Exeter: University of Exeter Press, 258–274.

Guynn, William (2006). *Writing History in Film*. New York: Routledge.

Hales, Shelley (2003). *The Roman House and Social Identity*. Cambridge: Cambridge University Press.

Hall, Clayton M. (1923). *Nicolaus of Damascus' Life of Augustus: A Historical Commentary Embodying a Translation*. Northampton: Smith College Classical Studies 4.

Hallett, Judith P. and Skinner, Marilyn B. (eds.) (1997). *Roman Sexualities*. Princeton: Princeton University Press.

Hamer, Mary (1993). *Signs of Cleopatra: History, Politics, Representation*. New York: Routledge.

Hammond, Carolyn (trans.) (1998). *Caesar: The Gallic War*. Oxford: Oxford University Press.

Hannestad, Niels (1992). "The Deified Julius – or Caesar Renovated." In T. Fischer-Hansen (ed.), *Ancient Portraiture: Image and Message*. Copenhagen: Museum Tusculanum Press, 197–205.

Hare-Mustin, Rachel and Marecek, Jeanne (2001). "Gender and the Meaning of Difference." In Anne C. Herrmann and Abigail J. Stewart (eds.), *Theorizing Feminism: Parallel Trends in the Humanities and Social Sciences*. 2nd edition. Boulder: Westview Press, 78–109.

Hark, Ina Rae (1993). "Animals or Romans: Looking at Masculinity in *Spartacus*." In Steven Cohen and Ina Rae Hark (eds.), *Screening the Male: Exploring Masculinities in Hollywood Cinema*. London and New York: Routledge, 151–172.

Harris, William V. (1979). *War and Imperialism in Republican Rome: 327–70 BC*. Oxford: Oxford University Press.

Harris, William V. (1994). "Child-Exposure in the Roman Empire." *Journal of Roman Studies* 84: 1–22.

Hillard, Tom (1992). "On the Stage, Behind the Curtain: Images of Politically Active Women in the Late Roman Republic." In Barbara Garlick, Suzanne Dixon, and Pauline Allen (eds.), *Stereotypes of Women in Power: Historical Perspectives and Revisionist Views*. New York: Greenwood Press, 37–64.

Holliday, Peter J. (1997). "Roman Triumphal Painting: Its Function, Development, and Reception." *Art Bulletin* 79.1: 130–147.

Holliday, Peter J. (2002). *The Origins of Roman Historical Commemoration in the Visual Arts*. Cambridge: Cambridge University Press.

Hopkins, Keith (1980). "Brother–Sister Marriage in Roman Egypt." *Comparative Studies in Society and History* 22: 303–354.

Horsmann, Gerhard (1991). *Untersuchungen zur militärischen Ausbildung im republikanischen und kaiserzeitlichen Rom*. Boppard am Rhein: Harald Boldt.

Hughes-Hallett, Lucy (1990). *Cleopatra: Histories, Dreams and Distortions*. New York: Harper and Row.

Hunt, Leon (1993). "What Are Big Boys Made Of? *Spartacus, El Cid*, and the Male Epic." In Pat Kirkham and Janet Thumim (eds.), *You Tarzan: Masculinity, Movies, and Men*. New York: Palgrave Macmillan, 65–83.

Jones, Prudence J. (2006a). *Cleopatra: The Last Pharaoh*. London: Haus Publishing.

Jones, Prudence J. (2006b). *Cleopatra: A Sourcebook*. Oklahoma Series in Classical Culture, Volume 31. Norman: University of Oklahoma Press.

Joshel, Sandra R. (1992). "The Body Female and the Body Politic: Livy's Lucretia and Verginia." In Amy Richlin (ed.), *Pornography and Representation in Greece and Rome*. Oxford: Oxford University Press, 112–130.

Joshel, Sandra R. (2001). "*I, Claudius*: Projection and Imperial Soap Opera." In Joshel, Malamud, and McGuire, 119–161.

Joshel, Sandra R., Malamud, Margaret, and McGuire, Jr., Donald T. (eds.) (2001). *Imperial Projections: Ancient Rome in Modern Popular Culture*. Baltimore and London: Johns Hopkins University Press.

Joshel, Sandra R., Malamud, Margaret, and Wyke, Maria (2001). "Introduction." In Joshel, Malamud, and McGuire, 1–22.

Kampen, Natalie Boymel (1996). "Gender Theory in Roman Art." In Diana E. E. Kleiner and Susan B. Matheson (eds.), *I Claudia: Women in Ancient Rome*. New Haven: Yale University Press, 14–25.

Kaplan, Michael (1979). "*Agrippina semper atrox*: A Study in Tacitus' Characterization of Women." *Studies in Latin Literature and History* 1: 410–417.

Keegan, John (1976). *The Face of Battle*. New York: Viking.

Kennedy, Rosanne (1997). "The Gorgeous Lesbian in *L.A. Law*: The Present Absence?" In Charlotte Brunsdon, Julie D'Acci, and Lynn Spigel (eds.), *Feminist Television Criticism: A Reader*. Oxford: Oxford University Press, 318–324.

Keppie, Lawrence (1998). *The Making of the Roman Army: From Republic to Empire*. Updated edition. Norman: University of Oklahoma Press.

Keppie, Lawrence (2003). "'Having Been a Soldier': The Commemoration of Military Service on Funerary Monuments of the Early Empire." In J. J. Wilkes (ed.), *Documenting the Roman Army*. London: Institute of Classical Studies, 31–53.

King, Charles (2003). "The Organization of Roman Religious Beliefs." *Classical Antiquity* 22.2: 275–312.

Kleiner, Diana E. E. (2005). *Cleopatra and Rome*. Cambridge, MA: Harvard University Press.

Kraemer, Ross Shepard (ed.) (2004). *Women's Religions in the Greco-Roman World: A Sourcebook*. Oxford and New York: Oxford University Press.

Kraus, C. and Woodman, A. J. (eds.) (1997). *Latin Historians*. Oxford: Oxford University Press.

Kronke, David (2005). "*Empire* Succumbs to Inevitable Decline." *Daily News*, Los Angeles (June 28): U7.

Lacey, W. K. (1974). "Octavian in the Senate, January 27 BC." *Journal of Roman Studies* 64: 176–184.

Landy, Marcia (ed.) (2001). *The Historical Film: History and Memory in Media.* New Brunswick: Rutgers University Press.

Lang, Kurt and Lang, Gladys Engel (2002). *Television and Politics.* New Brunswick: Transaction Publishers.

Langlands, Rebecca (2006). *Sexual Morality in Ancient Rome.* Cambridge: Cambridge University Press.

Latimer, John C. (1952–1953). "An Early Experiment in Latin Teaching." *Classical Outlook* 30: 80–81.

Lefkowitz, Mary R. (1993). "Influential Women." In Averil Cameron and Amelie Kuhrt (eds.), *Images of Women in Antiquity.* Revised edition. Detroit: Wayne State University Press, 49–64.

Lehman, Peter (2001). "Crying Over the Melodramatic Penis: Melodrama and Male Nudity in Films of the 90s." In Peter Lehman (ed.), *Masculinity: Bodies, Movies, Culture.* New York and London: Routledge, 25–42.

Lendon, John E. (1997). *Empire of Honour: The Art of Government in the Roman World.* Oxford: Oxford University Press.

Lendon, John E. (2005). *Soldiers and Ghosts: A History of Battle in Classical Antiquity.* New Haven: Yale University Press.

Levinson, Richard and Link, William (1986). *Off Camera: Conversations with the Makers of Prime-Time Television.* New York: New American Library.

LiDonnici, Lynn R. (1999). "Women's Religions and Religious Lives in the Greco-Roman City." In Ross Shepard Kraemer and Mary Rose D'Angelo (eds.), *Women and Christian Origins.* Oxford and New York: Oxford University Press, 80–104.

Lindenberger, Michael (2007). "Should Incest Be Legal?" *Time,* www.time.com (April 5).

Lo, Malinda (2005a). "Sweeps Lesbianism a Mixed Bag." *AfterEllen,* www.afterellen.com (February 23).

Lo, Malinda (2005b). "Back in the Day: The Kiss Heard Round the World." *AfterEllen,* www.afterellen.com (March 1).

Luhmann, Niklas (2000). *The Reality of the Mass Media.* Cambridge: Polity Press.

Lukacs, Barbara Ann (1995). "Julius Caesar." *Shakespeare Bulletin* 12–13: 19–20.

McCullough, Colleen (1996). *Caesar's Women.* New York: Avon.

Macdonald, Marianne (2006). "Roman Invasion." *Evening Standard Magazine* (January 13): 29–31.

McDonnell, Myles (2006). *Roman Manliness: Virtus and the Roman Republic.* Cambridge: Cambridge University Press.

McGinn, Thomas A. J. (2004). *The Economy of Prostitution in the Roman World: A Study of Social History and the Brothel.* Ann Arbor: University of Michigan Press.

MacMullen, Ramsay (1984). "The Legion as Society." *Historia* 33: 440–456.

Malamud, Martha (2001). "Serial Romans." In Joshel, Malamud, and McGuire, 209–228.

Marc, David and Thompson, Robert J. (1995). *Prime Time, Prime Movers.* Syracuse: Syracuse University Press.

Marill, Alvin H. (2005). *Movies Made for Television: 1964–2004.* Lanham: Scarecrow Press.

Marincola, John (2003). "Beyond Pity and Fear: The Emotions of History." *Ancient Society* 33: 285–315.

Marincola, John (ed.) (2007). *A Companion to Greek and Roman Historiography.* Oxford: Blackwell Publishing.

Maxfield, Valerie A. (1981). *The Military Decorations of the Roman Army.* Berkeley: University of California Press.

Mayne, Judith (2000). *Framed: Lesbians, Feminists, and Media Culture.* Minneapolis: University of Minnesota Press.

Mazzoleni, Donatella and Pappalardo, Umberto (2004). *Domus: Wall Painting in the Roman House.* Los Angeles: J. Paul Getty Museum, Getty Trust Publications.

Mellor, Ronald (1999). *The Roman Historians.* London and New York: Routledge.

Milnor, Kristina (2005). *Gender, Domesticity, and the Age of Augustus: Inventing Private Life.* Oxford: Oxford University Press.

Morley, David (1995). "Television: Not So Much a Visual Medium, More a Visible Object." In Chris Jenks (ed.), *Visual Culture.* London and New York: Routledge, 170–189.

Mulvey, Laura (1975). "Visual Pleasure and Narrative Cinema." *Screen* 16.3: 6–18.

Mulvey, Laura (1989). *Visual and Other Pleasures.* Bloomington: Indiana University Press.

Munkelt, Marga (2004). "Recent Film, Stage and Critical Interpretations." In Spevack, 46–70.

Murnaghan, Sheila and Joshel, Sandra R. (eds.) (1998). *Women and Slaves in Greco-Roman Culture.* London: Routledge.

Nicolet, Claude (1980). *The World of the Citizen in Republican Rome.* Trans. P. S. Falla. Berkeley: University of California Press.

O'Connor, John J. (1977). "TV: Tour of Rome With *I, Claudius.*" *New York Times* (November 3): 74.

O'Connor, John J. (1997). "Perilous Journey Home Upon the Wine-Dark Sea." *New York Times* (May 16): D18.

Ogilvie, R. M. (1965). *A Commentary on Livy, Books 1–5.* Oxford: Oxford University Press.

Olin, Margaret (1996). "Gaze." In Robert S. Nelson and Richard Schiff (eds.), *Critical Terms for Art History.* Chicago: University of Chicago Press, 318–329.

Ostling, Richard N. (1977). "Franco Zeffirelli's Classical Christ for Prime Time." *Time,* www.time.com (April 4).

Ouellette, Laurie (2002). *Viewers Like You? How Public TV Failed the People.* New York: Columbia University Press.

Ozersky, Josh (2003). *Archie Bunker's America: TV in an Era of Change, 1968–1978.* Carbondale: Southern Illinois University Press.

Papazian, Ed (1991). *Medium Rare: The Evolution, Workings and Impact of Commercial Television.* New York: Media Dynamics.

Parker, Holt N. (1999). "The Observed of All Observers: Spectacle, Applause, and Cultural Poetics in the Roman Theater Audience." In Bettina Bergmann and Christine Kondoleon (eds.), *The Art of Ancient Spectacle.* New Haven: Yale University Press, 163–180.

Pelling, Christopher (2002). "Plutarch's *Caesar*: A Caesar for the Caesars?" In *Plutarch and History.* London: Duckworth, 253–265.

Pensabene, Patrizio (1988). "Scavi nell'area del Tempio della Vittoria e del Santuario della Magna Mater sul Palatino." *Archeologia Laziale* 9: 54–67.

Perigard, Mark A. (2005). "Discount *Gladiator*: Sitting Through Cheap Wannabe *Empire* Could Be A Fight To The Death." *Boston Herald* (June 26): 55.

Platner, Samuel Ball (1929). *A Topographical Dictionary of Ancient Rome.* Completed and revised by Thomas Ashby. Oxford: Oxford University Press.

Pomeroy, Arthur J. (2004). "The Vision of a Fascist Rome in *Gladiator.*" In Winkler, 111–123.

Poniewozik, James (2005). "Tearing Off the Togas." *Time* (August 22): 65.

Prince, Stephen (2006). "Beholding Blood Sacrifice in *The Passion of the Christ*: How Real is Movie Violence?" *Film Quarterly* 59: 11–22.

Raaflaub, Kurt A. and Samons II, L. J. (1990). "Opposition to Augustus." In Kurt A. Raaflaub and Mark Toher (eds.), *Between Republic and Empire: Interpretations of Augustus and His Principate.* Berkeley and Los Angeles: University of California Press, 417–454.

Rawson, Elizabeth (1986). "Cassius and Brutus: The Memory of the Liberators." In I. S. Moxon, J. D. Smart, and A. J. Woodman (eds.), *Past Perspectives: Studies in Greek and Roman Historical Writing.* Cambridge: Cambridge University Press, 101–119.

Rice, Lynette (2005). "When In Rome." *Entertainment Weekly* (August 26): 26–29.

Roller, Lynn E. (1999). *In Search of God the Mother: The Cult of Anatolian Cybele.* Berkeley and Los Angeles: University of California Press.

Rosenstone, Robert A. (2001). "The Historical Film: Looking at the Past in a Postliterate Age." In Landy, 50–66.

Royster, Francesca T. (2003). *Becoming Cleopatra: The Shifting Image of an Icon.* New York: Palgrave Macmillan.

Rutter, Jeremy B. (1968). "The Three Phases of the Taurobolium." *Phoenix* 22.3: 226–249.

Sabin, Philip (1996). "The Mechanics of Battle in the Second Punic War." In Tim Cornell, Boris Rankov, and Philip Sabin (eds.), *The Second Punic War: A Reappraisal.* London: Institute of Classical Studies, 59–79.

Sabin, Philip (2000). "The Face of Roman Battle." *Journal of Roman Studies* 90: 1–17.

Saller, Richard (1987). "Slavery and the Roman Family." In M. I. Finley (ed.), *Classical Slavery*. London: Frank Cass, 65–87.

Santoro L'Hoir, Francesca (1992). *The Rhetoric of Gender Terms: "Man," "Woman," and the Portrayal of Character in Latin Prose*. Leiden and New York: E. J. Brill.

Schultz, Celia E. (2006). *Women's Religious Activity in the Roman Republic*. Chapel Hill: University of North Carolina Press.

Sebesta, Judith Lynn and Bonfante, Larissa (eds.) (1994). *The World of Roman Costume*. Madison: University of Wisconsin Press.

Segrave, Kerry (1999). *Movies at Home: How Hollywood Came to Television*. Jefferson: McFarland.

Showerman, Grant (1901). *The Great Mother of the Gods. Bulletin of the University of Wisconsin*, 43. Philology and Literature series, 1.3. Madison: University of Wisconsin Press.

Skinner, Marilyn B. (1997). "Introduction: *Quod multo fit aliter in Graecia*. . . ." In Hallett and Skinner, 3–25.

Skinner, Marilyn B. (2005). *Sexuality in Greek and Roman Culture*. Oxford: Blackwell Publishing.

Sorlin, Pierre (2001). "How to Look at an 'Historical' Film." In Landy, 25–49.

Spacks, Patricia Meyer (1985). *Gossip*. New York: Knopf.

Speidel, Michael P. (1994). *Riding for Caesar: The Roman Emperors' Horse Guards*. Cambridge, MA: Harvard University Press.

Spevack, Marvin (ed.) (2004). *Julius Caesar*. Cambridge: Cambridge University Press.

Stanley, Alessandra (2007). "Friends, Romans, Countrymen, Lovers, Haters, Murderers, Barbarians. . . ." *New York Times*, www.nytimes.com (January 12).

Sterling, Christopher H. and Kittross, John Michael (2002). *Stay Tuned: A History of American Broadcasting*. Third edition. Mahwah: Lawrence Erlbaum Associates.

Strong, Anise K. (2005). "Incest Laws and Absent Taboos in Roman Egypt." *Ancient History Bulletin* 19.1–2: 31–41.

Syme, Ronald (1939). *The Roman Revolution*. Oxford: Oxford University Press.

Toher, Mark (2004). "Octavian's Arrival in Rome, 44 BC" *Classical Quarterly* 54.1: 174–184.

Toher, Mark (2006). "The Earliest Depiction of Caesar and the Later Tradition." In Wyke, 29–44.

Umphlett, Wiley Lee (2006). *From Television to the Internet: Postmodern Visions of American Media Culture in the Twentieth Century*. Madison: Fairleigh Dickinson University Press.

Vermeule, Blakey (2006). "Gossip and Literary Narrative." *Philosophy and Literature* 30: 102–117.

Versnel, H. S. (1970). *Triumphus: An Inquiry into the Origin, Development and Meaning of the Roman Triumph*. Leiden: E. J. Brill.

Walker, Susan and Ashton, Sally-Ann (2006). *Cleopatra*. London: Duckworth.

Walker, Susan and Higgs, Peter (eds.) (2001). *Cleopatra of Egypt: From History to Myth*. London: British Museum Press.

Wallace-Hadrill, Andrew (1987). "Time for Augustus: Ovid, Augustus and the *Fasti*." In Michael Whitby, P. Hardie, and Mary Whitby (eds.), *Homo Viator: Classical Essays for John Bramble*. Bristol: Bristol Classical Press, 221–230.

Wallace-Hadrill, Andrew (1997). "*Mutatio morum*: The Idea of a Cultural Revolution." In Thomas Habinek and Alessandro Schiesaro (eds.), *The Roman Cultural Revolution*. Cambridge: Cambridge University Press, 3–22.

Walters, Jonathan (1997). "Invading the Roman Body: Manliness and Impenetrability in Roman Thought." In Hallett and Skinner, 29–43.

Warrior, Valerie M. (2006). *Roman Religion*. Cambridge: Cambridge University Press.

Watermeier, Daniel J. (1994). "Julius Caesar." *Shakespeare Bulletin* 10: 9–10.

Watermeier, Daniel J. (1999). "Julius Caesar." *Shakespeare Bulletin* 17: 36–38.

Wheeler, Mortimer (1964). *Roman Art and Architecture*. London: Thames and Hudson.

Wheen, Francis (1985). *Television: A History*. London: Century Publishing.

Wiedemann, Thomas (1992). *Emperors and Gladiators*. London and New York: Routledge.

Willans, Geoffrey (1957). *Peter Ustinov*. London: Peter Owen.

Williams, Raymond (1990). *Television: Technology and Cultural Form*. Second edition. London and New York: Routledge.

Winkler, Martin M. (2001). "The Roman Empire in American Cinema after 1945." In Joshel, Malamud, and McGuire, 50–76.

Winkler, Martin M. (ed.) (2004). *Gladiator: Film and History*. Oxford: Blackwell Publishing.

Winkler, Martin M. (2007). "Introduction." In Martin M. Winkler (ed.), *Spartacus: Film and History*. Oxford: Blackwell Publishing, 1–13.

Wiseman, T. P. (1993). "Lying Historians: Seven Types of Mendacity." In Christopher Gill and T. P. Wiseman (eds.), *Lies and Fiction in the Ancient World*. Austin: University of Texas Press, 122–146.

Witherspoon, John and Kovitz, Roselle (1987). *The History of Public Broadcasting*. Washington, DC: Current Publishing.

Woodman, A. J. (1988). *Rhetoric in Classical Historiography: Four Studies*. London: Croom Helm.

Wyke, Maria (1994). "Woman in the Mirror: The Rhetoric of Adornment in the Roman World." In Leonie J. Archer, Susan Fischler, and Maria Wyke (eds.), *Women in Ancient Societies: An Illusion of the Night*. New York: Routledge, 134–151.

Wyke, Maria (1997). *Projecting the Past: Ancient Rome, Cinema and History*. New York and London: Routledge.

Wyke, Maria (2002). *The Roman Mistress: Ancient and Modern Representations.* Oxford: Oxford University Press.

Wyke, Maria (ed.) (2006). *Julius Caesar in Western Culture.* Oxford: Blackwell Publishing.

Yavetz, Zvi (1983). *Julius Caesar and His Public Image.* Ithaca: Cornell University Press.

Zander, Horst (ed.) (2005). *Julius Caesar: New Critical Essays.* New York: Routledge.

Index

CPSIA information can be obtained
at www.ICGtesting.com
Printed in the USA
BVHW08s0347190618
519379BV00007B/73/P